TEACHING CHILDREN TO WRITE, K–8

A Complete Guide to Developing Writing Skills

Robert L. Hillerich

Professor of Education
Bowling Green State University

PRENTICE-HALL, INC.
Englewood Cliffs, New Jersey

Library of Congress Cataloging in Publication Data

Hillerich, Robert L.
  Teaching children to write, K–8.

  Includes bibliographies and index.
  1. English language—Composition and exercises.
2. Children—Language.   I. Title.
LB1576.H43   1985   372.6'23   85-3588

ISBN 0-13-891771-X

10 9 8 7 6 5 4

PRENTICE-HALL INTERNATIONAL, INC., *London*
PRENTICE-HALL OF AUSTRALIA, PTY. LTD., *Sydney*
PRENTICE-HALL CANADA INC., *Toronto*
PRENTICE-HALL HISPANOAMERICANA, S.A., *Mexico*
PRENTICE-HALL OF INDIA PRIVATE LTD., *New Delhi*
PRENTICE-HALL OF JAPAN, INC., *Tokyo*
PRENTICE-HALL OF SOUTHEAST ASIA PTE. LTD., *Singapore*
WHITEHALL BOOKS, LTD., *Wellington, New Zealand*
EDITORA PRENTICE-HALL DO BRASIL LTDA., *Rio de Janeiro*

to Dottie

About the Author

Robert L. Hillerich has been an elementary teacher, elementary principal, and assistant superintendent for instruction. After earning an undergraduate degree in English and humanities, he went on to earn a doctorate in elementary education from Colorado State College. Currently a professor of education at Bowling Green State University, he teaches graduate courses in reading and language arts. Prior to coming to Bowling Green, he was chair of the Department of Reading and Language Arts at the National College of Education, where he established and directed the reading clinic.

Dr. Hillerich is the author of more than one hundred journal articles, four professional books, an elementary spelling/writing series, a readiness program, and a beginning reading program. In addition to teaching graduate courses in the teaching of reading and of written composition, he has been director of the Northwest Ohio Writing Project and is a regular speaker at national, regional, and state conferences of many different professional organizations, including the National Council of Teachers of English, the International Reading Association, and the National Association of Elementary Principals. He is also prominent as a director of inservice workshops for principals as well as teachers throughout the United States and Canada.

About This Book

THIS BOOK IS WRITTEN FOR anyone who wants to improve the teaching of written communication. Specifically targeted at inservice teachers of kindergarten through grade eight, it has implications for all levels of instruction.

Kindergarten was selected as the beginning level only because it is the first level in formal schooling; who is to say that writing doesn't begin even before that level? Certainly the composing process and dictated stories belong in any kindergarten language program. Conversely, important elements of the process of writing at the beginning levels continue to be essential at middle grades and junior high as well as at secondary school and college, albeit on an increasingly sophisticated level.

Certainly no one, layperson or professional, will question the need to improve skill in writing. This need has been amply demonstrated through each of the national assessments as well as through other research. Given the vast number of books on the subject, one might question the necessity for still another on the teaching of writing. However, this book meets an urgent need in that it bridges the gap between the two kinds of books currently available: those that offer summaries of research and those that serve only as a potpourri of ideas. Neither a cookbook of specifics to be followed blindly nor a summary of abstract research, *Teaching Children to Write, K–8* is based on existing research findings to serve as a practical guide to procedures, methods, and skills deemed essential for the development of proficiency in written expression of all kinds.

The cornerstone of this book is the belief that one learns to write by writing. Supporting this cornerstone is a prerequisite: that experience in writing must be enjoyable!

More specifically, one writes in order to communicate effectively with a reader. Students need to be made aware of this fact, and the writing class must be conducted in a manner that makes this purpose readily apparent. No one writes in order to put correctly spelled words on a page with proper punctuation and capitalization; however, if a writer is to effectively engage the reader, that writer must also handle mechanics correctly, lest resulting distractions interfere with the message. Hence, this book deals with improving all aspects of written composition, from such concerns as style and organization to correctness of format and other mechanics.

Whether used by the classroom teacher as a guide to instruction or by the prospective teacher as a college text, this book deals with the entire scope, with all areas of concern for the teacher of writing. With no intent to duplicate the table of contents at this point, I will briefly note some major elements of concern:

- How do I organize my class for instructions...when I deal with five sections of middle-schoolers per day?...when I deal with a restless group of six-year-olds?

- What does prewriting consist of? How can I capitalize on the oral language of my students?...or develop it?

- What are some ideas that I can use to stimulate more writing? What are the different kinds of writing that my students ought to experience?

- In elementary or junior high school, what needs to be taught about writing in the content areas? Is factual writing to be treated differently from "creative" writing? How do I involve others, such as science and social studies teachers, without implying that they should become "English" teachers?

- Do I merely give experience in writing, or can I do some "teaching"? If the latter, what skills can be taught?...in grammar?...in vocabulary development?...in spelling?...in other mechanics?

- What are the best methods for teaching these skills?

- *Conferencing* is a term connected with the process approach to writing. How can I hold conferences with immature six- or seven-year-olds?...with my junior high students when I see five sections per day?

- What are some techniques I can use to see that all writings get "published"?

• What are some effective techniques for evaluating students' writings?...on a day-to-day basis?...over a period of time?...to check the effectiveness of the process in my class?...to complete a school-wide evaluation?

Although this book is organized in a logical order, it need not be read chapter by chapter. After the first chapter, you may choose to skip about to pick up ideas on topics of most concern to you at present. After all, writing is a recursive act: It may be "logical" to begin with prewriting, but Sean is in the process of revising a first draft and Diana is now editing a final draft for publication.

At the risk of stating the obvious, I will also point out that the book was not organized in a developmental sequence, grade by grade, because most elements of a writing program cannot be assigned a grade-level designation. Part of the task in teaching writing is to determine the aspiring writer's major problem at the time and to work on that. Hence, the organization is a topical one, with implications in all chapters for all levels.

Finally, as demonstrated by the mere existence of this volume, I firmly believe that the basics of writing can be taught; there are certain skills and understandings that—if learned—will result in better writing. Nevertheless, an overriding belief is the demonstrated fact that individuals also learn to write by writing. There is no substitute for enjoyable practice in writing when that writing is done to communicate with a reader.

Have fun with your students in writing!

Robert L. Hillerich

Acknowledgments

I AM GRATEFUL to the many excellent classroom teachers with whom I worked as principal over the years. I am even more indebted to my graduate students at Bowling Green State University and to participants in the Northwest Ohio Writing Project for their probing questions and for sharing many of their good practices. A special thanks is due to Sue Simpson and Lois Stevens, who were particularly helpful through their careful reading and valuable comments on the manuscript of this text. All have been experienced, interested, and dedicated teachers, from kindergarten through twelfth grade, who not only teach writing but who also write.

Contents

1

Overview

If you wish to be a writer, write.
EPICTETUS, A.D. 110

THIS CHAPTER PRESENTS the basic viewpoint or philosophy that serves as the foundation on which the remainder of the book rests. In effect, it is also a summary of the practical elements that make up a good writing program and that are expanded upon in the ensuing chapters. First, however, it seems appropriate to take stock of where we are today in the teaching of this "second R."

HOW ARE WE DOING?

Criticism of education in this country is a popular pastime. It sells newspapers and magazines, usually by pointing out that educators are not doing their jobs as well as they did in the "good old days."

Many of the criticisms are overgeneralized complaints based on real problems in a limited number of situations and cannot be supported by facts of any kind when applied to the majority of schools in this country. On the other hand, when critics take aim at the teaching of written composition, they are right on target. Here we have to acknowledge the accuracy of the complaint that "Teachers aren't teaching children to write" and its corollary "Children aren't learning how to write."

The most significant measures of the status of writing in this country are the National Assessments of Educational Progress done by the Education Commission of the States in 1969 and 70, 1973 and 74, and

1978 and 79. Results with ages nine, thirteen, and seventeen offer little encouragement that writing is being taught well, if at all (NAEP, 1980–81). In fact, according to the latest assessment, all age groups declined in spelling, and both thirteen- and seventeen-year-olds declined in writing skill as evaluated either by holistic scoring or by number of words used per T-unit (any independent clause with all of its subordinate clauses and modifiers). About the only positive findings were that (1) urban teenagers showed some improvement over previous assessments, and (2) nine-year-olds showed improvement in the last assessment in both holistic evaluation and in number of words per T-unit.

Most disheartening among the National Assessments were two indications of what happens to students in writing. The first study (NAEP, 1972a) included young adults who had volunteered to participate. When asked to write in response to a picture, almost one-third of these volunteers refused that portion of the test, saying, "I can't write." Does this mean that they had been told so often in school how poorly they wrote that they were now convinced of it?

Second, when papers were sorted globally into above-average, average, and below-average quality, an even more tragic implication was appparent. At age nine, the above-average papers had more comma errors per hundred words than did the average, and the average had more of these mechanical errors per hundred words than did the poorest papers. However, by age thirteen this was no longer true. In fact, the investigators reported that the above-average themes of thirteen-year-olds were nearly perfect mechanically; the only concern with them was that they were written in short, simple sentences and used common, everyday words (NAEP, 1972b). This finding suggests what many of us have observed in classrooms: After a few years, students eventually learn that if they use short, simple sentences they will punctuate correctly, and if they use common words that they know how to spell instead of the more appropriate word they wanted to use, they will spell correctly, and their papers will not be returned with a "hemorrhage" of red pencil marks. Too often this is what we encourage, and we call it "teaching writing."

WHY AREN'T WE DOING BETTER?

Applebee and others (1981) surveyed 754 of the "best" secondary English teachers about their practices in teaching writing. These teachers reported that an average of 44 percent of their lesson time was devoted to writing. However, only 3 percent of that writing consisted of a paragraph or more, and that was usually done as a test of content. Students were using writing only as a means of displaying their knowledge of content studied.

Pettigrew and others (1981) observed teachers in grades three through six to identify the discrete behaviors involved in a writing lesson. They reported that a writing lesson is unlike any other kind of lesson and that teachers are not prepared to teach such lessons. For example, of nine discrete activities involved in a writing lesson, five seldom or never occur in other kinds of lessons. Furthermore, the great number of skills involved in writing resulted in a confusing mix of five or more different skills being taught in most of the lessons observed.

A failure to *teach* was also pointed out by Bridwell (1981), who found that 75 percent of college freshmen seldom or never had had a conference with a teacher about a piece of writing or had submitted a rough draft for opinion. Most writing was a one-shot activity.

Probably more telling was the investigation by Haley-James (1981), who reported how 319 fourth-grade teachers allocated their nonreading language arts time. The greatest portion of each period was devoted to grammar, with the next largest amount of time given to spelling. "Written composition" finished a weak third, barely ahead of listening and handwriting.

All of this suggests that a major reason students do poorly in writing is that we just don't *teach* writing. Observation of most writing lessons will reveal "teaching" such as is seen nowhere else in the world of education. Most often the lesson consists of (1) assigning or stimulating a topic, (2) having pupils write, (3) possibly admonishing them to proof-read their papers, and (4) going error hunting through the papers with a red pencil. In other words, no *teaching* takes place.

Of course, this point merely raises another: If the basic problem is a failure to teach, why don't teachers teach writing?

With each of my writing classes, I usually begin by asking that very question of the teachers participating. Responses are consistent from group to group. Outstanding among the reasons for not teaching more writing is usually the complaint about lack of time. A great deal of research has verified the importance of allocated time—and the even greater importance of time on task—as contributing significantly to achievement. With the crowded curriculum, time is a serious concern. However, reappraisal of priorities can often locate time, and increased efficiency can create time. On the latter point, two major thieves of time are irrelevant activities in spelling lessons and the feeling of teachers that they must be editors of every paper their pupils write. Suggestions for spelling instruction are presented in Chapter 9, and the teacher's role in evaluating is discussed later in this chapter as well as in Chapter 13.

Other reasons reported by these teachers can all be subsumed under the heading of "uncertainty"—uncertainty about what to teach, what to evaluate, ways of motivating, and so on. As Pettigrew pointed out, teachers have not been trained to teach writing. Again, this book, among others, can help to provide the needed guidance.

Leaving the area of research evidence, we can also point to some additional reasons why writing is so seldom *taught*. As teachers, we tend to be a bit reticent where criticism is concerned. It is much easier to evaluate children's writing in terms of mechanics—the errors of capitalization, punctuation, and spelling—than it is to deal with the more nebulous elements of style, word choice, organization, clarity, and so on. The former are either right or wrong! Furthermore, we can count up the number of errors and thereby justify that grade on the report card. That is safe!

A final point and another fact in education: We tend to teach that which is tested. Standardized achievement tests are usually administered to include reading, spelling, and math. Those we teach. Perhaps a positive result of the current concern about competency testing will be the addition of a test of writing skill. Whether or not competency testing becomes required, every school ought to make writing one of the regular areas to be evaluated.

In brief, it seems that pupils don't do a better job of writing because they usually aren't taught how to write. They aren't taught to write because many teachers have not been taught how to teach writing. On the other hand, research has provided enough direction for the teaching of writing that we certainly can do a better job. That evidence must be put into the hands of teachers so that they will no longer need to stay on that hard asphalt of right or wrong, so that they will dare to step into the less-charted marshlands of style and clarity.

SOME BASIC BELIEFS

Interest and research in writing have snowballed in this past decade. Although much of the evidence as to direction has existed for more than a quarter of a century, it has taken more recent and intensified efforts to bring it to the fore. What is your view of the writing process and the purpose for writing? What basic principles do you accept for teaching writing? Is there consistency in your beliefs about the writing process and its teaching as you evaluate pupils' writing? Let's consider a few general principles.

Approaches to Writing

While there is no intent to enter into an involved theoretical discussion, it seems appropriate to present briefly some of the models of rhetoric that have been developed, since they offer more insight into the writing process than do the traditional modes of discourse: narration, description, exposition, and argument. Considerations ought to be given to the thinking of Moffett, Britton and others, and Myers and Gray.

Moffett (1983) identified the universe of discourse as a tripartite entity: I, you, it. Someone writes to someone about something. Further explication indicated that writing develops in terms of rhetorical distance and abstraction. *Distance* refers to audience, which expands from the writer's own musings to self, to a close contact, to a general or unknown readership. *Abstraction* ranges from the immediate and known, to the past, and—ultimately—to the theoretical.

Similar considerations can be seen in the classifications of Britton and others (1975), who also go beyond the mere classification of types seen in the traditional modes of writing. Their classifications are expressive, transactional, and poetic, where they see the expressive as basic. This is a more personal writing to a close audience, explaining to self or to a reader close to the writer, with a more informal style and less need for amplification. Transactional writing is seen as directed to a more distant audience, more formal in style, and typified by informative or persuasive motivation. The poetic may be informative or persuasive, but it influences the reader more in terms of form and style as opposed to content.

Myers and Gray (1983) deal more directly with the theory of *teaching* writing, which they divide into processing, distancing, and modeling. Processing focuses on the sequence of stages in writing or the variation in strategies used by the writer. Distancing is concerned with the relationship between speaker and subject or between speaker and audience, and the modeling view makes use of imitation, text examples, sentence combining, and heuristics.

All of these views offer additional insights into the writing process; however, acceptance of or adherence to a particular approach in a purist fashion is not so important as using what is helpful from each to accomplish the goal of developing writers who can communicate clearly and effectively with a variety of readers for a variety of purposes and in a variety of modes. Hence, we must (1) focus on the process of writing, helping youngsters to become consciously aware of—to monitor—their own process; (2) gradually move pupils from the informal expressive mode—the "I" orientation—to the transactional— "it"—and the poetic; (3) develop a sense of audience and the ability to communicate effectively with diverse and more distant audiences; and (4) provide experience with every type of writing, from journals to diamantes, from news articles to byline columns, and from narratives to free verse.

Purpose of Writing

Basic to anything I might say in this book about writing is the belief that the purpose of writing is to communicate. One puts words in print to convey ideas, information, or feelings to a reader. No one writes (except, unfortunately, in some school situations) in order to string together correctly spelled words with proper punctuation and capitalization. Implied in this purpose for writing is the reader—an audience—who will receive and react to the content of the message, whether mentally or overtly. Pupils need to understand this viewpoint, through demonstration with their writings, from the very beginning of their writing experience.

Consider a parallel situation in oral language. Individuals develop their skill in oral language by using it in interchanges with others. What happens to the language development of the young child whose every statement is corrected for the manner in which it is stated? That youngster quickly learns that no one is interested in *what* he or she is saying, only in *how* it is said. Hence, the child's reaction is to stop talking to people who correct. Fortunately, most children discover from their earliest experience with oral language that its purpose is to communicate. They learn to talk, and, with similar emphasis, they can just as well learn to write.

Process *vs.* Product

As stated earlier, the "teaching of writing" too often consists of little more than assigning and then error hunting after the fact. While I truly believe—and can demonstrate from research—that children also learn to write by writing, such experience must include feedback of an audience reacting to the content of the message rather than merely to the form of that message.

This concern for content *vs.* form is often discussed in terms of process *vs.* product. Traditionally, teachers of writing have been concerned with product. They have collected that finished product and evaluated it with emphasis on the number of quantifiable errors. Some of the more "enlightened" have given two grades, one for mechanics and one for ideas.

In contrast to this product emphasis, enough evidence has existed for many years to indicate that if teachers will place their concern with the process of writing, the product will take care of itself (Hillerich, 1973). Of major import in this process is the precept that teachers must help children become aware of the intuitive knowledge of language that they already possess and then help them enjoy the manipulation of that language on paper. Enjoyment comes from reaching an appreciative audience and from finding more enticing ways to attract that audience. This subtle shift of responsibilty from teacher back to author is another theme that pervades this book.

All this does not imply an abdication of teaching; we've done that too often in the past. Quite the contrary, there is much to teach in the writing class. Such teaching is usually done through demonstration and example, through discussion and models, through exploration and sentence manipulation, or through direct teaching in the case of mechanical elements such as spelling, capitalization, or punctuation. This basic philosophy of writing and the teaching of writing is probably most clearly implemented through the criteria that teachers use in evaluating writing on a day-to-day basis.

Evaluative Criteria

There are many purposes for evaluation: for diagnosis of needs, for "grading" of students, for determining the quality of the program within the classroom, school, or district, for communicating the effectiveness of the school program to parents or community, and so on. Each of these may require different methods. Both the purposes and methods will be discussed in detail in Chapter 13. At this point, let's merely clarify the working criteria that teachers and pupils should have in mind for any piece of writing attempted. These criteria are a natural outgrowth of the philosophy of writing already stated. Listed very simply, the criteria are three:

1. clarity
2. interest appeal
3. correctness

Clarity. First of all, if the purpose for writing is to communicate, the major priority must be clarity: "Did I say what I wanted to say?" If not, communication has failed and the writer has wasted time in putting pencil to paper.

Application of this criterion involves consideration and examination of many aspects of a piece of writing, including organization, sequence, word choice, some of the mechanics, and—at the extreme—even handwriting itself.

Interest Appeal. Related to the first criterion and to the basic philosophy is this second concern: "Did I say it in an interesting manner?" If not, the reader will not continue reading, and again the writing effort has been in vain. Although clarity is still basic, here we express added concern for word choice, organization, style, creativity, specificity, and so on.

Correctness. Despite accusations to the contrary, current interest in process has not resulted in an "anything goes" attitude toward correctness. Correct mechanics are still important, but they must be placed in perspective. Most items of mechanical correctness are matters of *courtesy to the reader* and they are of concern during the final cleaning up of the paper *when that paper is going somewhere* outside the confines of the immediate close group.

Traditionally this criterion has been a major focus, possibly because it is so "objective" and quantifiable—we can count up the number of errors. Hence, it has also been the direction given to writing, to the point where "correct" inanities resulted in a higher evaluation than a much more creative and interesting paper that was riddled with mechanical errors.

We might add, also, that even this traditional approach did not eliminate the mechanical errors on pupils' papers. In fact, research indicates that it may have done just the opposite. Comparisons of pupils who wrote and received reactions to the ideas instead of corrections of the mechanics consistently demonstrated that they wrote better and had fewer mechanical errors than did those who received corrections on their papers. Perhaps these results are reminiscent of some home situations: After the fifteenth time Mother says "Close the door!" the child doesn't even hear it anymore.

Placing correctness as a third priority in the list of criteria does not mean, either, that all mechanics are relegated to this position. Some are matters of first priority as items of clarity. Consider, for example, the following two identically worded sentences:

Women, who are vain, love mirrors.
Women who are vain love mirrors.

In this case, the addition or omission of commas is a matter of clarity: What did the author mean? If commas are included, the author might be trampled as a male chauvinist, whereas omission of the commas results in a sentence that almost anyone would agree with. Hence, in this case, the mechanic is an item of first priority—clarity.

This shift in emphasis from the almost exclusive concern with mechanics to placing higher priorities on other aspects of written expression reflects what most people imply when talking about writing. Usually they refer to the "art" of writing. In contrast, it has been the "science" of writing that has been evaluated. Consider a school open house for parents. Those parents will make loving comments about the kindergartener's drawings. Anyone who criticized the kindergarten teacher for not "correcting" the misshapen or disproportionate figures would be considered strange, if not stupid. Yet, those same parents who "ooh" and "aah" about the drawings might go to the third- or eighth-grade class where the teacher has posted one of the best pieces of writing she has managed to get from their child. What do those parents say? They don't say, "Look at how well organized it is" or "Isn't that a clever way of saying it." Instead, they are more likely to say, "Look at that word in the third line. It's misspelled, and the teacher didn't even correct it." Too often we as teachers use this science model of right and wrong instead of the art model in evaluating children's writing.

Who ever *masters* the art of writing in a lifetime? Some individuals may think they have, but writing is an art that can be continually refined. Certainly no elementary pupil—or even a high school student—can be expected to master it. And where else can these people have a better opportunity to try their wings in language and to receive the positive encouragement and guidance they deserve?

"Teaching" Writing

Perhaps we'd best begin with a major area that we don't have to teach. We don't have to teach children their native language. Research is abundant to indicate that the average five-year-old comes to school with an intuitive knowledge of the language, its patterns and grammar, as well as with an extensive vocabulary. Despite this fact, too many teachers set out to teach children "English" as if it were a foreign language. (Even this is a poor analogy, since teachers of a second language realize that language is best taught through behaving in it rather than by talking about it.)

Kohl (1971) made some telling comments on this point:

> Imagine a mother worrying about how to teach her child to talk. The child is six months old; the sounds he makes are just beginning to be intelligible. He wants to communicate and is straining himself to be understood. And his mother worries about how to teach him the whole of language. She wonders whether she ought to start with grammar or vocabulary, whether to correct his mistakes or let him do it himself. She

worries about the dialect he will learn, about his ability to talk in full sentences, to distinguish vowel and consonant sounds. She might even wonder how to reduce the whole thing to developmental stages and teach him programed talking. [© 1971 Saturday Review Magazine Co. Reprinted by permission.]

Obviously, under such circumstances, most children would never learn to speak their native language! In other words, a major job of the teacher is to provide the environment—the stimulation, guidance, and audience—that will free children to use language in writing as they have learned to use it in speech. The real job of the teacher of "English" is to truly *educate* in the original sense of "drawing out" to a conscious level that wealth of language that most children bring to school with them.

One aspect of the writing environment to be considered is the interrelationship of the total language arts: reading, writing, speaking, and listening. Integration of the language arts is a positive and a popular theme these days, but it too can be carried to extremes. In an excellent summary of research on the interrelationships, Stotsky (1983) reported that teaching reading *skills* will result in improved reading but will not influence writing skill; teaching writing *skills* will result in improved writing but will not influence reading skill. In other words, skill instruction in either subject area will increase skill in *that* area only. Does it come as any surprise that children learn what we teach and do not learn what we do not teach?

On the positive side, however, Stotsky indicated that additional reading experience is as good as or better than grammar study for increasing writing skill. In fact, she found that additional reading is also as good as or better than *additional* writing practice for increasing writing skill. Wide reading has long been recognized in the research as the best means of broadening vocabulary, and we at least strongly suspect that it also develops an awareness of style, the variety of ways of expressing ideas.

Perhaps the teaching of writing would have no greater stimulus than if teachers themselves would write. It is a known fact that most teachers do not write. Recently, a number of teachers in several midwestern school districts admitted that they would like to improve their ability to teach writing, but they refused to participate in a planned workshop on writing because they themselves were going to have to write every day. They felt—like the young adults in the national assessment—that they "couldn't write."

Unless the teacher writes, how is that teacher to understand the problems faced by the writer? Actually, as the "Perfessor" said in the comic strip "Shoe,"

> Writing is simple, Muffy. First you have to make sure you have lots of paper, sharp pencils, typewriter ribbon, and you put your belly up to the desk. You roll a sheet of paper into the typewriter and you stare at it until beads of blood appear on your forehead. [Reprinted by permission: Tribune Company Syndicate, Inc.]

Nobody ever said that writing would be easy. Nor is the *teaching* of writing easy. However, experiencing the process will provide the teacher with deeper understanding of the problems and concerns and will certainly result in better teaching of the process. Such experience will probably result in understanding that the writing itself is not really so much fun; it is sometimes painful. The pleasure begins to creep in as the writer plays with that finished first draft—the end is in sight. The true pleasure is in viewing the finished piece and is doubled when someone reads and reacts to the product.

In guiding fledgling writers, the teacher may be helped in understanding their difficulties by using a distinction made by Moffett and Wagner (1983). They point out two discrete aspects of writing: composing and transcribing. Composing consists of determining the content and selecting and organizing the ideas and ultimately the words; transcribing is a matter of converting this equivalent of speech into print and includes mechanics such as letter formation, spelling, capitalization, and punctuation. For example, if an executive dictates a letter to the stenographer, who then types it, who "wrote" that letter? Both had a hand in the letter: The executive composed it, and the stenographer transcribed it.

The major point here is not to place a value judgment on the two activities, although that too has implications. Which is more important, the composing—the content and style of the message—or the transcribing—the correct format and mechanics? Even more pertinent in teaching, by recognizing the two distinct elements the teacher may unearth and remove the stumbling blocks for some children. For the youngster whose problem lies in transcribing, the teacher may work around that to encourage composing through dictation while working to strengthen some of the mechanics that cause the problem. Conversely, if the problem is in composing, models, guidance, and practice on that aspect can lead to improvement.

In addition to providing an appropriate environment to stimulate and to free writing, there is some teaching to be done. What are the components of a good writing program for any classroom? Let's consider the major elements briefly here in what amounts to a summary overview of the balance of this book.

ELEMENTS OF A WRITING PROGRAM

As implied in the Preface, I was faced with the same dilemma that you, as a teacher, face: Where does one begin in dealing with the myriad of skills, understandings, and attitudes that must be developed—and taught—if pupils are to learn to write well? As Ciardi once said, "The good writer has mastered thousands of particulars." Perhaps this is another reason for some of our problems in teaching writing: We want to do everything at once, and, as a result, we do nothing well.

Not only are there thousands of particulars, but these particulars are recursive: The writer goes back and forth from one aspect to another. Composing might seem a logical first step, but composing takes place throughout the process of writing, even in revising. And some revising may take place during the writing of the first draft. Certainly skill instruction may occur before, during, and/or after the actual writing. Nevertheless, since everything can't be discussed at once, let's proceed with a somewhat logical sequence. That sequence should include:

> prewriting and composing
> writing
> skill instruction
> editing
> publishing
> evaluating

Prewriting and Composing

No one takes out a piece of paper and immediately begins writing on a subject not deliberated upon prior to that moment. Consider what you do with even such a basic type of writing as making out a grocery list. Do you merely take paper and pencil and begin listing? Of course not. You may mentally consider what is in the cabinet, freezer, refrigerator, and so on as you methodically examine your needs. Or you may keep the paper handy and add as the needs arise.

So it is with other kinds of writing. It takes time for thoughts to jell. With older students that time may be spent in quiet staring at the paper or the walls; with younger ones it may be a matter of group discussion or brainstorming. Ideas and techniques for the prewriting stage are discussed in Chapter 3.

During or before this prewriting, children often need to be stimulated with ideas about which to write. Although the best pieces of writing usually come from the ideas of the children themselves, those thoughts can be triggered by suggestions from the teacher. Of course, the teacher's problem is that the "well" eventually runs dry. Chapter 4 contains a wealth of ideas for stimulating writing.

Writing

One of the secrets of a well-ogranized writing class is that it may appear somewhat chaotic. If all are doing the same thing at the same time, something is wrong. No two individuals are likely to be at the same stage in a piece of writing at a given time. Some will be revising or proofreading their papers; others may be engaged in a final draft; still others will be at the prewriting or initial writing stage. Classroom organization for writing is discussed in Chapter 2, as well as in Chapter 8 as part of conferencing.

The time that students are engaged in actual writing is not a time for the teacher to be grading the math papers. It is a valuable time also to be participating in writing and to be circulating within the classroom, holding conferences with students about their pieces of writing, providing guidance on problems, or just showing an interest in the content of some of the writing. Procedures for conferencing are discussed in Chapter 8.

Skill Instruction

Instruction on the many skills required for good writing may take a variety of forms. At times, it may be on an individual basis for some specific problem that can be handled quickly during the conference. Most often it will be in small groups with youngsters who have the same difficulty. At other times the total class may benefit from certain experiences.

Throughout the year, wide reading and the sharing of reading must be part of the program. Youngsters may share from that reading about unusual or interesting ways of expressing an idea, different techniques for describing characters or scenes, or even unusual word choices. This topic is explored in Chapter 4.

Students need to gain skill in sentence flexibility. Here the entire class may benefit from instruction and practice with sentence combining, an activity discussed in Chapter 7.

The effective writer is a fluent writer: The words flow smoothly in the process of writing. Furthermore, that writer must have an adequate vocabulary with which to express the ideas intended. Wide reading, stimulating an interest in language for its own sake, and use of a thesaurus are among the means suggested in Chapter 5 to develop vocabulary.

Whenever one talks about skill instruction in writing, the role of grammar is bound to arise. Evidence on the lack of effectiveness of teaching formal grammar is abundant, and that evidence, along with some activities that may be more beneficial than traditional approaches to grammar, is presented in Chapter 7.

Among the mechanics to be taught, spelling is a major consideration by most teachers. Chapter 9 presents a research-based approach that will not only improve pupils' skill in spelling correctly but, through greater efficiency, also will provide some much-needed additional time for the teacher.

Since there is already a wealth of information and exercises dealing with the mechanics of format, capitalization, and punctuation, Chapter 10 is brief in providing some direction on those elements.

Editing

Chapter 11 deals with two major and often neglected aspects of writing, the editing tasks of revision and proofreading.

Most often, students, whether in elementary school or high school, consider a first draft the final draft of a piece of writing. They need to realize that even the most experienced writer goes back over a first draft and revises. Often the teaching of revision can begin with group revision of a piece placed on the overhead projector. Revision itself deals with style, word choice, organization, and like details.

In contrast to revision, proofreading deals with mechanics, the correctness or courtesy involved in writing. This too needs to be taught, not merely admonished to children as too often happens. Mere knowledge of a particular skill of mechanics does not ensure its use in proofreading. The skill of proofreading for each specific element must be taught and practiced in order for those skills to be applied to writing.

Publishing

"Publication" is the final stage for a finished piece of writing. The term is used here in its broadest sense, that is, in the sense that ultimately someone is expected to read and to react to the content of the writing. One of the major points on this topic is that the reader need not—in fact, should not—always be the teacher. If youngsters are writing as much and as often as they should be, it will be impossible for the teacher to read everything. Other options for "publication," as well as sources for publication in the more limited sense of commercial outlets, are discussed in Chapter 12.

Evaluating

Finally, Chapter 13 presents techniques for evaulating the success of the writing endeavor, both with individual students in the classroom and with the wider school community of total class, school, or school district. This topic is a broad one, encompassing both the variety of purposes for evaluation and the assortment of means that might be used to accomplish those purposes.

SUMMARY

This chapter has presented the basic philosophy of writing that underlies the entire book, a viewpoint that defines writing as an act meant to communicate a message to a reader. Growing out of the philosophy was a set of prioritized working criteria to be shared with pupils and to be used on a day-to-day basis for evaluating writing: clarity, interest appeal, and correctness.

Following a review of some of the reasons writing is not well taught—a documented fact—the elements of a writing program were presented and briefly commented upon. These elements, always recursive and repetitive in actual writing, include: prewriting and composing, writing, skill instruction, editing, publishing, and evaluating. The remainder of the book presents procedures and techniques to implement the program.

SUGGESTIONS FOR ACTION

(This section will be found at the end of each chapter. In remaining chapters most items will refer to activities you may want to do with your pupils. The collection of suggestions is really a potpourri from which to choose; it is not a list of items to be accomplished.)

1. Think back on the last "writing lesson" you taught. What were the elements included? Did some teaching take place, or was it another of the assign–write–evaluate lessons? (If you are not teaching at present, visit a class and observe.)

2. How does writing rank with other subject areas in your classroom in terms of time allocated? If writing is not given a major share of time, do your reasons match with those given in this chapter? If not, what are your reasons for not devoting more time to writing? Check with others in your school to see how much time they devote to writing.

3. Try a little informal survey of yourself and colleagues. Inquire as to the major purpose for writing; then ask how writing is evaluated. Is the means of evaluation consistent with the stated purpose?

4. The next time your pupils write, *you* write with them. Share your writing too. What are the reactions?

5. What is your major concern in teaching writing, recalling that you can't do everything at once any more than children can? Review "Elements of a Writing Program" (a few pages back) to pick the chapter that you feel will help you the most. That's the place to start.

6. Finally, do you at least have access to, if not subscribe to, *Language Arts?* This monthly publication of the National Council of Teachers of English will keep you abreast of the latest in teaching written expression.

REFERENCES

APPLEBEE, A. N., F. LEAR; and A. AUTEN, *"Learning to Write in the Secondary School: How and Where," English Journal,* 70 (September, 1981), 78–82. Reports a survey of recommended secondary English teachers, identifying what they did in writing.

BRIDWELL, L. S., "Rethinking Composing," *English Journal,* 70 (November, 1981), 96–99. Expresses concern, based on research, for having students move beyond the "first and only draft" in their writing.

BRITTON, JAMES, TONY BURGESS, NANCY MARTIN, ALEX McLEOD, and HAROLD ROSEN, *The Development of Writing Abilities (11–18).* London: Macmillan Education, 1975. (Distributed by National Council of Teachers of English.) Reports results of a study of the classification of writing into expressive, transactional, and poetic.

HALEY-JAMES, SHIRLEY (ed.), *Perspectives on Writing in Grades 1–8.* Urbana, Illinois: National Council of Teachers of English, 1981. Presents evidence and current thinking on improving skill in writing.

HILLERICH, ROBERT L., "Evaluating Process and Product in Children's Writing." Presentation at National Council of Teachers of English National Convention, November 23, 1973. Published in *Kansas English,* 60 (December, 1974), 2–7. Summarizes evidence to support the position that emphasis on the process of writing will improve the product.

KOHL, HERBERT, *Saturday Review,* March 20, 1971, pg. 55. Comments critically on the teaching of "English" in a review of several books about language.

MOFFETT, JAMES, *Teaching the Universe of Discourse.* Boston: Houghton Mifflin, 1983. Presents Moffett's theory of discourse, including all areas of reading, writing, and speaking.

MOFFETT, JAMES, and BETTY JANE WAGNER, *Student-Centered Language Arts and Reading, K–13.* Boston: Houghton Mifflin, 1983. An excellent presentation of theory and practice in the total language arts.

MYERS, MILES, and JAMES GRAY (ed.), *Theory and Practice in the Teaching of Composition: Processing, Distancing, and Modeling.* Urbana: National Council of Teachers of English, 1983. An excellent collection of articles on the three aspects of the subtitle.

NATIONAL ASSESSMENT OF EDUCATIONAL PROGRESS, *Writing Objectives for 1973–74 Assessment.* Denver: Education Commission of the States, 1972a. Discusses procedures for developing the writing objectives.

——, *Writing: National Results—Writing Mechanics, Report No. 8.* Denver: Education Commission of the States, 1972b. Reports results of the first assessment in terms of mechanics of writing.

——, "NAEP Newsletter," 13 (Winter, 1980–81), 1–3. Compares results of the three national assessments in writing for nine-, thirteen-, and seventeen-year-olds.

PETTIGREW, J., R. A. SHAW, and A. D. VAN NOSTRAND, *"Collaborative Analysis of Writing Instruction," Research in the Teaching of English,* 15 (December, 1981), 329–41. Describes the unique qualities of writing, based on observations in eight classrooms.

STOTSKY, SANDRA, "Research on Reading/Writing Relationships: A Synthesis and Suggested Directions," *Language Arts,* 60 (May, 1983), 627–42. Summarizes research on the interrelationships of reading and writing instruction on achievement in the two areas.

2

Organizing
the Classroom
for Writing

He is a great teacher who practices what he teaches.
COLUMBANUS, A.D. 600

LET'S FACE IT: Of all the questions teachers might have about any subject area, the most persistent, most pervading, and most difficult have to do with classroom management. I don't believe I have ever conducted an inservice session on any aspect of language arts without having teachers bring to the fore their serious concerns about organization and management.

Unfortunately, this is also an area where research has failed, and probably will continue to fail, to provide answers. A basic reason for this failure, I believe, is that so much of classroom management relates to teacher personality: What works for you might prove utter disaster for me. Of course, what works for you today might not work too well for you tomorrow; children are also a variable in the mix.

This chapter no doubt will also fail to provide "the answer," but it will present ideas that have proven successful with different teachers capable of varying degrees of individualization. Hence, we will present three stages in classroom management, ranging from the traditional, from which all teachers should be moving, to the ideal, toward which we should all strive. First, however, let's review a few basic principles on which any classroom plan should rest.

BASIC PRINCIPLES

The following might be considered a recall of Ed Psych 101, yet a refresher on these points is always in order:

1. Children want to communicate. Humans are social animals who learn language naturally—if not instinctively.

2. Children want to learn. Ask any parent for a tabulation of the preschooler's expressions. The most common are questions: Why? When? Where? How?

3. Children want to please. Research on the question of cheating has revealed that youngsters don't cheat merely to raise grades or to avoid punishment; they cheat in order to please an authority figure, whether teacher or parent.

4. Children possess a wealth of language. Research (see Chapter 4) reveals that the average five-year-old has mastered the sentence patterns of English and has an impressive oral vocabulary of several thousand words. It is up to us to capitalize on this store of language and to help the child use print as well as voice to express ideas.

We could continue with an expanded list, but what more do we need? These four principles—the desire to learn, to communicate, to please, and the ability to communicate—provide the perfect foundation for a classroom writing program. All we need to do is to make the most of them.

THE TRADITIONAL ORGANIZATION

Classroom visitation reveals the traditional to be the most common approach to the teaching or writing. Let's observe the situation and then offer a critique of it.

The Classroom Procedure

"All right, boys and girls. Please turn in your math papers and have your pencil and paper ready. It's time for writing."

With math papers dutifully collected, the teacher introduces the topic for today's writing assignment. Perhaps Halloween is approaching, so the topic is "One scary night..." With the teacher, youngsters are encouraged to talk about scary things they recall. In the process, some will contribute almost entire stories; others will participate very little.

Once the preliminary discussion is completed, youngsters are told to write their stories. While the writing is being done, the teacher will grade the math papers or the spelling test from earlier in the day, interrupted frequently by "How do you spell...?"

Keeping one eye on the group, the teacher determines by the degree of restlessness that it is about time to discontinue the writing, so she says, "You have five more minutes. Be certain to proofread your papers before you turn them in."

Once the papers are collected, the class moves on to another subject. The teacher is left with a pile of papers to grade. That grading may take place in the teachers' lounge, during the faculty meeting, or at home that night. The next day, some papers may be shared, and/or some with smiling faces may be posted as examples on the bulletin board.

What Happened? First of all, this traditional approach is known as a *product* emphasis, as opposed to a *process* emphasis. Stress is on the outcome, the finished product, as opposed to the techniques or procedures for writing. The objective is to evaluate finished papers for correctness.

At the beginning of this lesson, math stopped and writing started, as if one could press a button marked "writing" and things would automatically begin happening. Have you found this to be true in your own experience, even with all of the practice you've had? If so, you belong to a very special—and very limited—class of people. Most of us need some warm-up; most of us suffer from what I call "blank-paperitis." Writers need some time to think, to mull over, before they can begin to put ideas on paper. This kind of prewriting is discussed in detail in Chapter 3.

The teacher did engage in some prewriting activity, however. She encouraged some discussion of the topic before youngsters wrote. She did not, however, list any words on the board and, as a result of this omission, was interrupted frequently for spellings. Of course, the interruptions for spellings were symptomatic of another problem with this kind of writing class—a problem that could have been avoided if the teacher had established a climate in which youngsters knew that correct spelling was a concern in the editing stage of the writing.

A topic was *assigned* by the teacher, as if everyone in the group were interested in that topic today. Meanwhile, Cari was excited about her visit to the zoo, Erin had narrowly avoided missing the bus, and Sean was bubbling over to tell about his new baby hamsters. Evidence is clear that children—not to mention adults—will write more and write better on a personal topic, one they know and are interested in.

Any prewriting activity that involves group discussion of the topic is a double-edged sword: It has its good and bad sides. On the positive, such discussion does get ideas flowing and suggests appropriate word choices. However, it may also lead to carbon copies of the story: Many children will merely put down what they heard discussed. Likewise, listing words on the board will avoid some of the questions about spelling, but it may also entrap some children in the story of others.

While pupils were writing, what did the teacher do? Anything but write or teach. In other words, children were merely given an opportunity to practice what they knew. While practice in writing is important in itself, we certainly can do more. At the very least, we know that adult modeling makes an important contribution to children's interest and skill in writing. Why didn't the teacher let youngsters know that writing is important by engaging in that activity with them?

In addition to the worthwhile option of writing, the teacher might have taken advantage of the time during which pupils wrote as an opportunity to offer individual help on problems, to encourage ideas, to judge needs, or merely to become familiar with some of the pieces of writing those youngsters were doing at the time.

The lesson was concluded abruptly, as if all writers finished at the same time. Worse, children were then admonished to "proofread" their papers without any direction as to what to proofread for or how to do it. What does such an admonition mean to a second-grader—or even to an eighth-grader, for that matter? If anyone is to be successful in proofreading, that individual must first have been taught the mechanical skill or skills involved and must then be taught how to proofread for the item or items. At any K–8 level, certainly direction must be more specific than merely to "proofread your papers."

Finally, the teacher collected the papers. For what purpose? So she could go error hunting with the red pencil! This is evaluation of the product. From such an evaluation youngsters learn nothing about how to improve their writing. They look at the grade and possibly glance at the red marks before discarding the paper. They do learn that the purpose of writing is to put correct spellings and punctuation on the paper. Worse, they learn—as demonstrated in the national assessment—that they should use "easy" words so that they will spell correctly, and they learn to write less so that there will be fewer opportunities for error.

We might ask again, what was the purpose in this writing? It was not to communicate ideas to any reader; it was to satisfy the demand of the teacher. This is not an ideal purpose for any kind of writing.

In summary, we had a typical writing lesson in which the major elements were assign, write, and error hunt. More specifically, we can see at least the following problems:

1. The group was in a lockstep in terms of time for writing.
2. The teacher determined the topic.
3. Prewriting was a group process.
4. Youngsters called out for spellings.

5. Writing took place without teacher participation.

6. Proofreading was admonished, not taught.

7. The teacher error hunted after the writing.

8. There was no "publishing," at least for most papers.

Let's see if our next teacher can improve on this approach.

A FEW STEPS FORWARD

Many teachers have improved on the traditional approach. They have kept up on professional reading and have followed some of the evidence on how to improve skill in written expression. Although these efforts are still not ideal, we see some definite improvements over the traditional classroom writing session.

The Classroom Procedure

"All right, boys and girls. Please turn in your math papers and have your pencil and paper ready. It's time for writing."

When the math papers have been collected, the teacher introduces several topics. Again, "One scary night..." might be among them, but the teacher adds, "Some of you wanted to talk about the trip we made to the zoo last week. Maybe you'd like to write about that. José, you said your grandmother was visiting; did you want to tell us about the visit?

"Remember to think about what you want to write. If you have trouble with a topic, you might want to choose one from the list I have on the board. I haven't decided what I want to write about yet myself."

As youngsters and teacher begin their writing, quiet is expected. After the teacher has written for about five minutes, she gets up and begins moving about the classroom, noticing what children are writing, offering help on topics, clarifying with them some of the ideas they are considering, and so on. At this stage, her focus is not on mechanics but on the organization and presentation of the ideas the children want to express.

When a youngster signals for help on spelling, the teacher jots the word on one of the scraps of paper she carries and puts it on the child's desk. Others signal with questions about the content of their writing, and the teacher is there to offer help.

As some pupils finish writing, the teacher reminds them to read aloud softly what they have written to hear how it sounds, or they may exchange with others to see if the reader has any questions where ideas may be unclear or incomplete.

Having finished this stage, children understand that they are to hand their papers over to the "editors-for-the-week" to be checked for mechanics before being shared with the group, added to the bulletin board collection, or returned to their individual writing folders.

Periodically, this teacher reviews an element of mechanics she has taught, demonstrates how to proofread for that item, and then has youngsters proofread for that item on one of their completed papers. These papers are collected immediately after so that she can examine them to determine which children have now mastered that particular skill and which ones need further instruction. Even here, the teacher does not put the corrections on the papers; she notes who needs reteaching and plans to bring them together in a small group to provide that instruction.

Every paper is shared in some fashion. Some are exchanged with buddies for reading, some shared in a small group, and a few shared with the entire class. The teacher also collects the writing folders on a staggered basis to get an overview of the contents, make comments on the ideas presented, note progress, and identify an outstanding item or two on which a given child needs instruction. Most of that instruction takes place in small groups brought together because of a common need.

What Happened? In this classroom the teacher has moved toward breaking the lockstep. Even though a given period of time was still allocated for the entire class to engage in writing, all were not expected to be at the same point at the same time. Some of the children were involved in evaluating or editing while others were in the stage of initial writing.

In introducing the topic, the teacher did make some suggestions on what to write about, but she also left the options open. Children were free to select their own topics. This teacher knew that children did best with topics of their own choosing, but she also felt that some would sit until a topic was provided for them. Hence she compromised, trying to stimulate thinking about several topics so that chidren could choose what suited them.

During the writing, the teacher performed two important functions. First, she modeled writing: She wrote. If the teacher writes too, then writing must be pretty important. We might also hope that she shared that writing—especially an early draft—with the group. In fact, one of the most impressive situations I know was that of an eighth-grade English teacher who accepted a writing assignment from her class, stood in front of the class at the overhead projector, and began writing on that assignment. She held the attention of that group for the entire period as they saw her, an experienced English teacher, suffer through the process of composing, rethinking, scratching out, and just plain struggling to get something worthwhile on paper. Certainly that was a memorable experience for those students who previously must have thought that writing was easy for everyone but themselves.

Second, during the writing the teacher circulated about the class offering individual help and talking with pupils about what they were writing. This practice not only enabled that teacher to discover what individuals needed at the time, it also kept her in touch with what they were writing about and how they were doing it, and it enabled her to show a personal interest in their writing. Even if conferencing goes no further than this demonstration of personal interest in content, it makes a great contribution to children's enthusiasm and interest in writing.

Although interruptions to ask about spellings were done quietly, they were still an unnecessary interference that we hope the teacher is working on. She has been attempting to get her youngsters to realize that spelling concerns belong in the editing stage of writing and that they can get help on all words at once at that point. During the writing they need merely to underline (or in some other way identify) words they are uncertain about so that those items can be cleared up in the final stage of editing. And this teacher carried about a small pad of scratch paper to write the spellings on, thus avoiding the need to go to the board to write each word—or worse, to repeat a spelling ten times orally before the youngster got the entire word down.

The suggestion of soft oral reading to edit their papers for content was a good one. Further, sharing the paper with a friend for suggestions was an excellent idea. Oftentimes we think ideas on paper are clear when we reread our own work, but another may not find it so. It is much easier for us—and for children—to catch poor word choice, confusion, fragments, or what have you in the writing of another than it is to see it in our own.

The rotating team of editors can be helpful in ensuring that all youngsters get experience in the task of proofreading. Fortunately, this teacher has not left full responsibility for this task in the hands of the "editors." She reviews mechanics taught and teaches her children to proofread for them. As in the case of adults, the writer is expected to do his or her own proofreading before the final stage, wherein editors repeat the process. You will notice that this teacher took herself out of the role of editor in this class. In the process, she was not only free to do more important things, she also undoubtedly has children writing more because the papers will not be stacking up for her to mark.

In terms of the mechanics, teaching takes place before the writing, specific items are to be proofread for, and a check for those items leads to clues for reteaching of certain individuals.

"Publication" takes place in a variety of ways and with all papers. After all, the purpose of writing is to communicate ideas to a reader. Furthermore, the fact that the teacher does not edit the papers is not to suggest that she doesn't react to them. The individual language folders— or language "logs," as we'll call them—are collected periodically, a few at a time. Examination of these enables the teacher to react to writings and to evaluate progress. It also enables a more realistic approach to arriving at that *not* necessary—but *usually* required—evil, the report card grade. No individual progresses or regresses that much from day to day, or even from week to week. It is from a collection of writings that the teacher can arrive at a realistic assessment of how each child is doing in written expression.

In summary, we might contrast with the previous class a number of important items about class organization for writing:

1. Within the lockstep of time the group members had some flexibility in terms of what they were doing.
2. While still supplying suggestions or stimuli, the teacher allowed great freedom in the selection of a writing topic.
3. Prewriting became more individual within the given time frame.
4. Interruptions requesting help in spelling were less obvious.
5. During the writing, the teacher also wrote and circulated about the class to offer individual help.
6. Revision was modestly addressed by having pupils orally read their papers and/or exchange with a friend.
7. Proofreading was taught rather than merely admonished.
8. The teacher used demonstrated difficulties in content, organization, or mechanics as clues for reteaching or individual help.
9. All papers were "published"—that is, they were all read by someone.

Obviously this teacher has moved a long way from the traditional approach, but there is still a way to go. One of her problems is that writing is not a school-wide priority. She has had considerable reorienting to do and has some future goals in mind for her class organization. Let's see what she is working toward, a level she might already be working at with her children had she been in a school where writing was stressed from kindergarten on.

CLASS ORGANIZATION IN A WRITING SCHOOL

Because somewhat different activities take place in kindergarten and early first grade—the "pre-handwriting" stage—we'll look at several classes in this school where written expression is a priority. Or do you question that "writing" can take place before children learn to form letters or spell words?

At least two elements of writing occur with most children in the preschool years and certainly by kindergarten age. First, considering Moffett and Wagner's (1983) distinction between composing and transcribing, kindergarteners can and do compose. In fact, even in telling a story from pictures, kindergarten children will often stop midway, mumble to themselves as they compose, and then proceed with their narration.

Second, writing is a matter of encoding ideas in print. As others have pointed out, if you ask a preschooler, "Can you read?" that child will usually reply, "No." But if you ask, "Can you write?" most often the answer is "Yes." Kindergarteners will often caption their drawings with some scribbles or even with random letters to represent a title or idea. This kind of representation is an important step toward writing.

The Classroom Procedure in Kindergarten

Mr. Smith has twenty-five kindergarteners in his class. He's found that parent volunteers or senior citizens, as well as older pupils in the school, provide him with the extra "ears" to keep his youngsters talking. Even when no help is available, he manages to work with small groups, since he's established a rotating procedure. While he's working with Lea's group, Jack's group is at the puzzle table and Sherry's group is in the book corner. Meanwhile, Jan is in the back talking to that untiring pair of "ears," the tape recorder that Mr. Smith taught the children to use when he is busy and there's no one else around to hear what they have to say.

Today Jack's group is listening while Pete "reads" a story from a wordless picture book. As often happens with some of their show-and-tell experiences, the youngsters decide that they want to "write" the story to share with the rest of the class. If so, it will become a language experience story, with Mr. Smith serving as recorder. Sometimes the children decide each to do their own drawing from the story, and Mr. Smith helps them put a label or description under the illustration.

These youngsters have also become skilled listeners. They expect what they hear to make sense. Mr. Smith repeatedly asks if anything has been left out, and the youngsters are beginning to make good use of "Why?" "When?" "How?"

The Classroom Procedure in Other Grades

With an oral language foundation well established from kindergarten on, writing is a daily activity in all classes. Every classroom has its writing center, usually next to the library shelf. It may be a collection of desks, or it may be a table and chairs. Always it is inviting and well stocked with pencils, pens, and markers—colored as well as black—paper, and all kinds of story starters, from old greeting cards to magazine pictures. Everyone knows that it is a place for quiet work.

In most classes, a common time frame is still observed for writing, but writing is also a "free time" activity and has replaced many of the duplicated worksheets that used to be so commonplace. Mrs. Kohl, a first-grade teacher, has found still another way to impress her children with the purpose and value of writing. Since February, she has had a weekly period during which all communication is in writing. She, or any child who wishes to say something to the group, must do so on the chalkboard. Individual communiques are by note. Her children look forward to the weekly "silent" time.

In every classroom each child has a language log. Although it takes different forms, it is often a type of notebook or folder in which writing is kept and notes are made. From second grade on, this is also the last item to be used each day, when pupils are given a few minutes to collect their thoughts and to note the important happenings of the day. In examining some of these logs, we find a considerable collection of writings, some very tentative and others in a second or third draft. Inside each cover is a chart on which the teacher has recorded specifics that the youngster has mastered, along with the date when mastery was demonstrated. Some of these charts reveal quite a record of progress, and even the poorest student could point to this as concrete evidence of some accomplishment.

Most upper-grade teachers, like Miss Thompson, also use the language log to have students record the major learnings from science or social studies. In fact, many of these teachers have found this to be better than a review to help students find out what they do or don't know and better than a test to help them determine students' understanding or lack of understanding of the day's work.

Although these teachers may provide stimuli for writing, most of the writing is done on topics of the children's own choice. The fact that few are writing on the same topic adds incentive and interest in hearing what each wrote about.

In Miss Taylor's class it seems common practice for children to pass notes to one another. When questioned about her apparent oblivion to this activity, Miss Taylor only laughed. "Can you think of a better way to stimulate writing or to help children realize that the purpose of writing is to communicate a message to a reader?" All teachers are not quite so tolerant, but many provide mailboxes for the exchange of notes during class breaks.

Mrs. Walsh's fourth grade might be typical of the other classes. Upon entry, a visitor will be aware of a busy hum as students cluster in pairs or small groups while some quietly work on their own. Mrs. Walsh has just finished a haiku she was attempting and is now holding conferences. She schedules her more lengthy conferences during part of the writing time, but she always allows some of that time to move about the class, talking for a minute with individuals about their progress.

We notice that the conference in progress deals with Michele's completed first draft. Michele has long been accustomed to writing on every other line so that there will be room for revision, and she knows that a finished first draft is not a final product. Mrs. Walsh has raised a point about an unclear sequence in the story, and Michele seems to agree that it needs to be reorganized. Noticeably, Mrs. Walsh does not put a mark on the paper. She knows that the minute she takes over she has relieved Michele of the responsibility: As the teacher she will then have taken over "ownership" of that story. Furthermore, she respects Michele's right to tell her own story, not the story that Mrs. Walsh might like to tell.

Meanwhile, several children have gotten together in a small group to share some of their stories. They agree that one needs some more work, but another is so good that they ask Mrs. Walsh if it could be read to the entire class. Further, they know that all of their stories will be read by someone and that periodically they may choose a favorite to be posted, put in the class newspaper, or added to the class anthology.

Several of the youngsters are using the first-grade vocabulary to write "books" for first graders to read themselves. This has proven to be a popular activity and is beneficial to both the writers and the readers.

As time begins to run out, Mrs. Walsh reminds her pupils to get to a stopping point for now and to put their materials in their logs. She also asks three of them for their logs for her to review that evening.

We missed some of the important activities that take place in Mrs. Walsh's class. For example, the day before, she brought the entire class together to participate in group revision. Using one of the better pieces of writing from her class, she put it on a transparency, and together the youngsters found its strong points. Some identified excellent word choice, the clear organization, and even an unusual manner of stating an idea. Youngsters tried different sentence patterns to decide if those used were the best for the ideas expressed.

Tomorrow Mrs. Walsh plans several small group instructional sessions on different aspects of mechanics that have presented problems to the individuals concerned. She also plans a total group activity dealing with proofreading. Here she will make up the poor example herself rather than risk embarrassing any individual.

Except for the small and ever-changing instructional groups for specific skills, most teachers have found that ability groups of any kind are unnecessary in the writing class. Children at all grades work most of the time independently or in small clusters. A natural result is that all children are working on their own level and at their own rate.

What Happened? It was obvious in this school that language—oral and written—had a high priority and that the key was flexibility. Emphasis was on the process of writing, with the conviction that the appropriate process would result in superior products. Individualization was not seen as merely one-to-one instruction; flexible groups were based on need, and at times total group instruction was appropriate.

Oral language experience, with an interest in ideas and words, began in the kindergarten and continued from there. Children learned very early that language should make sense and that they may need to question.

Although a fixed time frame was also apparent, writing went beyond that period and was standard procedure for much of the day. It was used to communicate with others, and it was used to consolidate and summarize learning. Furthermore, flexibility within the time frame allowed for each child to be working at a different stage in the development of a piece of writing.

Ever-present language logs served as a method of collecting writing and related items. They also provided a convenient means for the teacher to review a child's work over a period of time, as well as for children to summarize what they had learned during the day. Assessment and diagnosis came from a collection of materials and was not dependent upon daily "grading" of writing.

"Teaching" took many forms in these classrooms. At times it was with the total group on a common need, as in the case of group revision and proofreading practice. At other times it was on a small group basis as several children were brought together because they shared a common instructional need. Refinement and smaller or more personalized points were accomplished in the brief conference time with each child.

Probably most important of all the observations were the facts that youngsters retained "ownership" of their writing—Mrs. Walsh did not redo their work in her own fashion—and all materials were read by someone, a reader who was interested in the content rather than only in the mechanics.

In summary, classes in this school have taken the next steps toward improving the teaching of writing:

1. Within the time frame, children had great flexibility in terms of their own activities.
2. Most writing ideas came from the children themselves.
3. Prewriting was completely individualized.
4. Interruptions for help in spelling were nonexistent.
5. During the writing, the teacher also wrote and circulated about the class holding conferences.
6. Language logs served as depositories for writing as well as records of progress.
7. Proofreading and revision were taught.
8. Youngsters retained responsibility for their writing because teachers did not take over their papers by marking on them.
9. The teacher used demonstrated difficulties as clues for reteaching or individual help.
10. All papers were "published" in that they were all read by someone.

In comparison with the better class in the previous section, it is clear that the major changes were the school-wide emphasis on oral language as a foundation for writing, greater flexibility of activity during the writing time, broader use of writing, and the more intensive use of conferencing. This last point is most important, and conferencing will be discussed in detail in Chapter 8.

Perhaps I should conclude here with a word of clarification. Nothing here is meant to imply that the traditional mechanics of capitalization, punctuation, and spelling are not important. What is meant—and is clearly supported by the research—is that the traditional approach had not improved these mechanics. In fact, evidence comparing groups whose papers have been corrected with groups where only the ideas have been reacted to indicates that the latter not only wrote better but, in three-fourths of the studies, made fewer errors in mechanics. One-fourth of these studies reported that there was no significant difference. *Not one study* has reported that "correcting" the papers decreased the number of mechanical errors as compared with groups whose papers were not so corrected (Hillerich, 1979).

SUMMARY

This chapter began with four basic tenets: Children want to communicate, want to learn, want to please, and have a vast store of language ability when they begin school. Suggestions for classroom organization of a writing program were then presented through three stages, from traditional, to improved, to the kind of situation suggested by current thinking and research.

Traditional writing classes kept all youngsters doing the same thing at the same time and focused on assigning, writing, and correcting, with the admonition to proofread sometimes included. Improved organization came through more flexibility during the writing time, teaching of skills instead of "error hunting," teacher participation in writing and conferencing, and emphasis on "publication," that is, someone's reading and reacting to the content of the papers.

The goal is even more flexibility within the writing period, turning that period into more of a workshop, writing at many other times and for other purposes, peer participation in revision, and conferencing as a focus for determining needs, recording progress, and giving individual help. In essence, we know that putting the focus on improving the process will ensure improvement of the product.

SUGGESTIONS FOR ACTION

Just as children are at different stages in their development, so too we as teachers are at different levels of growth. Assess where you and your students are now and, from that point, try some of the ideas you may not have considered to date. As you well know, no new activity is going to have an impact on your pupils overnight; stay with it for a few weeks, at least, before expecting change.

1. Set up and outfit a writing center in your classroom. Stock it with ample writing supplies and with pictures, story starters, and even with some examples of writing from your pupils.

2. Have youngsters keep a language log for their writing. Then see how flexible you can get. Can they all be at different stages in a piece of writing? Maybe you'll begin with just a few of the better writers and expand as others show the ability to take responsibility.

3. Clarify with students the three criteria discussed in Chapter 1. Then you and your children apply them to examples of writing. Raise questions when necessary about the clarity and interest appeal of that initial draft, to get the focus on content rather than on mechanics.

4. If you don't already do so, begin conferencing on an informal basis by merely circulating around the room during writing time and showing an interest in the content of what your pupils write. You'll be surprised at the interest this generates.

5. Use peer groups for sharing writings. With emphasis on the suggested criteria, pupils can do an excellent job with one another's writing.

6. The oral language example in this chapter was based on kindergarten, but be aware that even eighth-graders are not too old to enjoy and profit from wordless picture books and other devices for stimulating oral language development and the composing process. Try some.

7. If you have not already done so, restrain yourself from the "correcting" of pupils' papers. Instead, after discussing your procedure with them, only react to the content in terms of the ideas expressed. Then keep notes on errors for reteaching. (Inform parents as to your purpose and justification if the papers go home!)

8. You might want to read Chapter 11, "Editing: Revising and Proofreading," before you try some of the ideas on group revision or proofreading.

9. Establish mailboxes in your class and encourage children to use them for purposeful writing to one another.

10. Especially at the first-grade level, you might like to duplicate the practice mentioned in this chapter of having a silent period during which all communication is done in writing.

11. If you work with older students, have them try their hand at writing stories or poems for first grade, using a basic word list for the vocabulary. Use the words from the first-grade reader or the basic list provided in Chapter 9. You might even want to bind these into little books for the first-grade library, as suggested in Chapter 12.

12. Are your children writing at least every day? If not, this is "square one," where you need to begin.

REFERENCES

HILLERICH, ROBERT L., "Developing Written Expression: How to Raise—Not Raze—Writers," *Language Arts,* 56 (October, 1979), 769–77. In the process of summarizing writing instruction, points out evidence on the detrimental effects of "correcting" papers.

MOFFETT, JAMES, and BETTY JANE WAGNER, *Student-Centered Language Arts and Reading,* K–13. Boston: Houghton Mifflin, 1983. Presents theory and practice on the total language arts.

ADDITIONAL SOURCES

DUKE, DANIEL L. (ed.), *Helping Teachers Manage Classrooms.* Alexandria: Association for Supervision and Curriculum Development, 1982. An excellent collection of readings on both the principles and the practice of classroom management.

RHODES, LYNN K., "Organizing the Elementary Classroom for Effective Language Learning," in Hardt, Ulrich H. (ed.), *Teaching Reading and the Other Language Arts.* Newark: International Reading Association, 1983, pp. 83–103. Outlines a classroom organization based on *using* the language arts.

SEALEY, LEONARD, NANCY SEALEY, and MARCIA MILLMORE, *Children's Writing: An Approach for the Primary Grades.* Newark: International Reading Association, 1979. A somewhat structured approach to developing writing skill, including specific activities for primary children.

TURBILL, JAN (ed.), *No Better Way to Teach Writing.* Australia: Primary English Teaching Association, 1982, distributed by the National Council of Teachers of English. An excellent presentation of class organization and conferencing for primary writing.

3

Beginnings
in Prewriting and
Oral Language

Tom Birch is as brisk as a bee in conversation; but no sooner does he take a pen in his hand, than it becomes a torpedo to him, and benumbs all his faculties.
SAMUEL JOHNSON, 1743

IN THIS CHAPTER I'll present some ideas for getting young children started in writing, considering both their inner motivation to engage in communication and the means—oral language—with which they begin to express themselves. In addition to this concern for initial and continued oral language development, it is appropriate to present direction for prewriting activities at all levels. We'll begin, however, with oral language, which might be considered the *pre*-prewriting.

THE ROLE OF ORAL LANGUAGE

In some respects, we are trapped within our language. Language determines not only what we can talk and write about but also what we can think about. Try thinking about something for which you have no word. You can no more do that than you can describe something unseen or invisible.

Just as language sets the parameters for all speakers of that language, so too the amount of language an individual possesses sets the outer limits for that person. How well one functions in a society is determined in large part by how much control the individual has over the language of that society, and—in the society we are concerned with—that language is English.

Any individual's "English" is not a singular entity. More appropriately we should use the plural to indicate that we all possess "Englishes."

34

For example, the receptive understanding of a young child far exceeds the expressive, and the style and sophistication in written language of an experienced writer usually exceed that same person's oral language, since the writer has added time for thought, revision, and even thesaurus searching if necessary. Furthermore, the language style an adult uses in one situation is not necessarily that used in others.

In the Beginning:
Typical Children

Numerous research studies have revealed that the average five-year-old comes to school having mastered all the basic sentence patterns of the language. Further, such youngsters have a vocabulary of at least several thousand words. This fund of vocabulary, incidentally, represents more than 50 percent of all the words anyone writes in a lifetime. The basic job with such children—over half of a typical kindergarten class—is to capitalize on this control of oral language as it is now turned to interpreting (reading) and representing (writing) ideas in print.

Of course, part of the job is to continue expanding facility in the oral language as well. Concurrently, more basic activities are necessary for those other children who are not typical in their oral language development. Oral language activities for the atypical will be discussed in the next section.

Traditionally, children have been taught to read before they are taught to write, just as they naturally learned to understand speech before they produced it. Some researchers (Clay, 1975; Graves, 1983) have suggested that this might be backwards: Children can understand print better if we teach them to express themselves in writing before we introduce reading. As an experienced fence-straddler, I don't feel that we need to take an either/or position here. Until more evidence is in, why don't we recognize that both reading and writing have to do with the printed form of the oral language and acquaint youngsters with both at the same time?

At the most basic level, for example, children usually learn in kindergarten—in fact, come to kindergarten in most cases, already *able*—to distinguish *m* and *n*. Practice in this discrimination will be enhanced if they also trace or form the letters on paper. Usually next they learn, in reading instruction, that *m* represents the sound they hear at the beginning of *moon* or *monkey*. Why not also let them know that they can use this knowledge to write the first letter when they want to identify a picture or idea whose name begins with that sound?

Many classrooms, kindergarten and first grade, use language experience. Children, individually or as a group, decide on some experience or story they want to write. They dictate (compose) and the teacher records (transcribes) for them and reads back what is written. This is a very natural step toward writing as youngsters engage in selecting ideas, getting them organized, and dictating them. It can include all aspects of writing except the transcribing. Even revision may take place as the teacher reads back and children add, delete, or change elements.

Unfortunately, some teachers, in order to provide material simple enough for use in beginning reading, will paraphrase, condense, or substitute and repeat words. Then the value of language experience is lost. Literally recorded and read back to children, the recorded piece clearly demonstrates that what is said can be written and what is written can be read. This clearly demonstrates too that the written language is the same language the child has been hearing and using for years.

This last statement, while not controversial, has an implication that seems too often forgotten: We should *expect* young writers to write the way they speak. In fact, to attempt otherwise is to defeat the point of the statement and to send confusing messages to the child. First, we must free the child to write.

Positive effects of freeing children to write were clearly demonstrated in the 1960s as a result of research with i/t/a. In this approach to reading, words were essentially spelled phonetically and youngsters were encouraged to write. Of course, teachers could be little concerned about the traditions of writing and spelling, so children wrote and received few or no "corrections" on their papers. As a result, one of the few positive results of i/t/a was that by second grade these children were writing more and enjoying it more than children in traditional programs. Teachers certainly do not need to adopt i/t/a in order to reap the benefits of freeing children to write!

Initially, the preschool child learns something about writing through scribbling. The youngster learns that pencils or crayons are tools that can leave marks on paper—or on the wall. Eventually, the child gains some control over the scribbles, and they begin to represent thoughts about the real world. Anything from a malformed circle, a circle with a stick or two attached randomly, or an identifiable drawing of a human may represent a person. Most children function within this category when they enter kindergarten. They have identified the tools of writing, and they use drawings to represent their thoughts.

Since drawings are "writing" for these children, time must be allowed for "publication" here as much as with any other writing. Children need to "read" their drawings to the teacher or others. This verbalization of the drawing is an important forerunner of that language on paper which we call conventional writing.

As any kindergarten teacher knows, the next step is captioning or labeling the drawings. Many youngsters will attempt random letters and should be encouraged to continue with this experimentation. These pictures should be "read" whenever youngsters are ready to share them.

Labels will be requested and should be supplied by the teacher. Often such labels are traced over by children as they develop more interest in writing. In some classes, youngsters will even copy one another's labels if the teacher is too occupied.

As Dyson (1983) reported, "Talk surrounds this early writing, investing the labels with meaning. Eventually talk permeates the process, providing both meaning ... and the means ... for getting that meaning on paper." In fact, Clay suggested that the oral takes control of the printed message in this later stage.

If there is adequate sharing and discussion, soon adjectives will be added to the noun label. *Flower* becomes *red flower.* A natural development will be to add the marker *the,* a development more likely if the usual labels about the room are in sentences instead of merely single words: "This is the door." "This is a window."

By first grade, these children are eager to write. Some will move very quickly from drawing before labeling to writing before illustrating, a reverse of their kindergarten process.

To avoid having children overly concerned about the spellings of words at this stage, two techniques will be helpful. First of all, introduce them to rebus writing. Let them know they can use pictures in the same sentence with words: "I saw a (picture of a cat) in the (picture of a tree)."

Second, let them know that, as they are writing and don't know how to spell a word, they should write a few letters they know and draw a line under that word. When they or you read the story, there will be enough information to identify the intended word. They can also get help from you after they are finished writing if they want the full spelling of the word. Of course, older students must follow this same procedure, but, upon completion of the writing, they will use a dictionary to check their spellings.

This technique of identifying words whose spellings are not known is an important one to establish early. Few writers know how to spell every word they use. In order not to interrupt a train of thought, most have learned to identify the word in some way—by circling or underlining—and continue with the writing with the plan to check the spelling when the writing is completed. Although not many first-graders are known for extensive trains of thought that we must avoid derailing, the habit is an important one for a more serious reason. If pupils get into the other habit of writing a phonetic spelling, at more mature levels many will not remember their uncertainty when they go back to proofread. Therefore, this awareness of uncertainty is important to establish from the beginning.

Primarily, however, the job is to remove the mechanical blocks to written expression. We know that the very young child learned oral language through the desire to communicate. Why don't we encourage the development of written language in the same manner, rather than try to teach it through a highly structured series of steps? Young children need to use symbols—and drawings as well—to experiment and to express ideas of interest to them. We've learned that emphasis on the message—*what* the young child says—encourages further use of language; emphasis on correcting—*how* the child speaks—encourages silence. That same point applies to written communication. The first step in developing writing skill is to free the child to write.

Almost every kindergarten classroom is well stocked with materials for play: a household corner complete with table, chairs, dishes, "stove," and so on; trucks, cars, and other toy vehicles; blocks, puzzles, balls, and other manipulatives. All of these are conducive not only to play but also to oral language development. Further, books, labels, charts, and signs provide an environment for reading. Yet, very few kindergartens provide the props in a center for writing.

Why not have a "writing corner" in the kindergarten as well as in first grade? Stock it with all kinds of writing materials: pencils, black and colored; felt-tip pens; a few small chalkboards or a section of the mounted chalkboard, and a box of chalk of all colors; paper and card stock of all kinds, including envelopes; and perhaps an old typewriter or two. Let children experiment as they will. They might draw, scribble, form letters, make signs for some of their toys, and so on. An environment to encourage writing is as important as that environment which fosters interest in reading.

In the Beginning:
Children Limited in Oral Language

Barring physical or emotional trauma, very few children come to school without language. Unfortunately, some children are labeled as having "no language"—or, in the case of children from non–English-speaking backgrounds, as being "illiterate in two languages." These children may appear to have such handicaps, but it is usually because they learned very early that the language they have been using is not the acceptable language of school. Teachers who themselves came from non–English-speaking backgrounds recall their early years in school when they learned that it was easier to pretend they did not understand than to respond and be corrected for the way they spoke.

The first step in developing greater skill in oral language is to accept and encourage whatever language the child brings to school. Instead of "correcting" the way a young child speaks, we must react and respond to the ideas expressed. A second step, while expanding oral language for all children in the early grades, is to identify—at the *beginning* of kindergarten or nursery school—the specific oral language needs of the atypical child. Such children cannot be expected to express themselves in writing—or learn to read, for that matter—in a language in which they cannot function.

For non–English-speaking children, we must begin by providing an intensive oral English program. As we've known for decades, this is best done by immersing the child in the second language. The learner must engage in the language in normal sentence patterns; the second language is not learned through labels. There are many oral English programs available, including *Understanding English* by Louise Lancaster (Houghton Mifflin) and *English Around the World* by William Marquardt and others (Scott Foresman). Obviously the classroom teacher does not have the time required to devote to a child or two in these kinds of programs; but a little direction and the teacher's manual will enable an adult volunteer to provide the practice necessary to help such children.

For other youngsters who are deficient in oral language development, teachers can quickly determine specific language needs. The following items are arranged in some order of priority. Based on research with more than 900 children (Hillerich, 1978), the entire sequence can be tested in about fifteen minutes per child.

Auditory Discrimination. Any child who speaks English already hears a difference of one phoneme in words. If not, that child would not know if you were speaking of a *rail, nail, pail, sail,* or *tail* when you used one of the words. However, non-native speakers of English may not have experienced some of the sounds of English in their native language and therefore might not "hear" some of those sounds.

Check this by collecting, for example, pairs of pictures of objects such as *rock/sock* or *wing/ring.* Name the two pictures and ask the child to point to one of them. Any child who has difficulty in distinguishing between the two words can be given practice in the same manner with other pictures or with objects.

Merely because a child has immature speech—for example, says "wabbit" for *rabbit*—does not necessarily suggest an auditory discrimination problem. Most often this is a productive, not a receptive, difficulty. Likewise, the Hispanic child who begins to confuse items such as *sh* and *ch*, referring to *ship* as "chip" and *chair* and "shair," is in the same position.

Ability to Follow Oral Directions. Again pictures can be used while asking the child to perform basic acts, such as "Point to the (dog, cat)" or "Close the door and then touch the window." You may want to check on the ability to follow one-, two-, and even three-step oral directions.

Children who have difficulty in understanding such directions need to be given appropriate practice, beginning with one-step directions if that is where they are in their functioning.

Understanding Vocabulary. You might consider two kinds of vocabulary here: the words used in instructional directions, such as *in, under, same, different*, as well as general vocabulary: words that name animals, household items, foods, clothing, and so on.

You may test the former with directions to "Put this block *in* (*on, under*) the box." The latter can be tested by merely asking the child to name objects whose pictures you have collected.

Instruction is obvious: It requires experience with the kinds of items youngsters do not identify, and that experience must be with verbal mediation; that is, the appropriate word must be used with the object.

Expressive Language. In order to get a sample of the child's expressive language, it is ideal to engage that child in informal conversation on a subject he or she is interested in. However, this is very time-consuming. For purposes of identifying the child with a serious deficiency in oral language, a set of three or four simple sequence picture cards will serve the purpose. Lay out the cards, turn on the tape recorder, and ask the child to tell the story from the pictures. Then evaluate the language sample.

The best single measure of sophistication in oral language—or written, for that matter—is the number of words used per T-unit (Hunt, 1965; Loban, 1976). A T-unit—standing for "minimal terminal unit"—is any independent clause with all of its subordinate clauses and modifiers. Basically, a T-unit differs from a sentence in that a compound sentence is one sentence, but it is more than one T-unit. If one were to count words per sentence used by a kindergartener, the count might be more than one hundred, since the typical kindergartener connects each thought with "and then."

Following are three samples of kindergarten language, taken from testing for *Ready Steps* (Hillerich and Johnson, 1981). In each case, the T-units have been marked off with slash marks, and garbles (interruptions, repetitions, and so on) have been circled so they would not be counted. The number of words per T-unit is arrived at by dividing the total number of words by the number of T-units.

> *Low Kindergartener:* I see a boy / see a wagon / see a boy / rolling down the hill / he falled down. /
> (17 words divided by 5 T-units = 3.4 words per T-unit)
>
> *Average:* The boy's getting dressed / and he's running out to play. / He got in a wagon. / He's going to a hill. / He's riding his wagon down the hill. / He fell down. /
> (30 words divided by 6 T-units = 5.0 words per T-unit)
>
> *Superior:* Once upon a time there was a little boy named (named) Joey. / He went outside to get his (to get his) wagon and play. / He got in his wagon and (and) rolled down the hill / and he fell out of his wagon. /
> (37 words divided by 4 T-units = 9.2 words per T-unit)

According to a number of studies, the average kindergartener speaks in about five words per T-unit. Any child who speaks in fewer than four words per T-unit has a serious deficiency and needs intensive help.

Instruction is a matter of practice in language. That practice implies having some worthwhile things to talk about or, as any good primary teacher knows, providing experiences that stimulate children to talk—and then providing the "ears" to listen. Those "ears" may again be adult volunteers, senior citizens, or older students. The tape recorder, once children have been taught how to use it, has been found to be very helpful in some kindergarten classes.

Listening Comprehension. How well do youngsters under-stand when they are read to? Read a simple story (a paragraph in length) to the child and ask what it was about. If the child cannot recall most of the story, you might assume little experience with this kind of language activity. Once more, implications are clear: This is a youngster who needs two or three times the amount of reading-to that you might do with the others.

Sequencing. Is the child aware that there is a sequence to activities normally engaged in? You might check this by using a simple set of sequence cards. Ask the pupil to indicate the order in which the cards should be placed in order to tell a story.

You will probably find a good number of youngsters who have some difficulty in sequencing. In fact, some kindergarteners apparently do not realize that there is a sequence in normal activities. With these, you might begin by asking questions such as "When you get up in the morning, what do you do first? Do you get out of bed or do you eat breakfast?" Other experiences to further develop this sense of sequence might be to take a walk about the building and then recall what was done first, next, and so on. Field trips, especially with photographs to be arranged in sequence after the trip, can be helpful.

Using Oral Context. Most five-year-olds think along with a speaker and anticipate words that will make sense. However, those with limited language experience may not. Check each child by first explaining that you will say something but will not finish what you start to say. "You tell me what you think I was going to say.... 'I'd like a cold drink of _____.' What do you think I was going to say?" After this kind of clarification, give some other examples for the child to complete.

For any youngster who has difficulty, provide experiences ranging from basic nonsense sentences, where the child is to decide if what is said makes sense, to examples such as that suggested in the preceding paragraph.

The kind of diagnostic procedure suggested in this section will provide you with information about the level of language development of each child. Some specific activities were suggested, but interested involvement in language of all kinds is the key. In fact, after culling out seventy-eight research studies dealing with oral language development, I've found that studies dealing with oral language treatments are clear on at least one point: Intense informal involvement in oral language activities is significantly more effective than highly structured drills, sentence pattern repetition, and so on. In fact, teacher-directed intensive oral language experience or the kinds of informal language activities found in the *Peabody Language Kit* (American Guidance Service) or in *Ready Steps* (Houghton Mifflin) were the types that made a difference in the later achievement of youngsters.

Black Dialect

I might have titled this section "Dialects," but—at least as I see it—the major educational concern is with Black Dialect (BD) as opposed to "Standard" English (SE). There are various geographic dialects, as well as social dialects, in the United States. However, with the exception of BD, and possibly Southern dialect in some regions, most of the others—if not prestigious—are at least accepted and sometimes considered "cute."

A dialect is a variation in language style *within* a language community. It is not a different language. Hence, speakers of different dialects can and do communicate with each other. This is true of black, Bostonian, Texan, Midwestern, or any other dialect.

Basically, what was said about accepting the language of every child applies here. What Midwestern teacher would attempt to change the dialect of a Bostonian child—trying to get that child to pronounce *r's* where they "should be" instead of where they aren't? Yet, that same teacher is likely to "correct" the BD child for not pronouncing the plural marker or the past marker.

In addition to *accepting* the child's language, it seems to me that every teacher has a responsibility to *understand* that language. Teachers who work with children who use BD have an obligation to understand the characteristics of that dialect. Space does not allow adequate treatment here of the pronunciation and syntactical differences between BD and SE, but excellent and very readable background may be found in Smitherman (1977) and Dillard (1972).

Some of the highlights, in terms of pronunciation, can be listed. These include dropping of final *r* and *l,* so that *tore* and *toll* both are pronounced "toe." Weakening or loss of the final consonant /t/ and /d/ results in omission of past markers, so that *past* and *passed* both become "pass." The *th* in initial position often becomes /d/ and in final position becomes /f/, so that *this* may be pronounced "dis" and *Ruth* as "roof."

Implications for writing are apparent as a result of these differences. Spelling is likely to be affected. Although that is not—or at least should not be—a concern at the beginning stages of writing, it can be at higher levels. The solution, as discussed in Chapter 9, is to teach spelling the way research suggests, that is, not to rely on "sound" spelling of words. Even though the Bostonian may "pak the ca," that speaker puts the *r's* in when writing.

Dialects also differ in terms of vocabulary and syntax. The former is not much of a concern in reading or writing, but the latter is. Syntax is the grammar of the language, the way words are strung together to make legal English sentences.

In terms of syntactical differences, BD has eliminated some of the redundancies of SE. For example, plural and possessive markers are usually dropped. Hence, "ten cents" becomes "ten cent," since the BD speaker doesn't need to indicate plurality with two words. Likewise, "Sue's hat" becomes "Sue hat."

Use of the copula *be* is evident in the response to the question "Is your mother home?" The response "No, she working" and "No, she be working" indicate different meanings in BD. The former, with zero copula, suggests that the fact that she is working is unusual, whereas the latter indicates that it is the normal or usual behavior.

Repetition of the subject—not restricted to BD—is also evident in "Jim he sick." And, of course, there are many other differences between BD and SE. However, in none of these should communication suffer if the listener is concerned with the meaning instead of the form of language.

Back to application in writing: We should *expect* young writers to write the way they speak. The syntactical constructions used in speech will be the ones used in writing. Furthermore, if linguistic studies are to be believed, that oral language—and the resultant written language—is not going to change until the individual wants to imitate a different dialect group. This usually will not happen before the teenage years, when social pressures have an influence.

We know that traditional methods of trying to change children's manner of speaking have failed. And it's just as well. Imagine the inner-city child who walks out of school speaking the way the teacher wanted! That youngster would be in trouble the minute he hit the street.

All this is not to say that anything goes. Nor is it to ignore the fact that certain dialects are more socially and economically advantageous than others. Teachers must still provide a "standard" model and go further in upper grades by providing experience in the *various* ways of saying the same thing so that students will be aware of the options when they reach an age where change is desirable to them.

Upper-grade teachers have this responsibility to acquaint students with the fact that we all have a "wardrobe of language." As an educated adult, do you use the same language style at a friend's picnic that you use in a formal social setting? At the picnic, you might very appropriately call out across the field, "Hey, Fred, toss me the ball!" At dinner, you would hardly call across the table, "Hey, Fred, toss me the rolls!"

Acquainting these students with this "wardrobe of language" includes discussion of the *ways* of expressing an idea, translating to appropriate language for different settings, and providing both the oral and the written model of "standard" English. It also includes demonstrating and discussing the fact that oral composition is usually less formal than written composition.

PREWRITING

Of all the elements in the writing process, prewriting is the most lauded, least understood, and certainly the least explicated. What is prewriting? When does it take place? What behaviors make it up? Is it something to be taught or merely to be experienced?

Most authorities agree that prewriting is the heart of the writing process, but few have offered concrete direction. A few writers claim to be able to write by the clock, but most acknowledge prewriting pains. As Thomas Wolfe once claimed, "Writing is easy. Just put a sheet of paper in the typewriter and start bleeding." It is the prewriting that is so difficult.

Prewriting seems to be somewhat individual and idiosyncratic in its specifics, but there are some general considerations that can be pulled out of personal experience and that of others. This is just one more reason teachers of writing must write: They must write in order to better understand the process.

Outside the constraints of the classroom, prewriting may extend over longer periods of time. Does this have implications for *inside* the classroom as well? For example, my own prewriting for this book took place at some very unlikely times, while cutting the grass, grocery shopping, and so on. Some ideas needed time to incubate and to jell. In order to have this time, many of us will do almost anything but write. My wife always knows when I'm in the throes of prewriting: I even straighten my otherwise permanently littered desk.

How many of your students have to sharpen pencils, borrow paper, or go to the lavatory when they are supposed to start writing? This apparent procrastination is not necessarily an act of rebellion; oftentimes it is a matter of wrestling with the problem.

What Is Prewriting?

If pushed for a definition, I'd suggest that prewriting is a *process to be taught.* Here brevity is not the soul of wit but of impoverishment when it comes to direction for teaching. Nonetheless, the point is important: Prewriting requires more than allocated time. If students are going to become proficient in the process of writing, they must develop skill in basic procedures, and the most basic are those involved in prewriting. Effective efforts here make the actual writing relatively easy.

One element of prewriting is exploration leading to discovery. The exploration may take place in order to identify a subject or, with a subject already in mind, to further define and clarify the particular topic to be written about. At least beyond primary, this exploration will also involve consideration of the audience to be addressed.

As Smith (1982) has pointed out, however, prewriting consists of more than discovery. It also includes incubation and rehearsal. In other words, thoughts on the subject need to gestate, while the writer often engages in internal composing.

Partially too, prewriting may serve the purpose of helping the writer get into the mood or loosen up. Even the function of getting thoughts organized may contribute to this easing into writing, since jotting notes or rehearsing will keep that writer from worrying about how to get started.

Furthermore, the very term *prewriting* may be a misnomer if it leads one to believe that it is an act that takes place only *before* writing. It is recursive, cycling through the entire process, often occurring even in the revision stage of editing as the writer considers or rehearses some element in the piece of writing.

Some Prewriting Activities

There is no prewriting activity that will be helpful to all individuals at any time, nor is there one that will be helpful to any individual all the time. Nevertheless, there are a number of examples that can be beneficial if young writers are aware of them.

Any writer will do a better job when writing on a subject that he or she has had personal experience with or is personally interested in. All students, from young to more mature, need ideas, but usually they should not be given a single topic on which to write; they should be presented with options, provocative possibilities that also allow for their own interests and innovations.

At the beginning stages, younger pupils usually benefit from preliminary discussion that relates possible writing topics to their personal experiences. In the process, the teacher may stimulate with open-ended questions and ideas for expansion of the subject. Some teachers have found that writing pertinent words on the board is helpful, although others report that it channels thinking too much. Possibly the solution is in listing a great enough variety of words to keep the topic open.

Written language has its foundation in the oral. Hence, many elementary prewriting activities may begin with oral exchange. This exchange provides opportunities for exploring and discovering, the first stage of prewriting. We might arbitrarily distinguish two additional stages of prewriting: organizing and rehearsing. Certainly there is no clear demarcation between stages. They too are recursive, since the organizing stage may lead to new discovery, just as the rehearsing may result in both new organizational ideas and new discoveries.

Exploring and Discovering. The exploring and discovering stage is basic to all prewriting. It may be the most time-consuming, and it provides the greatest opportunity for variety in many activities. Decision making here relates not only to topic but also to method, format, and content.

Some of the activities here are private, as students are encouraged to think about the topic and to reach back into their memories or personal experiences in order to develop the topic. They may imagine, recall, or otherwise explain to themselves about the subject.

Many activities may be group processes as youngsters stimulate each other. Among these are the following, which can be used at any level:

discussing and reacting

observing

brainstorming

listening

using films, art, photos

interviewing

experimenting

reading and researching

role playing or dramatizing

Brainstorming has been a popular and effective technique for generating ideas. However, Rodrigues (1983) raised some concerns about its potential superficiality as well as the danger of lack of total participation by the group. He suggested "brainwriting" as an alternative. He also suggested a number of variations, but the basic idea of brainwriting is to divide the class into small groups. Each group member, independently, will list three or four ideas on the topic and exchange the list with another, who will add his or her ideas. As the papers pass around the group, each student will get new thoughts from others' lists. Finally, the small groups may share their lists with the entire class.

This idea of jotting down ideas can also be beneficial in preparation for a group discussion, whether in a writing or a reading class. Too often the teacher may raise a question and one student will quickly supply "the answer." If all are expected to jot down a few notes in response to the stated question, the discussion will be based on more careful consideration of the question, thinking time is allowed, and all participate.

A number of other methods can be taught to students to assist them in developing a topic. They might make a simple list of ideas or random responses to the subject, or they might use word associations or group and classify ideas in order to discover new relationships. Such classifications can also be expanded to identify similarities or differences among events or objects. Grouping, as opposed to mere listing, can be used to relate words or ideas to a central subject. For example, the word *round* might elicit the following cluster from primary children:

big

hard   fat

balloon   happy

face   *round*   sad

square   circle

head   soft

ball

In addition to grouping or classifying, the reverse can be helpful. Have students consider how the subject under consideration *is not like.* ...Then, *How could it be like...?* For example, "How is a piece of candy not like a hammer?" One eats the candy but pounds nails with the hammer. "How could they be alike?" If the candy is hard enough, it might be used to drive a small nail (which is better than eating the hammer!). Even analogies can be used as follow-ups with older students.

More formal devices, such as the five *W*'s or other heuristic models, can be used in discovering at upper levels. A heuristic model, based on Pike's particle-wave-field theory from physics, has become popular for descriptions. First the writer views the object in isolation, a "particle," then as a dynamic process, a "wave," and finally as part of larger system, a "field." For example, extensive lists for each of the three categories could be made in describing a chocolate-chip cookie:

1. "particle": brown, oval shape, bumpy surface,...
2. "wave": sticky mix, swelling while baking, crumbling,...

3. "field": mix of flour, sugar, chocolate, etc.; tasty treat; classifies with sugar cookies, spice cookies....

Organizing. Once ideas have been assembled, students need to organize them in some fashion. This requires planning in terms of purpose and audience as well as in terms of method and format.

Although a formal outline is seldom used, it is one possible technique. More helpful, usually, are less structured means, such as grouping of related ideas collected in the exploration stage. Webbing or mapping can be used to show relationships. For example, if students plan to write on the topic "Animals I Know," they might begin by constructing something that looks like Figure 3.1.

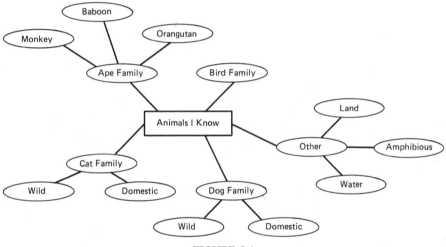

FIGURE 3.1.

Mapping is an aid to thinking, enabling the writer to focus on the organization of ideas rather then on the language used to express them. It is a visual process more than a verbal one, with entries kept to a minimum and usually consisting of one word. Furthermore, it is a categorizing process, as the writer moves from the topic to major components of the scheme, considering and elaborating on each of these subtopics with additional detail.

Selecting from among the grouped ideas is also necessary. Here students can be guided, through private consideration, conferencing, or group discussion, to evaluate and to delete the irrelevant. In the process they may give the ideas priorities, narrow the topic, or be guided in making judgments about how they will expand their topic: through cause/effect, enumeration of facts, supported generalizations, sequence, comparison/contrast, classification, problem/solution, and so on.

Likewise, decisions on sequencing are important at this stage. Acquaint students with the various methods through discussion and examination of previous class works, as well as through published models. Methods of sequencing will include chronological, logical, spatial, and so on, depending upon subject matter and purpose.

Rehearsing. Rehearsing is usually private, although with young children it may take place during exploration. With most writers rehearsal takes place throughout the process of writing, from prewriting through revision. It is a matter of talking to oneself, testing expressions, and otherwise "composing" the piece.

Fluency

Fluency has at least two components. One is the matter of keeping the words flowing on the paper; the other is the battle to overcome the merciless exchange of stares that takes place between writer and empty paper—that "blank paperitis."

In the first instance, there is no substitute for experience in writing. The more one writes, the more likely are words to appear on that paper. However, at least one additional specific contribution can be made to develop fluency.

Most elementary teachers are familiar with SSR, sustained silent reading. Have you tried SSW, sustained silent writing? Ask your pupils to get pencil and paper ready, and you also do the same. Tell them that when you say "go" you will all start writing and write for three minutes until you say "stop." If at some point they can't think of anything to write, they should keep writing their last word or write "I can't think of anything to write" until they get another thought.

If you engage in SSW daily, you will find that fluency—the number of words written in a given period of time—will show a definite increase. Not only will fluency increase, some teachers have reported that the organization and content of the writing during SSW have improved.

Although that last point is not necessarily a claim for SSW, the only complaint I have heard was from a sixth-grade teacher who was skeptical and tried SSW for three weeks in her class. She acknowledged that fluency did increase greatly but complained that mechanical errors showed no change! Well!

Of course, the amount of time devoted to SSW may vary by grade level and experience. Two or three minutes seems to be a good starting point, and few elementary teachers would carry a given experience beyond about five minutes. However, *daily* practice is essential.

The second block to fluency, "blank paperitis," will be eased by appropriate prewriting activities. Even more, teachers can help by avoiding the usual admonition of English texts about having a "good beginning sentence." Most writers don't know what will be a good beginning sentence until *after* they have finished the writing. The first step is merely to get started, to get something down on the paper. Once a few words have begun to flow, others follow more freely.

One third-grade teacher demonstrated an excellent example of how to get her youngsters started. The children were excited as they noticed the season's first snow falling heavily. Enthusiastically, the teacher suggested, "Let's write about snow!" She had hardly gotten the words out when Terrie whined, "I hate snow!" "Good," said the teacher, "that's a great beginning sentence! Put it down." About that time Steve shouted out, "You know, one day last winter..." "Terrific!" the teacher exclaimed. "Put it down. That'll make an excellent beginning." In other words, *put anything down* to get started. After the writing is completed, that beginning sentence may be modified or discarded for a "good beginning sentence."

SUMMARY

Writing has its base in the oral language. Typical five-year-olds come to school with a wealth of language. With these, the job is to relate that oral language to print and to bypass for the time the difficulties presented by lack of spelling ability. Techniques for doing this include rebus writing and putting down only a few letters to represent the word intended.

For the atypical youngster, suggestions were offered to help the teacher identify specific language needs and to follow up with their remediation. Whether language-deprived or from a non–English-speaking background, the child must be able to function in the oral language before being expected to engage in the printed form, whether in reading or in writing.

A dialect is not a different language. Hence, in the case of Black Dialect—or any other dialect—children can function if teachers will (1) understand their dialect and (2) accept it. As such children mature, experience with the "ways" of speaking and writing, along with the "standard" English model from the teacher, will enable them to become bidialectal.

Prewriting was presented as a process to be taught. Suggestions were made for three stages of prewriting: exploration/discovery, organization, and rehearsal. As part of prewriting needs, fluency was discussed in terms of getting words to flow on paper and of overcoming "blank paperitis."

SUGGESTIONS FOR ACTION

1. If you teach kindergarten or first grade and have not already done so, check the oral language of your children. You might begin with those you suspect of having some weaknesses, using the specific techniques suggested for atypical pupils. Then, of course, follow with the indicated instruction.

2. Provide a wealth of words in print for pupils. Encourage them, from the beginning, to name their pictures and further label them as they develop more skills.

3. Try some rebus writing with those beginners. Also don't let them worry about the spellings of words; encourage them to put down a few of the consonants that they know and go on with the writing.

4. How many words per T-unit does your "average" child use? Get an oral language sample and use it as a benchmark with which to compare your class. Sometimes "verbal" children are not always the most sophisticated in their use of language; they can deceive us with a torrent of words.

5. At any level, if you work with children from other language backgrounds, be certain that they are developing in oral English. Get the help you need from adult volunteers or senior citizens, using one of the references cited or a similar program.

6. If you work with children who speak Black Dialect, be certain that you know the nature of that dialect. If not, use one of the references to get acquainted with its characteristics. You might, with older students, also try some translating to different levels, from their extreme informal, through "standard," to extreme formal.

7. Which of the suggested prewriting activities have you tried? Investigate the effectiveness of some of those that might be new to you. Since individuals may vary in their prewriting habits, students will benefit from learning a variety of ways of exploring and organizing ideas for a writing task.

8. Write a short piece and reflect on your own prewriting feelings and behaviors. Whether or not you get some additional clues about the elements of prewriting, you will certainly develop some appreciation of its importance.

9. When did you last write with your pupils? Model writing with them and don't forget to share your piece too!

10. With older students, try the "particle-wave-field" heuristic. You should find that they can greatly expand on a topic with this kind of experience behind them.

11. Try SSW daily for a few weeks. You might want to have students count the number of words they write after the first trial and compare with the number written after several weeks, using the same amount of time for both trials.

REFERENCES

CLAY, MARIE M., *What Did I Write?* Exeter, New Hampshire: Heinemann Educational Books, 1975. Examines the beginnings of writing in young children.

DILLARD, J. L., *Black English.* New York: Random House, 1972. Provides the history and characteristics of Black Dialect.

DYSON, ANNE HAAS, "The Role of Early Language in Early Writing Processes," *Research in the Teaching of English,* 17 (February, 1983), 1–30. Analyzes the role of oral language in early writing activities.

GRAVES, DONALD H., *Writing: Teachers and Children at Work.* Exeter, New Hampshire: Heinemann Educational Books, 1983. Describes Graves's work with first graders in writing.

HILLERICH, ROBERT L., "A Diagnostic Approach to the Early Identification of Language Skills," *The Reading Teacher,* 31 (January, 1978), 357–64. Reports techniques and effectiveness of a diagnostic approach to the language needs of kindergarteners.

HILLERICH, ROBERT L., and TIMOTHY G. JOHNSON, *Test for Ready Steps.* Boston: Houghton Mifflin, 1981. Diagnostic test for identifying oral language needs of nursery school and kindergarten children.

HUNT, KELLOGG, *Grammatical Structures Written at Three Grade Levels.* Urbana, Illinois: National Council of Teachers of English, 1965.

Reports results of analysis of writing skill at grades four, eight, and twelve, including use of the number of words per T-unit as a measure.

LOBAN, WALTER D., *Language Development: Kindergarten through Grade Twelve.* Urbana, Illinois: National Council of Teachers of English, 1976. Reports results of a longitudinal study, following the same group from kindergarten through grade twelve. Loban's use of a "communication unit" is the same as a T-unit.

RODRIGUES, RAYMOND J. "Tools for Developing Prewriting Skills," *English Journal,* 72 (February, 1983), 58–60. Suggests "brainwriting" as an alternative to brainstorming.

SMITH, FRANK, *Writing and the Writer.* New York: Holt, Rinehart and Winston, 1982. A thorough analysis of the process of writing.

SMITHERMAN, GENEVA, *Talkin and Testifyin.* Boston: Houghton Mifflin, 1977. Explains the background and characteristics of Black Dialect, using Black Dialect as part of the explanation.

ADDITIONAL RESOURCE

KOCH, CARL, and JAMES M. BRAZIL, *Strategies for Teaching the Composition Process,* pp. 25–63. Urbana, Illinois: National Council of Teachers of English, 1978. Teachers of upper grades will find many specific strategies for prewriting activities, each described in detail.

4

Stimulating
Writing

To know how to suggest is the great art of teaching.
HENRI AMIEL, 1864

THIS CHAPTER MIGHT BE considered an extension of the previous one. Here are a variety of ideas for stimulating writing, ranging from lists of kinds of writing and topics for writing, to specific activities that can be conducted in classrooms at any level. Not one suggestion is worth using if it is *imposed* on students; any one is valuable if it triggers the individual's imagination or touches a preexisting emotion or attitude in that student.

STIMULATING *VS.* MOTIVATING

The word *stimulating* in the above heading was chosen deliberately. Most teachers of writing do not expect to have to "motivate" young writers. Just as the desire to talk is natural, given the situation, so too humans will write if they have reason to. Further, individuals will write with more enthusiasm, clarity, and reader appeal if their inner motivation is tapped.

In other words, the writing children do must be purposeful: It must be done because the writer has some information that he or she wants to communicate to another. Unfortunately, in school much writing fails to meet this criterion on two counts: First, the only purpose for writing is that the teacher assigned it; second, the teacher already knows what the writer might be able to say about the subject.

Edelsky and Smith (1984) discussed this concern in terms of "authentic" and "inauthentic" writing, the latter being what most often is done in school. They point out what many of us have observed. The assignment of inauthentic writing results in groans, mechanical questions ("How many words?"), and so on. In contrast, youngsters are self-motivated, interested, and remain on task when writing about something that interests them and that they want to communicate to others.

This is not to say that topics can't be discussed in order to trigger ideas in the students. No one develops in a vacuum. In fact, child or adult is usually stimulated by some external situation that then initiates the expression of ideas which were previously internalized. Hence, although topics may be suggested by the teacher or generated by the class, youngsters should *always* have the option of choosing their own subjects.

In Chapter 1 you read an overview of the elements in a writing program. This chapter deals with the two jobs that are prerequisites to success in any writing program: freedom to write and experience with all types and styles of writing. The former demands opportunity and stimulation; the latter presumes some instruction or demonstration. Both also require considerable practice, which—to be worthwhile—must be enjoyable. Hence, humor and nonsense have a definite place in any writing program.

CATEGORIES OF WRITING

You will recall from Chapter 1 that English teachers have traditionally referred to four categories of writing: description, narration, exposition, and argument. As Britton and others (1975) pointed out, this system was based on prescription—how one *should* write as opposed to how writers *do* write. Further, it was based on analysis of products rather than on the writer's intent or mode. Of practical significance is the classification they arrived at, presented here in greatly oversimplified form:

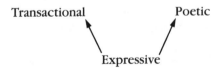

The point is that the expressive is basic. This is the more personal kind of writing, where writer and audience are close. It is less structured and more revealing of self, and it includes personal letters, diaries, and a limited audience. This is where children begin.

Transactional and poetic usually have more distant audiences, and both may be used to inform or control. The major difference lies in style:

Transactional places emphasis on the content, whereas the poetic places emphasis on the style, format, or language used. Within the transactional category are reports, directions, arguments; within the poetic are literary pieces of all kinds, some of which might also be expressive.

Although I have not attempted to classify suggestions for types of writing under either Britton's or the traditional scheme, it seems worthwhile for the teacher to have this distinction of Britton's in mind in discussing writing with older students. In fact, one of the many teaching tasks is that of moving students beyond expressive writing to the transactional in terms of both audience and subject distance. One means, suggested by Kreeft (1984), is through use of a dialogue log. This is a notebook in which the student and teacher both write, responding to each other's entries. Kreeft has found that appropriate questioning reactions written by the teacher gradually move the student to structure and amplify statements, to make them more understandable to a less personal audience.

It is most important, of course, that students engage in every kind of writing we can think of. The following types are not classified according to grade, since many can be used at any level. The difference is that the ten-sentence "All About Me" of first grade becomes the ten-page "Look Out World, Here I Am" of eighth grade.

Warm -Ups

analogies	palindromes
announcements	posters
billboards	proverbs
bumper stickers	puns
captions	riddles
commercials	slogans
definitions	spoonerisms
epitaphs, humorous	telegrams
graffiti	tongue twisters
idioms	travel brochures
jokes	"wanted" posters
malaprops	word origins

Longer Pieces: Literary and Factual

allegories	journals
autobiographies	legends

biographies
books for beginning readers
book jackets
character sketches
descriptions
diaries
directions
essays
fables/folktales
fairy tales
fantasies

mysteries
myths
nursery rhymes
outlines
parodies
plays
reports
reviews (book, movie, TV)
short stories
tall tales

Newspaper Types

ads
advice columns
cartoons/comics
classified ads
editorials
gossip columns

headlines
letters to the editor
news articles
sports articles
TV guides
weather reports

Poetry

cinquains
concrete (form) poems
couplets
diamantes
free verses

haiku
limericks
quatrains
tankas

Letters, Social

apologies/regrets
friendly letters
invitations
requests
thank-you letters

Letters, Business

applications
complaints
inquiries
requests/orders
subscriptions

Literary Devices

alliteration
dysphemisms
euphemisms
hyperbole

metaphors
oxymorons
personification
similes

IDEAS FOR WRITING

One of the greatest contributions any teacher can make to the writing skill of youngsters is to develop in them an interest in language for its own sake. One way to develop awareness of and enthusiasm for language is to have a bulletin board section marked off for the "Sentence (or Paragraph) of the Week." Here pupils can compete to find the best statement they can in terms of word choice, sentence structure, clarity, brevity, or whatever your emphases are at the time. Various entries might even be defended by their sponsors at the end of the week.

      The following ideas are very loosely categorized, and each may have many variations and be used at any grade level. All are skeletal and require prewriting discussion and preparation. Additional ideas for writing will be found in Chapter 5.

Warm-Ups

Activities are presented in no intended order. Some are merely short exercises for their own sake, whereas others, such as similes or alliterative pieces, provide practice with elements that might be used later. Still others, such as the imaginative combinations, encourage children to think in more creative ways. These are the kinds of little notes and tidbits that your students might store in their language logs. Especially at kindergarten and first grade, many of these will prove to be helpful oral language activities.

      1. *Sensory Words.* Have pupils list all of the words they can think of that relate to sights, sense of touch, sounds, smells, and tastes.

      2. *Onomatopoeic words.* Pupils might collect words that imitate the sounds they represent: *splash, buzz,* and so on.

      3. *Similes.* Begin by calling attention to similes and having pupils collect them from their reading materials. Then have them write their own similes.

      4. *Metaphors.* Once your children are familiar with similes, show them how a simile can be converted to a metaphor. For example, "The airplane looked like a gnat" becomes "The airplane was a gnat." Have them convert similes to metaphors and then have them write their own metaphors.

      5. *Alliteration.* Introduce a few examples, such as "a slippery, slithering snake" or "a tart, tangy tangerine." Have pupils make up their own examples.

6. *Rigmarole.* This medieval roundelay is a further expansion of alliteration. The first line begins with alliterative words for *one,* the next line for *two,* and so on, with all lines in the same sentence pattern. Example:

> *One weary wanderer watching walruses;*
> *Two tiny tads tasting tarts;*
> *Three…*

7. *Expanded uses.* Exhibit a common object such as a block, brick, paper clip, or rubber band. Have students write all the different uses they can for the object in five minutes.

8. *Malaprops.* Provide a few examples of misused or transposed words: "My friend really depreciated the lovely gift" or "The speaker received a standing ovulation." Let pupils enjoy making up their own malaprops.

9. *Addled adages.* Provide a list of old maxims. Have pupils take the first part of each and write a new ending. Examples: "A bird in the hand is worth a good dinner." "Silence is no talk."

10. *Elevated adages.* From the list of maxims, have pupils select several to rewrite at an extremely formal level. Example: "Their intense occupation was analogous to hymenopterous insects."

11. *Imaginative combinations.* Let pupils take off from some of Koch's (1970) unusual combinations, such as "I was wrapped in a blanket of happiness," "a crowd of friendliness," and so on.

12. *Puns and riddles.* Youngsters can enjoy collecting and making up these bits of nonsense to share with others after they've added them to their language logs. Some of the comic pages of the newspaper are a good source of puns.

13. *Graffiti.* Graffiti comes in all forms, including bumper stickers. Provide some examples or have pupils find them: "Stop air pollution—quit breathing" or "When in doubt, worry." Then have pupils write their own.

14. *Humorous epitaphs.* These can be anything from one-liners—

> Epitaph for an old baseball: This is my last out.
> Epitaph for a pencil: I've made my last point.

to humorous ryhmes:

Here lies a joker, Moe Fry,
Who loved to play tricks and to kid.
Then he'd laugh till we thought he would die,
And he did.

15. *Grab bag.* Have each student bring a small common object to school in a paper bag. After exchanging bags, each recipient is to describe the object received (without naming it) so clearly that others can guess what it is. As a variation, you may prefer to have descriptions done in stages: First the writer is to smell only and record reaction, then feel and describe, and finally look and complete the description.

16. *Be Thumb Kid!* Have pupils write what they would do if they were as small as their thumbs. Example: "I'd go on a treasure hunt under the sofa…"

17. *Bug list.* Pupils may write sentences—or even paragraphs—indicating "It really bugs me when…" Example. "It really bugs me when I put my money in the soda machine and nothing happens."

18. *Compound daffynitions.* Have students collect compound words and make up literal definitions for them: "Pineapple—a new kind of fruit made from grafting apple branches onto pine trees." As a variation of this, have pupils make silly questions: "Did you ever see a horse/fly?" "Did you ever see a board/walk?"

19. *Homophone hazards.* To help youngsters realize the dangers of homophones—and possibly to help them get some, such as *there* and *their,* sorted out—have them deliberately write sentences using the wrong homophone: "Eye no a reel arrow plane when eye sea won."

20. *Mnemonics.* A good follow-up for #19 is to have youngsters think of mnemonic devices to help them keep confusable homophones apart, especially *there/their, to/too/two,* and others you find. Example: "*There* contains *here* (a place); *their* contains *heir* (a person)."

21. *High/low.* Children may write rhyming sentences beginning "Is there anything…" Examples: "Is there anything as high as the moon in the sky?" "Is there anything as low as your toe in the snow?"

22. *Strange comparisons.* Initially you might provide the strange comparisons in question form and have youngsters write answers in one or two sentences. Later, they can write their own questions and answers. Examples: "Which is heavier, a smile or a grimace? A grimace because it pulls my face down." "Which is noisier, the sun or the moon? The sun because it scares me awake."

23. *Strange uses.* You might list a few items, such as a leaf, a seashell, a blade of grass, a piece of glass. As a heading, have pupils write "What can you do with a ...?" Then have them list, in phrases or sentences, the uses for the item.

24. *Captions.* Use photos of faces or have youngsters bring in snapshots of their own babyhood. Post a few at a time and have students write one-line captions indicating what the individual might be saying, based on the facial expression. (Animal pictures also work well for this activity.)

25. *Would you ...?* Given a question, children are apt to reply in one sentence with a reason: "Would you like to be as soft as a feather?" "...as big as an elephant?" "...as fast as a jet?"

26. *What is ...?* Encourage pupils to use adjectives along with their nouns in responding to questions such as "What is soft?" "...smooth?" "...hard?" and so on. Example: "What is soft? Furry little kittens."

27. *"Liar's club."* Have pupils pretend to take part in a "Liar's Club" contest. See who can make up the most outrageous fib.

Story Starters

As students mature in their writing, they need to become aware of the questions they must ask themselves about what they are writing. Basic, of course, are the five *W's: who, what, when, where, why.* These can begin to be developed as early as in the first grade.

Later, youngsters also need to become aware of audience distance. One writes differently to a close audience, one familiar with and to the writer, from the way one does—using the more formal mode—when an audience is more distant and unknown personally to the writer.

Following are a few ideas to stimulate thinking about different topics. Additional suggestions can be found in references at the end of this chapter.

1. Suppose you were trapped in a candy store (art museum, toy factory, etc.). Use the five *W's* to tell your story.

2. Look at the world from another's viewpoint. How would a fish consider a fisherman? How would an extraterrestrial view your activities? How would a mouse picture cheese in a trap?

3. Suppose you were "Super Boy/Girl." "What would you do? How would you feel? Why?

4. Imagine that you are a pencil. Write what you think and feel in a day in your life. (Alternatives are many here: a shoe, tennis racquet, paint brush, etc.)

5. Be a reporter. Interview a parent, baby brother or sister, paper carrier, or even a tiger at the zoo. Write your article.

6. If you were _____ for a day, what would you do? (Options are unlimited: school principal, teacher, parent, president, and so on.)

7. If you had a whole day to do just as you pleased, what would you do?

8. Write the most *un*tempting recipe you can think of. Give all of the directions. Use words to describe how the senses of taste and smell might be offended.

9. Invent an object. Describe it, telling what it is made of, why it is important, how it is used.

10. If you could make three changes in the world (your town, our school), what would they be? Why do you think they are important?

11. Create and describe a mixed-up animal. For example, there is *the beefalo,* a combination of cow and buffalo. What would a tigerouse (tiger/mouse) be like? ... a rabbiphant (rabbit/elephant)?

12. Compare group nonsense stories. On three separate slips of paper, have each student write a phrase, on one slip answering the question "Who?" on the second "Did what?" and on the third "Why?" Scramble each category of phrases in a separate box. Have each student draw out one copy of each phrase to read a full sentence. Example: "A lazy old man ... flew through the air ... because the eggs were scrambled."

Titles for Writing

Following are titles selected from actual writing of students in an elementary school district. These are offered in the hope that some might strike your fancy and that of your pupils. All kinds of variations are possible, and the titles have not been organized in any fashion other than to identify a few possible categories: Fact or Fiction, Personal, Character

Sketches, Descriptions, How to, and Argument. Even these can take different directions in the handling.

Fact or Fiction

One Upon a Time There Was...

A Mouse in the House

The Big Fire

The Day I Painted the House

If I Were a Pilgrim

If I Were a Parent

If I Were a Raindrop

If I Were a Sock

If I Were President

I Wish I Were an Elephant

What a Day to Play Baseball!

Leprechauns I Know

Lost in My Own House

When I Went Fishing

Vacation Time

One Day I Saw Trouble Coming

The Dog That Couldn't Sleep

The Cat That Could Do Anything

One Day I Woke Up Late

If I Were a Computer

Through the Looking Glass

Running Down the Street,...

Adventure of a Falling Star

My Face Was Red!

When Abe Lincoln Was Little

I Was a Baby Dinosaur

The Cat Who Liked Waffles

A Place I'd Like to Visit

As Dark as...

As Noisy as...

Why I Like School

How I'd Change Our Classroom

Fun in the Rain

A Cold Day in May

When the North Wind Blew

A Foggy Day

Rain Keeps Coming Down

Snow...I Hate Snow!

Lost in a Storm

If the Sun Quit Shining

If Snow Was Applesauce

I Know Summer Is Coming Because...

My Friend the...

Who's at the Zoo

When the Circus Comes to Town

The Bunny That Forgot Easter

A Mixed-up World

The Magician

Something New

The Spooky Shadow

A Funny Dream

The Flying Cup

The Cookie Jar

What a Bike Ride!

The Funny Secret

The Silly Day

The Big Hotel

If I Were a Mouse

The Three Friends

Dear Mr. President:

If I Were a Fish

The Kids Next Door

My Toy Came Alive

A Special Pet

Everything Went Wrong Yesterday

We Had a Tiger at Breakfast

Terry (Tillie) the Tiger

Once I Was an Old Shoe

The Hamster That Caught Cold

The Travels of a Mouse

A Hamster Named Harry

If I Were One Inch Tall

If I Were a Chicken

What Was That Noise?

A Ride in a Jet

Why My Pet Would Choose Me

What Makes Me Smile

The Fastest Kid in School

If I Could Be a Worm

If I Could Fly

Searching for Treasure

My Friend's House

The First Buds of Spring

A Genie in a Jar

The Hardest Job I've Had to Do

Terry and the Flying Carpet

A Parade Is...

A Lost Arrow

The Broken Wheel

A Strange Valentine

How the Easter Bunny Came to Be

Clothes of the Future

Travel in the 21st Century

The Cordless Telephone

If I Were an Astronaut

The Grandfather Clock

A Skeleton in the Closet

What Table Manners!

An Important Decision

I Know What You're Thinking!

When I Got Lost

A Toy That...

The New Girl (Boy) in School

Our Mail Carrier

Fun Is...

The Police Officer

A Fire Fighter

A Mystery

The Talking Fish

Something New

Never-Never Land

A Loose Lizard

Lost in the Forest

February 16, 2002

The Lost Kitten

The Lighthouse

My Favorite Color

Me and My Shadow

What Is It?

I Am a Nickel

My Magic Wand

Colors

The Friendly Dragon

My Pet

A Silly Seal

The Flying...

A Day in the Park

An Unusual Gadget

My Trip Through Space

My Greatest Invention

The Olympics

A Strange Dream

The Alarm

Habits

Borrowing

Humor is...

I Was in a Big Hurry When…	I Knew It!
White Clouds in a Blue Sky	Confusion!
The Big Event!	And Then It Happened!

Personal

All About Me	My Name Is…
What I Like about My State/City/Town	My Favorite Sport
Why I Like My Hobby	My Book of the Month Is…
My Favorite Subject in School	I Want to Be…
What I Like to Do on Vacation	When I Grow Up
If I Had Three Wishes	My New Year's Resolution
If I Had a Million Dollars	The Narrow Escape
My Memory of the Year	My Ambition
A Book Character I'd Like to Meet	My Pet Peeve
The Cat in My Family	I Was Frightened
I Am Thankful for…	People I Remember
If I Could Do It over Again	My Favorite Color
The Animal I'd Like to Be	What I Like to Do
My Least Favorite Season	My Ancestors
My Favorite Relative	Our Family Tradition
Moving into a New House	What I Think of…
My Favorite TV Show	I Made an Important Decision
I Changed My Mind Because…	My Most Important Day
How I Use My Allowance	My Favorite Christmas Present

Character Sketches

Someone I'll Never Forget	A True Friend
The Personality of a Rock	My Mom/Dad
A Person Who Influenced Me	A Family Portrait
The Kindest Person in the World	Me, Myself
Snow White's Eighth Dwarf	The Daydreamer
An Important Ancestor	The Babysitter
My Favorite Historical Character	The Gum Chewer
The Best Person I Know	Brown Eyes
A Book Character I'd Like to Meet	My Grandma/Grandpa
The People Next Door	A Typical American

Descriptions

The Lonely Road	My Pet
A Strange Stillness	Full Moon
Noises in the Night	A Thunderstorm
A Jet Takes Off	Snow Flakes
My Favorite Spot	A Cloud in the Sky
Main Street	The Haunted House
The Aroma of Thanksgiving Dinner	Words
A Busy Restaurant	Music
This Is a "Contraption"	Colors
The Sounds of School	November
A Quiet Place	A Summer Day

How to's

How to Care for Plants	How to Repair…
How to Build a Monster	How to Play…
How to Begin a _____ Collection	How to Cook…
How to Make New Friends	How to Bake…
How to Teach a Parrot to Talk	How to Use a Pen
How to Care for a Pet	How to Pick a Book
How to Get Along with Your Sister/Brother	How to Take Video Pictures
How to Make Something from Nothing	How to Set the Table

Argument/Persuasion

What Our School Needs Most	The Most Important Invention
Living on a Farm vs. Living in the City	Summer vs. Winter
The Advantages of Friends	The Best Book Is…
School Should be Cancelled	Before and After
I'd Rather Have a _____ Than a _____	The Best State Is…
Customs We Need to Borrow	America's Greatest Athlete
Everyone Should Have a Hobby	Sportmanship
Why I Like Poetry	My Favorite School Subject
Jet vs. Van Travel	Lunch Period Should Be Longer

We Should Make Spelling Easier   The Best Pet Is...

Everyone Should Learn a Second
Language   The Best Sport Is...

More Expanded Writing

Some kinds of writing require additional instructional preparation and are often aimed at specific kinds of skills. The following writing and language activities fit into this category.

1. Make youngsters aware that sometimes people say what they don't mean. Give them some examples, such as the following, and have them look and listen for others:

"I will remain firm! And where compromise is necessary, I will compromise." (President Carter on energy, April 20, 1977)

A local television station announced an "award" for "average citizens who have never done anything to win an award."

A legislative candidate (we'll call him Tom Smith) ran a radio commercial—only briefly!—stating: "You all know how the state wastes money. Tom Smith does too."

Such remarks might make one feel like the only person at the United Nations without earphones!

2. Find three or four pictures of similar subjects. Number them and post them for the class to see. Have each pupil select one (secretly) to be described as specifically as possible. Share descriptions to see if they are clear enough for the class to decide which picture is being discussed. (This also presents a good opportunity to justify revision.)

3. After a discussion of places of interest in their town, have pupils write brief descriptions such as a chamber of commerce might prepare for each site. You might want to compile these into a booklet about the town. You may want to begin this activity with an examination of travel brochures or publications received by pupils who write to chambers of commerce for information.

4. Just for fun, have each pupil jot down on a small card three unrelated nouns, with adjectives if you'd like. Randomly distribute the cards and have each recipient write a brief piece tying the three nouns together in a story.

5. Have students examine classified ads in the newspaper. Then have them use the format to write an ad of their own trying to sell some item of theirs. Remind them that they are limited to twenty-five words or fewer.

6. Examine other parts of the newspaper with your class. After pupils understand the characteristics of each kind of writing, have them attempt an editorial, an advice column, a column of opinion, a news article, or a sports column.

7. Initial instruction in using a dictionary can be assisted enjoyably if pupils make their own nonsense dictionaries, or the class prepares one with entries from each individual. For example, one entry in a third grade "Daffy Dictionary" was "jumetamlshan /ju mē 'tam l shan / a weird wizard."

8. Use of a dictionary for meaning can be enhanced if youngsters are given questions that include a strange word. They are to locate the meaning according to the context and answer the question. Examples: "Would you rather meet a person who is insipid or inspired? Why?" "Is a braggart more likely to talk about his expiration or his expertise? Why?"

9. Older students can use their knowledge of the dictionary to write serious definitions. Point out that a good definition must be specific, must identify the class to which the entry belongs, and must clarify characteristics that distinguish it from other members of the class. Use examples from dictionaries in your room.

10. Have students bring in old TV schedules and examine the descriptive blurbs for the programs. Then have them write one- or two-sentence blurbs to describe their favorite program so that others would want to watch it.

11. Older students may enjoy imitating some of the soap opera teasers by writing a concluding statement for one segment of a show. Example: "Will John return to Mary? Will Jody walk again? Who kept Jan from finding happiness in her new home?"

12. If students are interested in the *Guinness Book of World Records,* have them make up nonsense entries. Example: "Tim Smith, a fourth grader at Franklin School, balanced a marble on his nose for 17½ minutes."

13. After acquainting your group with the connotations of words (see Chapter 5), have them make new commercials for familiar cereals or other foods. They might also enjoy reversing the slant to "unsell" the products. They could also invent their own products to promote.

14. If you teach lessons on propaganda techniques, be certain to include experience in writing that makes use of some of the devices to argue a position. Actually using these techniques themselves is the best way I know to have youngsters recognize when others use them in running text. Too often, school experience with propaganda devices is limited to commercials and ads instead of recognizing that these devices are also used in connected discourse to persuade a reader.

15. Directions are among the most difficult kinds of writing. Ask students to write directions for how to do some very familiar activity, such as how to put on a sweater, how to tie a shoe, how to make a peanut-butter sandwich, or even how to get from class to the cafeteria. Once directions are written, follow several examples literally. Usually indications for revision are clear after only one or two examples.

16. A good "get acquainted" writing activity in any class is to distribute randomly the names of class members, making certain that no one gets his or her own name. Then, using "Blank" as the name, have each person write about the one whose name is drawn. See if the class can identify the individual being described. (You may need to censor some of these.)

17. Once students are acquainted, have them again draw names of class members and write an absence excuse for that person. These should capitalize on the characteristics of the person and be in exaggerated form. (As with #16, the class should realize that they are not to make fun of a person's dress, speech, and so on.)

18. From first grade on, youngsters need to realize that a good writer is observant. One first-grade teacher had her pupils observe every visitor to the room. As soon as the visitor left, they were to recall all of the details they could about that person. With older students this can be done in writing. (This activity has the added advantage of keeping the kids quiet while the teacher conducts business with the visitor!)

19. Social letter writing is a skill that needs to be taught. Too often letter writing instruction focuses on format instead of content. After initial instruction on format, keep that posted for reference and discuss the content of each kind of letter. Then have children write letters—and be certain that they are sent to the addressees! Letter writing should include invitations, social letters, holiday greetings, thank-you letters, and letters of regret—all done for appropriate situations.

20. Business letters are also important by the time students reach the middle grades. Here practice—preceded by instruction on appropriate content as well as format—should include subscriptions, requests/orders, letters of inquiry, complaints, and applications.

21. Unusual recipes might be concocted by older students. For example, one group suggested the following recipe for a good writing class:

Ingredients:	Interested Students
	Stimulating Teacher
	Free Flow of Ideas
	Topics to Write About
	Time to Write
	Respect for Other's Opinions
Product:	Students who enjoyed writing and who wrote.

Other recipes might be written for "Success," "Failure," or "How to make a teacher cranky."

Using Books as Springboards

As suggested in Chapter 1, additional reading is as beneficial as additional instruction in writing for improving writing skills. We might add that when the two are tied together they mutually stimulate each other. Following are some ideas that can be used.

1. Have pupils pick a favorite book character. Let them write what the character is like and why that one is their favorite.

2. Let pupils write a new adventure for a character or a new ending for a favorite book.

3. Have them write a diary of the character based on the adventures of that character in the book.

4. Have pupils challenge one another to guess a book from a headline they make. For example, what books might these be from: "Runaways Hide out in Art Museum" or "Life of Chief Cheese-Taster Endangered"?

5. Even older students can enjoy making up headlines for nursery rhymes. For "Mary Had a Little Lamb" one bright group came up with the headline: "School Board Says Baaa to Ewe."

6. After reading some of the *Just So Stories,* have pupils write their own "How the..." tales.

7. The class may appreciate a file box or cumulative folder to which anyone reading a book may contribute a brief note identifying the book, telling what it is about, and why they did or did not like it. Such a collection can be helpful to others looking for a good book to read.

8. Younger pupils may enjoy illustrating a book jacket and writing the blurb for a favorite book. Older ones might make jackets for the books *they write.*

9. Pupils can also make "wanted" posters, depicting a character and telling why and by whom that person is being sought.

10. Following experience with news writing, students might like to write a "news" article based on a book, as if the events in the book had taken place at the present time in their town. Even nursery rhymes can be used—imagine the story following the headline "Bears' House Vandalized."

11. At any level, students might enjoy writing a letter to their favorite author about a book or character they enjoyed. Send the letter to the author in care of the publisher, and you can expect a response to the class.

12. Letter writing can be expanded. What kinds of letters might be written between two characters, such as Anatole and Frederick, or between Henry Huggins and Romona? What might a character say in a letter to the author, and what reply might the author make?

13. Youngsters might also write a friendly letter to recommend a book to someone they know. These could even be to classmates and "mailed" through the classroom mailbox.

14. Have pupils write parodies of familiar tales, such as "Coal Black and the Seven Giants" or "Big Red, the Walking Hood" Reversals can also be developed: What would have happened if Jack's beans had not grown? What might have happened if the three bears had been home when Goldilocks got there?

15. Older students might compare/contrast two favorite characters or two different books on the same theme. The more sophisticated handling enables the use of primary books with older students. For example, students may compare the authors' attitudes toward work in the case of *Frederick* and "The Grasshopper and the Ant."

16. Youngsters might like to compile character sketches of favorite types of characters into booklets, such as "Clever Cats," "Crafty Kids," or even "Mighty Mice." More seriously, this could become a "Who's Who" of familiar characters.

17. After reading examples of myths, have pupils try their hands at explaining some natural phenomenon.

18. Read some examples of color poems from Mary O'Neil's *Hailstones and Halibut Bones*. This technique is appropriate for sensory poetry at any level and it was used by one first-grade teacher to develop an entire unit about color: listening, writing, mixing colors, listing objects and animals of the color, and so on.

19. Read a few poems from Eve Merriam's *It Doesn't Always Have to Rhyme* or from Shel Silverstein's *Where the Sidewalk Ends*. Your youngsters will certainly get some ideas from these!

20. After discussion of idioms—or reading some of the *Amelia Bedelia* books—have pupils write their own stories in which idioms are interpreted literally.

21. Read a few tall tales to the group. Have them write about when "It was so... (hot, cold, big, soft, etc.)."

22. Another use for nursery rhymes, fables, or fairy tales—at all ages—is to write updated forms. Suppose Mother Hubbard lived in a condo, or what might Jack and Jill fetch today?

Jingles and Poetry

Many of the "Warm-ups" previously suggested, including similes, metaphors, and creative thinking, are basic to writing poetry. This section presents ideas ranging from simple jingles to more sophisticated forms of poetry, most of which are appropriate for any age level after pupils have been given a few examples.

1. Simple rhyming couplets can be written:

If I were a cat
I'd find things to bat.

2. Youngsters might enjoy free verse in a five W's form:

Who	*Lena Lonely*
What	*Waiting for school to begin*
Where	*By Miss Taylor's door*
When	*Every morning*
Why	*Because no one will talk to her.*

3. Rhyming couplets can be expanded for older students. Have each one bring in a bag containing some small fruit or vegetable. Exchange bags and have recipients write a series of couplets describing the item. In reading their couplets, have pupils read one set at a time to see how many clues the group needs to identify the object. This activity can be helpful in pointing out the need for clarity and specificity in writing. Example:

> *White when fresh, brown if old*
> *Pungent and spongy, good warm or cold.*
>
> *Tasty on salad; alone, apropos.*
> *My cap is a treat; my stem, so-so.*
>
> *Tasty and mild, trust my white-capped guise,*
> *But beware of my brothers if you be wise.*

4. **Prepositional poems** are not only a nonthreatening type of introduction to writing, they also provide experience with that class of words. There is no rule other than that each line should begin with a preposition (and some poetic license is allowed!):

> A DIFFERENCE
> *During the summer*
> > *on a boat*
> > *in the breeze*
> > *over peaceful water.*
>
> *Instead of*
> *During the winter*
> > *on the bus*
> > *to the class*
> > *over icy roads.*

5. **Limericks** are nonsense forms that youngsters enjoy, although adults seem to find them frightening to write. Provide a sample of two, review the rhythm and rhyme, and turn the youngsters loose:

> *There once was a kitty named Scat*
> *Who fought with a much bigger cat*
> > *He said, "Though I'm small,*
> > *I'm loaded with gall.*
> *So I knocked that fat cat flat."*

(In demonstrating the first time, it is usually better to make the rhythm clear, using a last line such as "So I knocked that cat to the mat." However, pupils should understand that they can then make adjustments for effect.)

6. Definition poems or acrostics may or may not rhyme. The first letter of each line forms a word when read vertically from the top:

5 word: synonym for title

Where	*Perky in manner*
Anger	*Agile as a gazelle*
Reigns.	*Trustworthy of character.*

7. A cinquain is a five-line poem with specific rules as follows:

1 word: title	*Kitten*
2 words: description	*Furry bundle*
3 words: action	*Batting at shadows*
4 words: feeling	*Happy to be loved*
1 word: synonym for title	*Cat*

8. A haiku is a three-line Japanese poem usually dealing with nature and painting a concise word picture. The lines consist of five, seven, and five syllables:

Dew on the rosebud
Tiny jewel in the sun
Ice on red velvet.

9. A tanka continues a haiku by adding two more lines, each with seven syllables.

10. The diamante is a diamond-shaped poem in which the subject is reversed in the middle of the fourth line. It follows this pattern:

1 noun	*Love*
2 adjectives	*tender, gentle*
3 participles (*-ing* forms)	*smiling, warming, caring*
4 nouns	*closeness, happiness—gloom, distance*
3 participles	*sneering, gnawing, glowering*
2 adjectives	*harsh, cruel*
1 noun	*Hate*

11. Concrete poetry or shape poetry is a form where the words are put on the page to illustrate the subject of the poem. For example, a poem about sailing might be written in the shape of a saiboat. This same idea can be used with single words or phrases, such as:

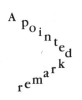

12. Interesting free verse can be developed as a collage of newspaper or magazine words and phrases.

13. For more serious poems, one way to help young writers get started is to have them decide on a subject, such as fear, love, beauty, or happiness. Have them list all the words they think of that relate to their subject. (You might even like to try group brainstorming for this.) Listed words will serve as a memory bank for writing the poem.

LITERARY MODELS

The use of models from literature seems to have fallen into disfavor as compared with its intensity of use in the 1960s. Used too strictly, models can become threatening: What student can hope to match the quality of an accomplished author? Further, a servile reliance on models turns the young writer into little more than a mimic. However, as mentioned repeatedly, reading and writing can be related, to the benefit of skill development in both. In addition to simple activities already presented under "Using Books as Springboards," children's books can become a valuable source of direction for the writing class.

Rather than being presented with "a way" of writing something, youngsters can compare and discuss "the ways" different authors handled a particular type of writing. From such examinations, they can realize different avenues for their own creative expression.

This book could present to you a list of citations—paragraphs from outstanding children's books—that illustrate characterization, action, description, and so on. However, I've found it better to turn that job over to the youngsters themselves. In fact, when I asked teachers to announce to their students that I was looking for good paragraphs of various types, teachers told me that many of their pupils, from third grade up, went to the library shelf, pulled out a book, and opened it almost directly to a paragraph that they remembered. Not only did they recall particular paragraphs, but their taste was apparent, as the same paragraphs were often recommended by children from different schools. Of course, the most often mentioned was the description of "It" from *A Wrinkle in Time*.

Begin by announcing to your pupils that you'd like them to be alert during their reading for the next week or so for any paragraph that is a particularly good example of something you've already decided upon. When they find one, they are to jot it down in their language log and present it for discussion at the specified time. (Or you might ask that they copy it for duplication at that time.)

Topics for the excellent-example paragraphs might be of your own choosing, chosen jointly by the class, or from the following list:

1. Opening paragraph of a story (or opening sentence)
2. Explanations or directions
3. Descriptions of characters, scenes, sounds, places, moods, animals, actions, objects, people
4. Use of literary devices.

At the appointed sharing time, discussion of the examples will reveal the many different ways authors accomplish their purposes. For example, the class might be comparing paragraphs describing characters. The paragraph introducing Henry Huggins provides a physical description—"His hair looked like a scrubbing brush," and so on—while the description of Junket reveals personality through actions. After discussing the different ways in which a character can be brought to life, youngsters may then attempt a description of a person they know.

SUMMARY

This chapter has presented a collection of ideas for stimulating writing in children of all ages. Although an awareness of the distinction in emphasis between transactional and poetic writing—as compared with the basic expressive mode—may be helpful, activities were not so tightly organized. Teachers were encouraged to *offer* ideas rather than to *impose* them on youngsters. Experience with every type of writing is essential, and that experience must be enjoyable if children are to develop as writers.

The close relationship between experience in reading and writing was demonstrated in several instances, and the use of literary models was suggested as one means of acquainting students with the *ways* of accomplishing various writing objectives.

SUGGESTIONS FOR ACTION

Since most of this chapter has consisted of suggestions, it seems pointless to repeat them here. Pick activities that appeal to you and your pupils. Then write—and you write with them! In fact, many teachers have enjoyed writing based on a number of the activities listed here while they were engaged as graduate students in writing classes.

If you teach grade three or above, try having your students collect exemplary paragraphs of a particular type to discuss and to provide additional ideas on method and style.

REFERENCES

BRITTON, JAMES, TONY BURGESS, NANCY MARTIN, ALEX MCLEOD; and HAROLD ROSEN, *The Development of Writing Abilities (11–18)*. London: Macmillan Education, 1975 (distributed by the National Council of Teachers of English). Reports results of a study of the classification of writing into expressive, transactional, and poetic.

EDELSKY, CAROLE, and KAREN SMITH, "Is That Writing—Or Are Those Marks Just a Figment of Your Curriculum?" *Language Arts*, 61 (January, 1984), 24–32. Defines and discusses the need for "authentic" writing as opposed to the "inauthentic" kind too often found in classrooms.

KOCH, KENNETH, *Wishes, Lies, and Dreams*. New York: Chelsea House Publishers, 1970. A collection of poetry written by children, accompanied by introductions as to methods used.

KREEFT, JOY, "Dialogue Writing—Bridge from Talk to Writing," *Language Arts*, 61 (February, 1984) 141–50. Suggests a dialogue journal to provide written interaction between student and teacher as a means of leading middle-grade students from expressive to transactional writing.

ADDITIONAL RESOURCES

BRANDRETH, GYLES, *The Joy of Lex*. New York: William Morrow and Company, 1980. A humorous collection of ideas for writing, including everything from puns to graffiti.

————, *More Joy of Lex: An Amusing and Amazing Z to A and A to Z of Words*. New York: William Morrow and Company, 1982. More of the same kind of fun with language.

HIPPLE, THEODORE W, ROBERT G. WRIGHT, JANE H. YARBROUGH, and BRUCE BARTHOLOMEW, *"Forty-Plus Writing Activities," English Journal,* 72 (March, 1983), 73–76. Ideas for stimulating writing.

KORENBLIT, JOAN B., and JUDY PRIVEN, *Language Arts Through Writing.* Chicago: Childrens Press, 1984. An extensive collection of "lessons" for developing skill in writing.

MOFFETT, JAMES, and BETTY JANE WAGNER, *Student-Centered Language Arts and Reading, K–13.* Boston: Houghton Mifflin Company, 1983. A professional text on the theory and practice of language arts instruction.

TEACHERS AND WRITERS COLLABORATIVE, *The Whole Word Catalog.* New York: Teachers and Writers Collaborative, 1972 (distributed by the National Council of Teachers of English). A collection of ideas for stimulating writing.

UNITED STATES POSTAL SERVICE, *All About Letters.* Washington: United States Postal Service, 1979 (distributed by the National Council of Teachers of English). Material to encourage and assist instruction in letter writing for teenagers.

————, *P.S. Write Soon!* Washington: United States Postal Service, 1982 (distributed by the National Council of Teachers of English). Material to encourage and assist instruction in letter writing for grades four through eight.

5

Developing
Vocabulary

*Words, when well chosen, have so great a force in them that a
description often gives us more lively ideas than the sight of things
themselves.*

JOSEPH ADDISON, 1712

THIS CHAPTER PRESENTS IDEAS and techniques for expanding the receptive
and expressive meaning vocabularies of students. This expansion is
accomplished through involvement in language, with some refinement
through use of the tools of the writer—the dictionary and the thesaurus.
(Discussion of the spelling vocabulary is presented in Chapter 9.)

The English language is made up of an enormous number of
words. *Webster's Third Unabridged Dictionary* boasts of more than
450,000 entries. If one were to consider the many variant and inflected
forms of these entries, well over a million words would make up the
lexicon. In fact, Olson (1983) claims that there are about 11 million
different words in the English language.

It's not only that we have such a number to consider; the lexicon
changes daily. In fact, between 1973 and 1983, Merriam-Webster claims to
have added thousands of *new* words to *Webster's Ninth New Collegiate
Dictionary.*

Faced with such facts, what words should be taught? Certainly no
one would suggest teaching even the 450,000 base words. To do so, in an
average lifespan of seventy years, would require learning an average of
seventeen and one-half words per day, or 122 words per week during that
entire life.

Fortunately, such a monstrous task is neither suggested nor
necessary. Let's begin by considering the different vocabularies possessed
by each individual. Then we'll proceed to discuss how many words are
important and how they might best be learned.

VOCABULARIES

Every individual possesses a number of vocabularies of different sizes. Those samples of the total English lexicon are depicted in Figure 5.1.

Probably no one has control of *every* word in the language. Beyond this fact, however, the proportions in Figure 5.1 will vary with the education and experience of the individual. Most limited will be the "recognition vocabulary," those words named and understood instantaneously upon seeing or hearing them, without need for context or further thought. This vocabulary is a subset of the larger receptive vocabulary.

For most people, the expressive vocabulary, that used in speaking and writing, is more limited than the next larger, the receptive. Within the former, it would be difficult to depict the relative size of the speaking versus the writing vocabulary: Obviously young children have a larger speaking vocabulary, whereas the educated adult might use a more

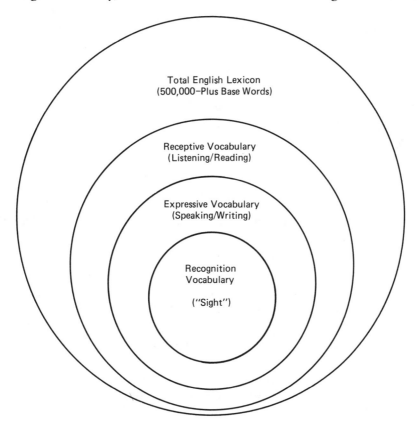

Total English Lexicon
(500,000–Plus Base Words)

Receptive Vocabulary
(Listening/Reading)

Expressive Vocabulary
(Speaking/Writing)

Recognition
Vocabulary

("Sight")

FIGURE 5.1. The Vocabularies of English

extensive writing vocabulary as a result of access to contemplation, dictionary, and/or thesaurus.

It is safe to assume that the receptive vocabulary of anyone exceeds that person's expressive vocabulary: A completely foreign word can often be understood because of the use of context, an aid not available for expression. Again, the relative size of the reading versus the listening vocabulary will vary with age and experience: The young child will understand more by listening than by reading; the educated adult will probably have a larger understanding vocabulary in reading than in listening because of the time allowed for review and analysis of context.

Figure 5.1 not only shows relative size, it can be used as an example of progression in vocabulary development. One moves from the total lexicon to incorporate a new word into the receptive vocabulary. With experience, that word eventually becomes part of the expressive vocabulary and ultimately may become automatic—part of the recognition vocabulary.

More specifically, the stages one goes through in meeting a word and adding it to the vocabulary are something like the following:

1. "That looks (sounds) like a word, but..."
2. "I've seen (heard) it before, but..."
3. "I think I know that word; use it in context."
4. "I recognize that word anywhere."
5. "I use that word myself."

As stated, no one needs to learn all of the words in English. A few words are used in almost every sentence, whereas there are many that will never be seen or heard by the average person. As an example, consider that three words—*I, and, the*—account for 10 percent of all the words on a page in English. The ten most frequently used words account for about 25 percent of all words used, and one hundred make up 61 percent of the words children use in writing (Hillerich, 1978) or 48 percent of the words in adult printed material (Kucera and Francis, 1967). In fact, fewer than 3,000 words account for 95 percent of all words used by children or adults. Obviously, one reaches a point of diminishing returns in trying to teach every word in English.

To consider this point from another view, Nagy and Anderson (1984) reported that the student in grades three through nine reads 20,000 to 40,000 different words, including 3,000 to 4,000 new words per year. They conclude:

Our findings indicate that even the most ruthlessly systematic direct vocabulary instruction could neither account for a significant proportion of all the words children actually learn, nor cover more than a modest proportion of the words they will encounter in school reading materials.

How, then, are we to develop vocabulary in students? Examination of more than 200 research studies on vocabulary development has led me to essentially the same conclusion as that arrived at in the discussion of oral language development: The best single way to develop vocabulary—receptive or expressive, and in adult or child—is through enjoyable exposure to words in a variety of contexts, with an interest in language.

Each phrase is important here. The exposure must be enjoyable if the individual is to participate actively. Contexts for a given word must be varied so that the rough edges are smoothed and the nuances of meaning become apparent. Finally, interest in language puts the icing on the cake; it causes the learning to continue for a lifetime.

What has just been stated is not all that can be said about vocabulary development, but it is the key. There are some specific techniques and activities that will help to provide this exposure and develop this interest. Furthermore, a second point gleaned from analysis of the research on vocabulary development is not only important, but it is also verified by common sense: Regardless of the techniques used, teachers who make a conscious effort toward increasing their students' vocabularies are more likely to accomplish this increase than are teachers who make no such effort.

TECHNIQUES FOR DEVELOPING VOCABULARY

There are two kinds of instruction dealing with vocabulary development: those activities that are generalizable to words other than those studied and those that are not generalizable. Some research studies fail to recognize this distinction. For example, it is foolhardy to teach *susceptible* or *supersede* and to test gains using *peignoir* or *carburetor.* Such learning is word specific. On the other hand, learning that *un-* reverses the meaning of the familiar words *lock* and *tie* should generalize to *un-* when it is affixed to other familiar words, such as *uncover* or *unearth.*

We'll discuss this latter type of instruction first. It should be the most important, but unfortunately it is also the most limited. In fact, what we have to say here is as much in the vein of what not to do (in order to avoid wasting time) as it is in suggesting what should be done.

Generalizable Vocabulary Instruction

Generalizable vocabulary instruction is limited to certain affixes—those prefixes and suffixes that can be used to alter the meaning of familiar words. In fact, it deals primarily with prefixes, since most of the suffixes are inflections that merely change the part of speech of the word without altering its semantic meaning: *play* to *played, dust* to *dusty,* and so on.

Often, time is wasted in teaching prefixes that are of no help to anyone. Deighton (1959) presented straightforward and sensible criteria for determining which ones to teach: In order to be worth teaching, a prefix or suffix must be (1) frequently used and (2) consistent in meaning. This latter point is especially pertinent from a reading standpoint. How is one to know, in the case of a prefix with six different meanings, which is the meaning in the particular unfamiliar word?

Following is a list of nineteen prefixes often suggested for instruction. Using Deighton's criteria and *Webster's Ninth New Collegiate Dictionary,* I've marked with an asterisk those that I believe are worth some instruction. Deighton is more stringent, and his choices are marked with a "plus" sign.

> **ad-** to, toward, near (also assimilates: *af, ac, ag, al, ap, as,* **at**).
>
> **com-** (has lost its meaning in most words)
>
> **de-** do the opposite of, reverse, remove something from, remove, reduce, something derived from, derived from something, get off of, molecule with one or more atoms removed.
>
> **dis-** do the opposite of, deprive of, expel from, the absence of, not, completely.
>
> **epi-** upon, beside, akin to, attached to, over, outer, after, related to, distinguished from.
>
> **ex-** out of, not, outside, former.
>
> + *in- not, in, into, (also used as an intensifier: *inflammable*).
>
> *inter- (has six meanings, but all are interrelated as "between")
> between/among: *interstellar*
> located between: *interfaced*
> occurring between: *interglacial*
> reciprocal: *interrelationship*
> carried on between: *international*
> shared by: *interfaith.*
>
> + *mis- bad, wrong, opposite of, not.
>
> + *mono- alone, one.
>
> + *non- not, the absence of.

ob- in the wrong way, against, toward, inversely.

***over-** so as to exceed or surpass, excessive.

***pre-** (has five meanings, but all relate to "before, in time or space")
in front of/before: *prehistoric*
in advance: *precancel*
front/anterior: *preabdomen*
preparatory to: *premed*
in front of: *premolar.*

pro- (based on two different prefixes, one from Latin, one from Greek) earlier than, projecting, rudimentary, in front of, in place of, favoring.

***re-** again/anew: *retell*
back/backward: *recall*

sub- under/below, subordinate/inferior, with repetition to deal with parts, less than completely/somewhat, less than the usual amount, basic, almost/nearly, adjoining/bordering on.

trans- on, to the other side of/across, beyond, through, such as to change.

+ ***un-** not, the opposite of.

As you see in this list, many prefixes should be excluded because they have too many meanings. I would provide instruction with some, such as *inter-, over-, pre-,* and *re-,* despite Deighton's omission of these. They can be taught with a general meaning, since their "different" meanings are all related.

Conversely, one might argue that *in-* falls into the same category as *ad-,* since both have several meanings and both assimilate. (*In-* is spelled *il-* in *illegible, im-* in *immeasurable, ir-* in *irreversible.*) However, the use of *in-* as an intensifier seems to be fading, and it is among the most frequently used of all prefixes. Hence, it probably deserves some instruction.

That instruction seems best initiated by jumping off from some receptive experience—reading or listening—where youngsters meet the prefix as part of a familiar word. From this experience, they can search for other examples of the prefix, and they may also attempt to construct new words by prefixing a familiar base word and checking with one another or the dictionary.

Suffixes that affect meaning and are consistent in their meaning are very limited. In fact, there are only two or three major items here: *-less,* in the sense of without or unable to act or be acted on (*fearless, helpless*), and *-able/-ible,* in the sense of capable of or liable to (*consumable, collectible*).

A third possible suffix is *-ful,* in the general sense of full of (*eventful, helpful*). Specific meanings may vary, as in the latter case, where one is not "full of help" but is characterized by or given to help.

Other than the suggestion not to waste time working with affixes that offer no insight to meaning, there is little more to say about them from a writing standpoint. However, since initial experiences are usually receptive, we might add the caution that, in reading, students should be taught always to note a base word before assuming that a given collection of initial letters represents a prefix. For example, *preach* may appear to have the prefix *pre-,* but one would certainly err in jumping to that conclusion. And there are about ten times as many of these anomalous "prefixes" as there are real ones.

Nongeneralizable Vocabulary Instruction: Specific

Usually your goal with students is to increase their receptive, and ultimately, their expressive, vocabularies. Most often you do not have a specific word in mind to "teach." Under such conditions, your efforts are devoted to increasing their interest in words and then to help them build associations for those words through classifying, relating to other words, finding other examples, or otherwise fitting those new words into the schemata or mental blueprints they already have.

At times, however, you may have a specific word in mind that you do want to teach, perhaps from science or social studies. Peters (1975–76) has reported successful accomplishment of this goal with the Frayer model, which includes four clarifying techniques: (1) state the relevant attributes (a *gnu* is a type of antelope; it has horns); (2) state irrelevant attributes (the size of the horns is irrelevant); (3) use non-examples (a *gnu* is not a fish or bird); (4) place in a hierarchy (size: elephant, *gnu,* fox).

Along the same—but less structured—lines, students might develop meaning for words by examining them from a variety of views, as suggested by Johnson and Pearson (1978). Using the words *caterwaul* and *feline* as examples, students could complete a chart such as the following:

	caterwaul	*feline*
Use:	We heard the *caterwaul* of a squirrel.	That manx is a typical *feline.*

	caterwaul	*feline*
Definition:	a harsh cry	relating to the cat family
Synonym:	wail	cat
Antonym:	sing	canine
Class:	sounds	animals
Example:	screech	Tabby

Another device reportedly helpful in developing specific word knowledge is the mnemonic keyword method (Pressley, Levin, and Delaney, 1982). Not only has this technique been found successful with students from second grade up, it transfers to use after instruction. In other words, with adequate instruction and practice in the technique, students will generalize to applications in similar situations. As an example of the technique, to remember the meaning of the word *caterwaul,* pupils might be helped by associating the *wail* of a *cat* on a *wall.* Especially with younger children, a picture is valuable, whereas older students can merely be encouraged to visualize the situation.

This technique has been most used in learning the vocabulary of a second language or in remembering two associated items, such as states and their capitals. For example, Ohio and its capital might be remembered by associating the "high" in the state name with Christopher Columbus, visualizing *Columbus* on the *high* seas. Further, whether teacher or student supplies the mnemonic device doesn't seem to make much difference.

Nongeneralizable Vocabulary Development: Nonspecific

Most vocabulary development will fit into the category of nongeneralizable vocabulary development, wherein concern is for broadening the meaning and useful vocabulary in uncontrolled directions. We'll begin, however, with some activities that seem to represent a hybrid, since they can be used with random words but also represent a technique that is helpful with specifics.

One such activity is that of having students classify words. Classifications may range from relatively simple words in categories such as sounds, smells, tastes, and so on, to more complex words such as the following, where students are asked to chart the words from this list into one of the columns that follow:

intransigent	mobile	meander
elation	adamant	hostile
enthrall	transitory	immobile

Feelings	*Movement*	*Lack of Movement*
_____	_____	_____
_____	_____	_____
_____	_____	_____

What has been variously called a semantic network, semantic mapping, or webbing can also be used to show interrelationships of words and to build further meaning for a specific word. For example, Figure 5.2 shows how the word *feline* could continue the following web indefinitely.

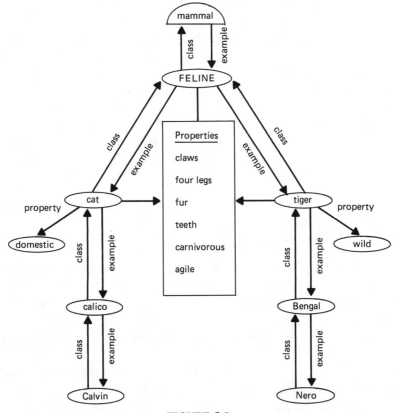

FIGURE 5.2.

Still another method of building meaning through identifying characteristics is what Johnson and Pearson (1978) call semantic feature analysis. Here students might take a collection of related words, such as what are called "fruits" in science, and identify their characteristics or features across the top of a chart, marking a "plus" sign if the item has the characteristic and a "minus" sign if it does not.

"Fruits"	vegetable	fruit	round	sweet	citrus	red	yellowish
apple	−	+	+	+	−	+	−
orange	−	+	+	+	+	−	+
beet	+	−	+	+	−	+	−
grapefruit	−	+	+	−	+	−	+
carrot	+	−	−	?	−	−	+
banana	−	+	−	+	−	−	+
lemon	−	+	−	−	+	−	+

Of course, this kind of classification may take many forms. Students can be given a classification such as "fruits," or anything from "jobs" to "vehicles" to "emotions," for which they can list all of the specific words they can find or think of. Likewise, the reverse can be used, where pupils are given a mixed list of words that they are to classify under common properties. They can also be given sets of four or five words, one of which is to be deleted because it does not belong with the others.

Another method of classifying words is to consider their origins. Many of our English words have been "borrowed" from other languages. Youngsters might like to sort words according to their sources, or they might see how many words they can collect from a given country. For example, in contrast to the Anglo-Saxon terms *cow, sheep,* and *pig,* the French have provided *beef, mutton,* and *pork.* Spanish has given us not only *chili* and *taco,* but also *mosquito, burro,* and *rodeo,* to name only a few.

(For any of these kinds of activities, the best technique is to provide an example or two for youngsters to complete. Then encourage those students to develop their own sets, following the model, for others to attempt to complete. After all, they need the thinking and digging experience more than you do. Anytime *they* build the exercise they are much more personally involved than when the teacher does it. However, it's only fair that you attempt to complete the exercise with the rest of the class.)

Getting youngsters involved in word and phrase origins will increase enjoyment and excitement about words. The collegiate or unabridged dictionary may be used at upper grades, and many books are appropriate at all grade levels. Following are just a few examples that lead to interest in word origins.

Asimov, Isaac. *Words from the Myths.* Houghton Mifflin Company.

Epstein, Samuel, and Beryl Epstein. *The First Book of Words.* Franklin Watts.

Ernst, Margaret S. *Words: English Roots and How They Grow.* Alfred A. Knopf.

Funk, Charles E. *Heavens to Betsy.* Warner Paperback.

————. *Thereby Hangs a Tale.* Warner Paperback.

————. *A Hog on Ice.* Harper and Row.

Funk, Charles E., and Charles E. Funk Jr. *Horsefeathers.* Warner Paperback.

Mathews, Mitford M. *American Words.* World Publishing Company.

Morris, William, and Mary Morris. *Dictionary of Word and Phrase Origins.* Harper and Row.

An authoritative reference that ought to be available to teachers in your school is *Origins* by Eric Partridge, published by The Macmillan Company.

Students can enjoy finding origins and challenging one another with them. They might also make up imaginary origins for words or phrases they use. Some imaginary origins might not be considered too strange when compared with the real ones. For example, we have a number of words that are really mistakes. The Canary Islands were so named because of the breed of large dogs (canines) found there. The dogs were long forgotten by the time the little songbird became known and was named after the islands. An even greater error is represented by our association of *sinistral* or *sinister* with left. The list could go on: *host* originally referred to a stranger or enemy; however, today the only remnant of that meaning is in *hostile.*

Eponyms can be enjoyed in the same manner. Two excellent sources for older students, or for reading excerpts to younger ones, are *People Words* by Bill Severn (Ives Washburn, Inc.) and *Word People* by Nancy Sorel (McGraw-Hill Book Company). A good example here is the word *maverick,* which was the name of a rather lackadaisical cattle rancher who never got around to branding his calves. Hence, when neighbors found an unbranded calf in their herds they knew it was a "Maverick."

The word *maverick* also demonstrates another point your students might be interested in following: Words change in meaning. Originally a *maverick* was nothing more than an innocent stray, whereas today that word is associated with rebellion. Obviously, despite the admonitions of Sydney Harris, Richard Mitchell, and other defenders of the English language who want us to use words only the way they "should be used," meanings do change. Encourage your students to follow the trail of some of the changes.

Students might find it interesting to classify words according to the type of change they have undergone. For example, *awful* has reversed its meaning from the original "awe-inspiring." Other words have gone through different kinds of changes in meaning, such as the following:

Narrowed Meaning:	a *deer* was any four-legged animal, even a mouse.
	poison referred to anything to drink.
	a *maid* was any female person.
Broadened Meaning:	a *journey* was a day's travel.
	a *neighbor* was a nearby farmer.
	a *lady* was the wife of a lord.
Upgraded Meaning:	a *mansion* was a farm house.
	lingerie refered to any linen garment.
Downgraded Meaning:	a *villain* was a farmer.
	sly meant skilled or wise.
	a *wench* was a small child.

Of course, youngsters can have fun in just considering the kinds of word usages they hear. How many people who ask for a "kleenex" really care whether they get a Kleenex, a Scottie, or a Puff? Or how often do you "xerox" something on A. B. Dick or IBM machines? Often trade names become generic, just as early refrigerators were called "ice boxes" and then "Frigidaires."

These kinds of investigations could go on and on. Nevertheless, good writing requires that the writer use appropriate words. In contrast, too often we do not say what we mean. People who want the "lion's share" of something think they are asking for the greatest portion; however, it's the hyena's share that they mean. How many times have you heard individuals say they will "dial" a number when the instrument they use is a pushbutton phone? Encourage your youngsters to report on some of the misuse they hear.

All of these kinds of activities—along with more to follow—make for involvement with words. They are also fodder for the language logs, to be shared at various times. Furthermore, that sharing can be done on a continuing basis if a section of the bulletin board is marked off for "Word Play."

Literary allusions offer fertile ground for tilling. Isn't it helpful, when a speaker refers to "the crash of Thor's hammer," for the listener to understand that the reference is not to the village blacksmith? Have youngsters collect these allusions from myths, from the Bible ("an eye for an eye"), or from other pieces of literature. For example, would your students understand if one were referred to as "a regular Peter Pan" or "a friend like Brutus"?

Allusions to parts of the body make up many metaphors in common use: "head in the clouds," "nose out of joint," "all thumbs," "all ears," "a heel," and so on. In the same vein, we make use of many animal references in our metaphors: "a clothes horse," "fishy," "make a hog of oneself," "dirty dog," "horsing around."

These metaphors, which have become idioms, can be introduced to students at any age through the primary books by Peggy Parish about Amelia Bedelia (Harper and Row), the maid who takes all instructions literally. Amelia literally puts the lights out (outside)), dusts the furniture, dresses the chicken for dinner, and so on. Make your students more aware of the proliferation of idioms we hear by letting them write—or draw in the case of younger pupils—literal interpretations of some of the common idioms. Some, too, are very local. For example, I was momentarily puzzled at one teacher's request that her children "pick up the floor."

Malaprops were mentioned in Chapter 4. In the same vein, spoonerisms might be collected or concocted. My own favorite is "It's kisstomary to cuss the bride."

Some time ago it was popular to combine spoonerisms with clichés to form humorous anecdotes, such as the one about the admiral who had everyone busy painting his fleet of ships until there wasn't a stern untoned. There were also the islanders who tried to drive the pesky flocks of birds away by throwing rocks at them. Of course, they continued until these wasn't a tern unstoned.

Although oxymorons—the combination of two apparently contradictory terms—might seem reserved to Shakespearean literature, they are all around us. The bard was noted for "tragic mirth" or "sweet sorrow," but it is not unusual to hear of "jumbo shrimp" or "authentic replicas," not to mention—as one comedian quipped— "military intelligence."

Another means of growth in language usage is through discrimination of the shades of meaning among "synonyms." Given a word, youngsters can find all of the related words and classify them on a continuum. For example, *walk* might lead to *stroll, meander, amble, mosey,* and so on. This might also lead to the choice of words that could be used by two individuals with differing opinions on the same point. For example, in referring to one who is unmoving on a subject, is that person *firm, inflexible,* or *stubborn?* Is you friend *cautious with money, frugal,* or *stingy?*

These kinds of activities lead quite naturally into concern for the connotations of words. In addition to their denotation—dictionary meaning—most words have connotations—emotional impacts on the reader or listener. Awareness of connotations can begin as early as third or fourth grade. To initiate the activity with younger pupils, put a word on the board that is familiar, such as *dog.* Then ask for other words they can think of that mean the same as dog, for example, "canine." You might develop a cluster such as the one shown in Figure 5.3.

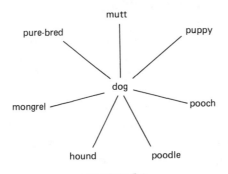

FIGURE 5.3.

Then ask children to classify these words by "positive" or "negative" connotation or, with younger pupils, as "good sounding" and "not-so-good sounding." Some might be neutral or indifferent, such as *dog.* Help pupils become aware that, although denoting the same, the choice of a given word makes a difference on the reader: Referring to a friend's *dog* as a *mongrel* or *mutt* is quite different from calling it a *dog* or *pooch.*

Older students might use nouns of more interest, such as *automobile,* leading to *car, limousine, jalopy, beater, wheels,* and so on. Verbs and adjectives can be used as well. At lunch, did your students just *eat,* or did they *snack, gorge, devour, inhale, wolf,* or *oink* their food?

After experience in classifying into positive and negative connotations, students can then write a brief story in which they choose their words to slant the story one way or the other. Have them also reverse the slant by merely substituting equivalent words with opposite connotations.

Some color words seem to have definite connotations. For example, *white* is often associated with fear: *white flag, white livered. Red* seems emotional: *red flag, red-faced, red herring.* Even the sounds of words may have an effect. Are all *sn-* words unpleasant? (Think of *sneer, snicker, snarl, snob, snare,* and so on.) Students might like to explore these possibilities.

Incidentally, experience with connotations is one of the best backgrounds for critical reading. Youngsters who have discovered the effect of connotation by using it are more likely to see how a writer is using it against them in slanting pieces of writing.

Many of the examples of word play suggested in Chapter 4 can also be used to develop an interest in words. Among these were simile and metaphor. Personification might also be introduced, wherein human qualities are attributed to nonhuman objects, as in "the trees blushed in the face of winter." Likewise, older students might enjoy discovering and making up examples of hyperbole (exaggerated statements), such as "I walked a thousand miles today." Its opposite, litotes, can also be fun: "We were not exactly a raving success."

Euphemisms are all around us. No one sells "used cars" anymore; they are all "predriven." Garbage collectors have been replaced by "sanitation engineers," undertakers by "funeral directors," and increased taxes by "revenue enhancement."

Of course, your students might be even more familiar with the opposite of euphemisms: dysphemisms, the substitution of a more disagreeable term for the one intended, for example *mongrel* for *dog, old lady* for *mother, heap* for *car, axle grease* for *butter,* and so on.

Students of any age can enjoy playing with homophones, words that sound alike but may have different meanings and spellings. Introduce this kind of activity with examples from one of Fred Gwynne's books, *The King Who Rained* (Young Readers) or *A Chocolate Moose for Dinner* (Windmill Books). Then turn your youngsters loose to make their own examples.

Homophones can be taken in another direction by serving as answers to riddles, as in the following examples:

> What do a prospective bride and the weatherman have in common? (showers)
>
> What do a rabbit and a writer have in common? (tails/tales)
>
> What do a tiger and a minister have in common? (preying/praying)
>
> What do an obese person and one who missed the bus have in common? (weight/wait)

Riddles can also be developed to which the answer is a pair of rhyming words. These are variously called hank-pank, hanky panky, and so on, depending upon the number of syllables to be used in the response. Examples are:

> What do you call a hard-of-hearing cook? (a deaf chef)

What do you call a gruesome tale? (a gory story)

What do you call a hat for sleeping? (a nap cap)

Portmanteaus are words formed by combining two words, such as *motel* from *motor hotel, chortle* from *chuckle* and *snort, brunch* from *breakfast* and *lunch,* and so on. Can your students invent useful portmanteaus?

Before the modern craze drowns us in alphabet soup, youngsters might make a collection of acronyms and their meanings. Newspapers are replete with such as NATO, NOW, MADD, and so on. Your students might even enjoy making up their own, or they might make riddles such as "Why did Geneva's Original Organization for Youth change its name?"

Simple word play might also include palindromes, words or sentences that are spelled the same forward or backward. *Mom* or *madam* are examples of the former, with *redivider* supposedly being the longest. Sentences include *Nat saw I was tan* or, the most famous, *Able was I ere I saw Elba.*

Acrostics can also be a challenge to vocabulary. These are word squares and may be made of words of any length. Of course, the longer the words, the more difficult the task.

PEA

EAR

ATE

Even very young children can engage in simple analogies in order to develop vocabulary. Provide them with starters to complete, such as "as round as _____," "as tall as _____," or "as heavy as _____."

A little word magic might be in order. Using a pair of antonyms with the same number of letters, have students attempt to transform the original word, changing only one letter at a time, into a new word until they arrive at the antonym. For example, ask them to change *cold* into *heat* in as few steps as possible. They might progress as follows:

COLD

HOLD

HELD

HEAD

HEAT

If you are fortunate enough to have a variety of dialects or students of diverse ethnic backgrounds in your class, you might have pupils compare terms for common objects or activities. For example, my wife and I still debate whether to prepare eggs in a *skillet* or a *frying pan.* A New Englander might add to the confusion by suggesting that the utensil is a *spider.*

If you are tired of having your youngsters use only *said* and *asked* with quotations, you might make them aware of other verbs by introducing them to the "Tom Swifty," where a quotation is followed by a verb describing or related to what is said:

> "You dirty dog!" he growled.
>
> "You snake," she hissed.
>
> "These slippers are soft as a kitten," she purred.

The preceding, along with ideas suggested in Chapter 4, are just a sampling of the kinds of activities that can involve youngsters in language in a manner that will create an interest in words and meanings. Further, the basic tools of the writer, the dictionary and the thesaurus, need to be introduced to and used by all students.

TOOLS FOR VOCABULARY DEVELOPMENT

Dictionaries do not serve as major sources for new words. Just as preschoolers learned to speak, so too older individuals add most new words to their lexicons by listening and reading. Experience with real language is still the most effective way to develop vocabulary. Nevertheless, that experience alone is not sufficient when the writer is searching for the precise word or has only a vague understanding of what seems to be the appropriate word. It is then that he or she turns to the dictionary or the thesaurus. These are the tools for refining.

The Dictionary

The dictionary is a basic, albeit sadly neglected, tool for everyone. Children should have access to picture dictionaries in kindergarten and first grade. Simple beginning dictionaries should be available in quantity by second grade. By third grade and on—if not before—every child should have his or her own dictionary.

There are many different publishers of dictionaries. Some excellent ones are listed below, along with the approximate level for use.

Grades K–2 (Picture Dictionaries)

My First Dictionary (600-plus words), Oftedal and Jacob (Grossett and Dunlap).

Picturebook Dictionary (1,000 words), Hillerich, English, Bodzewski, Kamatos (Rand McNally).

Grades 2–3

The Ginn Beginning Dictionary, William Morris (Ginn).

My First Dictionary (Houghton Mifflin).

Grades 3–4

Beginning Dictionary (Houghton Mifflin).

Scott, Foresman Beginning Dictionary, Thorndike and Barnhart (Scott, Foresman).

Webster's Beginning Dictionary (G. & C. Merriam [distributed by Ginn]).

Grade 5 and above

Scott, Foresman Intermediate Dictionary, Thorndike and Barnhart (Scott, Foresman).

Webster's Intermediate Dictionary (G. & C. Merriam [distributed by Ginn]).

The American Heritage School Dictionary (Houghton Mifflin).

Advanced, Grade 6 and above

Webster's Third New International Dictionary (G. & C. Merriam).

Webster's Ninth New Collegiate Dictionary (G. & C. Merriam).

The American Heritage Dictionary of the English Language (Houghton Mifflin).

Items to be taught about the dictionary include (1) locational skills, such as alphabetical order and use of guide words; (2) use of the dictionary for meaning, including organization of definitions, parts of speech, and run-on entries; (3) use of the dictionary for pronunciation, including use of the pronunciation key; and (4) use of the dictionary for spelling.

There is already adequate information available for teaching alphabetical order and the other locational skills. Suffice it to say that the major problem here is that too often the drill is in isolation, unrelated to *using* that dictionary. Try some dictionary "races" to see how quickly youngsters can locate a given word. You might also have them make their own nonsense dictionary, as suggested in Chapter 4, in order to become more familiar with the dictionary's format.

Of course, one aspect of teaching the use of a dictionary is to acquaint students with its content, as you do with any new book. Together, read and discuss the introduction in your dictionaries. Without the information contained there, the user has no knowledge of how definitions are organized, what are considered "regular" inflected endings, and so on. Dictionaries differ!

In teaching children to use a dictionary for meaning, most teachers begin with words that are familiar but used in a new sense. Third-graders know what a *clock* is, but are they aware that one can *clock* a race, *tree* a squirrel, or build a *run* for the dog?

Of course, any words given to practice using a dictionary for meaning must be in context. There is no excuse for using a list of isolated words, or worse—as I saw on one workbook page—asking pupils to find meaning #2 for a word! The practice can be more enjoyable and more beneficial if words are given in a question so that students must not only locate the meaning of the word but must also use that meaning in answering the question, such as in the following examples:

Would you rather have a predicament or a premonition? Why?

Is it better to be exonerated or expatriated? Why?

Do foxes wear foxgloves? Why or why not?

After some examples, encourage your students to make up others to challenge classmates.

Use of a dictionary for pronunciation is not directly a writing skill. However, I would like to make one point here, since this particular use is not well taught. Learning to use a dictionary for pronunciation is an oral/aural skill; it cannot be developed through pencil-and-paper activities. Students have little difficulty understanding where to find the pronunciation key, what it represents, and so on. Their problem is in isolating the sound they have identified in the key, carrying it up to the special spelling of the new word they are trying to pronounce, and inserting that sound in the context of the remaining letters. Only oral practice will overcome this difficulty.

Of course, the same can be said of pronunciation of a multisyllabic word, where accent comes into play. Here again the problem is an oral one. Until this point, children automatically accented correctly any new word they picked up in the oral language. However, in using the dictionary to pronounce a completely strange word, they must gain conscious control of where they put the stress. This is something they have never had to do in the past, and it isn't easy.

These uses of the dictionary are provided for in most reading and English programs, but it is difficult to find *any* program that teaches youngsters how to use a dictionary *for spelling.* Development of that skill is discussed thoroughly in Chapter 9.

By about sixth grade and above, students should have access to more sophisticated dictionaries so that they can also learn to use them for locating word origins. Several copies of the Merriam-Webster Collegiate ought to be in every classroom. Further, those youngsters ought to have access to—and use—the unabridged dictionary (often found gathering dust in the school office or library).

The Thesaurus

Once your pupils have become acquainted with connotations—the variations in meanings of "synonyms"—through some of the activities suggested previously, they can profit from a simple thesaurus. Teaching them how to use it is primarily a matter of demonstration and practice.

A thesaurus is used in almost the reverse fashion of a dictionary. The latter is used to gather more information about a word; the former, to find the most appropriate word when only the idea, expressed through a less acceptable word, is in mind.

For third- and fourth-graders, the appropriate book is *In Other Words: A Beginning Thesaurus* by Schiller and Jenkins (Scott, Foresman). The next higher level, *In Other Words: A Junior Thesaurus,* is available for fourth- and fifth-graders. By sixth grade, students should have access to, and be taught how to use, *Roget's International Thesaurus* (T. Y. Crowell).

Although it is possible to purchase an alphabetical thesaurus, many more entries will be found in Roget's because of its organization. About half of the book is devoted to the index, and this is where one begins in using the thesaurus. For example, in searching for a more precise word to express the intended idea of "to reject," the writer will begin in the index with the entry *reject.* Under that entry, the index subsumes seven major categories of verbs: *exclude, expel, be incredulous, repudiate, discard, refuse,* and *disapprove of,* each with a numeral after it, indicating a section and paragraph entry in the body of the text. Perhaps the verb *discard* best illustrates the general sense the user wants to express. The numerical reference after that term is 666.7, referring the user to section 666, paragraph 7. Turning to that paragraph in the body of the text, the reader will find two dozen "synonyms," including *jettison, eliminate,* and idioms such as *wash one's hands of.*

Given the interesting involvement in language and the tools to deepen their understanding of words, your students will have the means with which to better express themselves in writing.

SUMMARY

This chapter began with the consideration that individuals possess receptive and expressive vocabularies, which represent a sampling of the total lexicon of English. From the total words possible, fewer than 3,000 constitute 95 percent of all words used in English. To attempt to teach specifically each of the remaining words, from the collection of hundreds of thousands, would be inefficient if not impossible.

Although most vocabulary study is word specific and does not generalize to knowledge of unstudied words, a few affixes can be taught that will apply to a fair number of new words. Beyond that, many activities were suggested to provide varied experience in language with an interest in words. A few of the activities are helpful when the goal is to teach a specific word; most activities contribute to the general interest in words, along with their assimilation.

Finally, a writer's basic tools—the dictionary and the thesaurus—were discussed. Here the job is to make the tools available and to teach their use. Neither reference was seen as a primary means for learning new vocabulary, since that comes from experience with language, but both were presented as tools for refining that knowledge and for increasing precision in the use of words.

SUGGESTIONS FOR ACTION

1. With older students, you might engage in a discussion of the two receptive and two expressive vocabularies to make them more aware of words they use and how they add to them. Which do they consider larger for themselves? How would they rank them? How do they believe they developed such vocabularies?

2. Look again at the list of prefixes and suffixes that were suggested for instruction. Which do you teach? Are there some you teach that are not included in the list? If so, can you justify those? Are you omitting some important ones?

3. The next time you want to teach a specific word, perhaps from social studies or science, try one of the devices suggested. In fact, it would be advisable to try the different techniques: Frayer's model, the mnemonic keyword device, Johnson and Pearson's semantic feature analysis, or one of the other classifying techniques. Some youngsters may find one helpful; others, another.

4. How often have you jumped off from books in vocabulary work? Try one of the books on word origins, eponyms, homophones, or idioms to get your students to read further about words or to develop some of their own booklets in one of these patterns.

5. Changes in meaning, new words, or the imprecise use of words in daily speech might be avenues your students find exciting. Have a section of the bulletin board available for their use to challenge and amuse the group. Encourage older students to keep an eye on the newspaper for examples.

6. Once you have a section of the bulletin board established and all students keeping language logs, pick and choose from among the many other suggestions in this chapter as well as from those in Chapter 4.

7. In kindergarten or first grade, discuss the picture dictionaries that are available. Not only can your children become aware of the organization of a dictionary, they can find a wealth of ideas for further talking or writing.

8. To what extent are students in second grade and above using the dictionary? If they are not to a great degree, investigate what skills they need in order to make better use of that dictionary. Then teach those skills.

9. If you have not already done so in third grade and above, spend some time acquainting your pupils with the shades of meaning and connotations of common words. Then introduce the appropriate level of thesaurus and have copies available in the room for reference.

10. No matter when or where, in talking or in reading, call attention to that unusual word, that perfectly chosen word, that melodious word, or that new word. Awakening an interest in words is the key to vocabulary growth.

REFERENCES

DEIGHTON, LEE C., *Vocabulary Development in the Classroom.* New York: Columbia University, 1959. Reports prefixes, suffixes, and combining forms that are frequently used and invariant in meaning.

HILLERICH, ROBERT L., *A Writing Vocabulary of Elementary Children.* Springfield: Charles C Thomas Publishers, 1978. Reports frequency of use of words from a study of 380,342 words used in writing by elementary children.

JOHNSON, DALE D., and P. DAVID PEARSON, *Teaching Reading Vocabulary.* New York: Holt, Rinehart and Winston, 1978. Presents techniques for "teaching" vocabulary.

KUCERA, HENRY, and W. NELSON FRANCIS, *Computational Analysis of Present-Day American English.* Providence, Rhode Island: Brown University Press, 1967. Lists by rank and alphabetical order words most frequently used in adult print.

NAGY, WILLIAM E., and RICHARD C. ANDERSON, *"How Many Words Are There in Printed School English?" Reading Research Quarterly,* 19 (Spring, 1984), 304–30. Analysis of the number of running words and word types presented to students in grades three through nine.

OLSON, GENE, *Sweet Agony II: A Writing Book of Sorts.* Rogue River, Oregon: Windyridge Press, 1983. An entertaining treatment of serious points about the process of writing.

PETERS, CHARLES W., "The Effect of Systematic Restructuring of Material upon the Comprehension Process," *Reading Research Quarterly,* 11 (1975–76), 87–111. Describes the Frayer model for developing technical vocabulary and presents research to support it.

PRESSLEY, MICHAEL, JOEL R. LEVIN, and HAROLD D. DELANEY, *"The Mnemonic Keyword Method," Review of Educational Research,* 52 (Spring, 1982), 61–91. Describes and summarizes research on the effectiveness of the mnemonic keyword method of vocabulary development.

ADDITIONAL RESOURCE

DALE, EDGAR, JOSEPH O'ROURKE, and HENRY A. BAMMAN, *Techniques of Teaching Vocabulary.* Palo Alto, California: Field Educational Publications, 1971. An excellent collection of ideas.

6

Writing
in Content Areas

*Education is an admirable thing, but it is well to remember from time
to time that nothing that is worth knowing can be taught.*
OSCAR WILDE, 1891

MANY PEOPLE SEEM to believe that one writes in order to express knowledge. Yet it is probably more accurate to say that one writes in order to discover knowledge, for it is in the process of writing that we learn what we know and don't know. This is a major purpose of writing in the content areas.

The emphasis in this writing, as in any kind of writing instruction, should be on the process as opposed to the product. English teachers have been hearing this for twenty-five years. Science teachers are quite familiar with the "process" approach, wherein students *behave in* science instead of merely reading about it. Unfortunately, "back to basics" seems to have set us *back* in science instruction.

This emphasis on process is in no way intended to minimize the outcome or product. However, your students' need to learn about procedures and techniques for writing is much more important than the specific paper they do today: Finding out *how* to write is more valuable than *what* is written on a given day. Furthermore, enough evidence exists to assure us that, if we continue to improve the process skills, the product will take care of itself.

Some educators distinguish "creative writing" from "content writing." I believe that this is an arbitrary and misleading distinction. Although each writing task may involve minor differences in specifics, writing is writing. In the larger sense, I would consider *all* writing as "creative" except for literal copy work. Even though the student may collect factual information for that science or social studies report, the way that information is organized and put on paper is that student's "creative" work.

You will find this inability to distinguish content writing from other types of writing apparent in this chapter. In fact, were it not for the importance of content writing, it could well have been incorporated into the other chapters, since it too involves the same procedures: prewriting and instruction, conferencing, writing, editing, and publication. Hence, with some additional comments, you are also encouraged to consider those other chapters in connection with your concern about content writing.

WHY WRITE IN CONTENT AREAS?

A major reason for writing in the content areas is the fact that, just as one cannot read reading, so too one cannot write writing. The content areas provide interesting and challenging material about which to write.

More important to the content teacher, writing in the content area increases learning of that content. Through such writing, students will organize their thinking on the subject, solidify hazy understandings, and focus on important information. In order to flesh out their writing, they will be led to additional sources where questions raised in the process of writing can be answered. Furthermore, manipulation of the ideas and incorporation of another sense will contribute to remembering more of that content, if that is another goal of the content teacher. In other words, suggesting writing in the content areas is not an attempt to convert the science, social studies, or physical education teacher into a teacher of English.

A third reason for writing in the content areas is the long-term contribution to skill in writing of any kind. This should be a concern of all teachers because it is a lifetime skill needed in any field. For example, a survey of scientists asked how they spent a typical week. They reported devoting one-third of their time to reading and writing for peers; one-third to reading and writing for lay people; and only one-third to behaving "like scientists."

In addition, writing in the content areas promotes thinking skills. We don't fully understand an idea until we write about it. Writing helps point up what we do and don't know. Recall your own experience with college term papers or essay exams. On some you wrote fluently because you were prepared; on others, did you have to pad and try to fake it?

Finally, if writing in the content areas is handled somewhat along the lines suggested in this chapter as well as in other sources, a new spark of interest is added to that content study. The procedure is no longer the typical read-discuss-test sequence.

SOME GENERAL CONSIDERATIONS

Some schools have recognized that writing in the content areas should not be limited to science and social studies classrooms. It is just as important in industrial arts, physical education, music, and art. Although teachers in these performing areas have probably done a better job than most in teaching by doing instead of by merely talking about the subject, even their contribution can be enhanced with some writing.

At the primary level, most writing will be expressive. Young children should write from personal experience and interest. Even here, however, topics can be related to content, as youngsters write about a pet (science), a trip to the post office (social studies), foods they like (health), games they play (physical education), and so on.

By middle-school level—and in some schools, before this—departmentalization replaces the self-contained classroom. In such situations, too often students see writing as "English." Little writing, other than for a test, may be done in the other content areas, and what is done usually is accompanied by the question "Do you take off for spelling?" and so on. This separation of "English writing" from "other writing" is unfortunate and can be addressed in at least three ways.

First, perhaps English teachers need to be nudged a bit more in the direction of content teachers. The first and primary concern in any writing, "English" or content, ought to be with the content. If the content is worthless or unclear, perfection in mechanics doesn't make it any better. In the reverse case, clear content with poor mechanics, we must offer the indicated assistance and instruction to enable that student to correct the mechanics.

Second, if the staff believes in writing, the arbitrary separation that takes place in departmentalized organizations can be removed. That staff can get together and establish a common purpose or goal for each period of the year. The periods may be three weeks, a month, or whatever fits into the schedule. In each period, the group will agree—in *all* subject areas—to focus on *one* objective at a time, that *all* teachers will reinforce with those students. For example, one important goal might be to improve *organization* in writing. Other goals for different periods might deal with *sequence, transitions,* or different methods of supporting a topic, such as by *detail, examples,* or *cause/effect.*

Third, just as content-area teachers should be concerned about writing in general, language arts teachers should be concerned with writing in the content areas. Too often experience in writing in the language arts class is limited to narrative and poetic forms. Yet, such writing is quite different from the expository writing used in content material. In narrative writing, action builds smoothly to a climax, with the denouement swiftly ending the story. In contrast, factual and persuasive writing tends to buttress its main thesis on a series of lesser points, each supported by a foundation of details as shown in Figure 6.1.

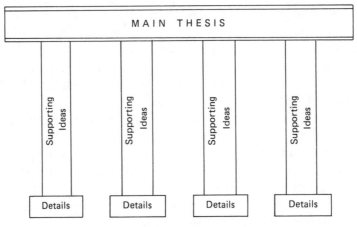

FIGURE 6.1. Expository Writing.

In addition, expository writing tends to be more abstract and impersonal than narrative, with the latter usually including personalized characters and dialogue. Narrative also tends to be sequentially ordered, whereas expository is more deductive, from general to specific. Elementary students need to become well acquainted with both kinds of writing, in language arts as well as in other subject areas.

If content writing is to be effective, students must move beyond mere summarization of information. They should be encouraged to work at higher levels of thinking: analysis, synthesis, and evaluation. Analysis involves breaking the topic into its elements or principles. Synthesis is problem solving in an original manner, putting the pieces back together in a new way. Evaluation involves making judgments about the topic, providing an answer to "So what?"

For example, in writing about the life of an important musician, artist, scientist, or historical figure, instead of summarizing the life, listing important contributions, and so on, have your students write a news article as if the person were alive today. They might also write a dramatic scene or an imaginary interview in which they make use of the information they have. Comparisons also enable use of that information: Would you rather have lived during that period than now? What problems did the individual face that might be avoided today?

Too often in the content areas, when there is writing beyond the test, it is one big term paper. This is the final *product,* and once it is written all you, as teacher, can do is error hunt. Instead of that term paper, why not have short weekly papers? Then you can assist in the growth of your students, and their writing can be focused on a specific purpose each time.

The immediate reaction to the suggested weekly paper is the lack of time teachers have to "grade" that many papers. Again, the point is to get out of the editing role. You should not grade each paper, any more than you should feel compelled to read every one. Peer evaluation, sharing in small groups, and compiling a log of those papers are steps in the right direction. Since grades are required, ask each student for the best two or three papers done during the grading period and base the grade on those.

PREWRITING IN THE CONTENT AREAS

I'll not repeat here the activities suggested for prewriting in Chapter 3, nor will I duplicate those suggested for vocabulary development in Chapter 5. Both of those chapters have numerous prewriting ideas relevant to content areas and should be examined from that viewpoint.

To begin with, youngsters cannot be expected to write in a content area if they lack the information to do so. Hence, some prior work is assumed. That work may include reading and researching, from a variety of sources rather than from a single textbook; observing and experimenting; interviewing and letter writing. Nowhere is there better justification for learning and doing than in letter writing. However, just as in any kind of writing, prewriting should include discussion of appropriate content for such a letter.

Vocabulary Development

One important portion of prewriting time in the content areas must be devoted to vocabulary development. As stated earlier, there are three aspects to vocabulary development: generalizable skills, dealing with affixes; nongeneralizable learning of specific words; and skill with the tools dictionary and thesaurus.

Although general writing makes use of a limited number of prefixes and even fewer suffixes for meaning, technical writing often involves words frequently formed from Greek and Latin combining forms. Hence, some instruction with the appropriate forms can be helpful for both writing and reading in the content areas. Among the most common prefixed forms with relatively invariant meanings are:

aut-/auto-	automatic, self-acting	automobile, autopilot
biblio-	book	bibliophile, bibliotherapy
bi-/bio-	life or living	biography, biologist
heter-/hetero-	other or different	heterogeneous, heterosexual
hom-/homo-	same, alike	homogeneous, homogenize
hydr-/hydro-	water, liquid	hydroelectric, hydrofoil
micr-/micro-	small, minute	microcosm, microwave
mon-/mono-	single, one	monarch, monotone
neur-/neuro-	nerve	neurosis, neurology
omni-	all	omnibus, omnivorous
phon-/phono-	sound, speech	phoneme, phonology
phot-/photo-	light	photoelectric, photometer
pneum-/pneumo-	air or lungs	pneumatic, pneumonia
pseud-/pseudo-	false or fake	pseudonym, pseudo
tel-/tele-	distant	telephoto, telekinesis
uni-	one	unilateral, unison

In addition to the foregoing, some noun endings are useful:

-chrome	colored	polychrome, monochrome
-cide	killing or killer	insecticide, genocide
-fication	making	electrification, certification
-graph	written, or instrument for	telegraph, pictograph
-ics	knowledge or skill	optics, electronics
-meter	means for measuring	odometer, barometer
-logy	theory or science of	geology, psychology
-phobia	extreme fear of	hydrophobia, claustrophobia
-phone	sound	homophone, xylophone
-scope	means of viewing	telescope, microscope

Other endings shed no light on meaning but can be helpful in building nouns from other known words. Among these are:

-ery   grocery, snobbery, thievery

-ism   proletarianism, fascism, communism

-ment   emplacement, fulfillment, management

-ness   happiness, sweetness, boldness

-ion/-tion   action, prescription, notation

-y/-ty   muddy, summery, seniority

-ship   apprenticeship , statesmanship, kinship

Numerous suggestions were made in Chapter 5 for developing nongeneralizable vocabulary, the meanings of specific words. This is particularly important in content areas, where content words such as *oligarchy* or *photosynthesis* can be crucial to understanding as well as to writing about a topic. Meanings are developed and enhanced through building as many associations as possible between the known and the unknown: comparing and contrasting, classifying, noting characteristics and noncharacteristics, and so on.

In addition to learning to use the tools of vocabulary—the dictionary and the thesaurus—students in content areas can benefit from building their own glossaries of words pertinent to that area, whether it be science, math, physical education, or industrial arts. Such glossaries should include not only definitions, but also example sentences or further explanation of the word.

Getting Organized for Writing

Among the best prewriting activities for content writing would be those involving research or class discussion to further develop understanding of the material. Then guide pupils to more advanced methods of handling that material, through analysis, synthesis or evaluation, as mentioned earlier.

Beck (1980) has also suggested an interdisciplinary approach as a means of broadening understanding and interrelating ideas. Just about any topic has ramifications for a variety of subject areas. For example, consider the Civil War in U.S. history.

History: What was occurring? When?

Geography: What were the crucial states?

Economics: What products and concerns helped lead to the struggle?

Math: What was the population? Compare it with that of the present.

Civics: What were the implications for civil rights, then and now?

Science: What were the limitations of technology? Compare with those of the present.

Industrial Arts: What tools and weapons were available? Compare.

Home Economics: How might nutrition have related to the war?

Language Arts: Who were some of the important people of the time? What did they contribute?

Music: What tunes were popular at the time? How were they listened to? What instruments were most popular?

Art: What were the effects of the war on creative production?

Although the above obviously is no attempt to write a unit lesson plan, it does indicate that each teacher, knowing his or her subject matter, can develop nearly unlimited possibilities to relate to any topic the staff seeks out. Tchudi and Tchudi (1983) have developed such an interdisciplinary lesson plan for all content areas on the topic of "The Elderly."

With more specific topics, planning can be assisted through the use of simple charts, identifying and interrelating information. Figure 6.2 shows three examples from "Intervention" (*Minimum Standards Implementation Series*, © 1983, Ohio Department of Education; reprinted by permission).

Outlining can also be an effective tool if students don't get bogged down on the mechanics of format. One technique to help avoid that problem is the use of mapping or webbing, as suggested in Chapter 5.

As part of any content writing, students should be encouraged to keep daily logs. The investment of five or so minutes at the end of a period produces many positive results. First of all, such writing will aid the student in identifying what is known and what questions remain. It also serves as an excellent summary of that learning and will provide for review as necessary. Finally, in the upper grades, teachers have found such logs beneficial to the student who was absent the day before.

Whether these logs remain personal or you examine them on a random basis is a matter for you and your students to decide. Certainly you can offer more assistance if you have an opportunity to examine the contents periodically. In any event, such logs should not be graded. They are an aid to the student and should never be considered a finished product for evaluation.

Chapter 3 contains a variety of additional techniques for assisting youngsters in getting started in their writing.

KINDERGARTEN–PRIMARY

	See	Touch	Smell	Taste	Hear
Thanksgiving Day	Grandma	Tablecloth	Fresh bread	Turkey	Talk
	Turkey	Bowls	Cranberries	Pumpkin pie	T.V.
	Dining room table	Plates			

INTERMEDIATE–SECONDARY
(Cause/effect)

SUBJECTS

What do we want to know about the causes/effects of the high cost of foods?	Coffee	Peanuts
Weather-cold Weather-rain Strikes/labor Shipping cost War/conflicts		

INTERMEDIATE–SECONDARY
(Specific Information)

SUBJECTS

What do we want to know about these three major battles of the Civil War?	Gettysburg	Vicksburg	Atlanta
Battle date Battle length Special problems Turning point Leaders—North Leaders—South			

FIGURE 6.2. Examples of Prewriting Charts

WRITING

As students begin their writing, you might want to try your hand at the same topic. This is one means of identifying problems your fledgling writers have. However, all of the writing time cannot be spent by you in writing, and it certainly should not be used to grade other papers. While students write, teachers should be moving about the room, providing assistance, showing interest, and getting familiar with what each student is accomplishing. This is conference time, and it is discussed more fully in Chapter 8. However, a few words ought to be said about it here.

Many conferences will take a minute or less, as the student is progressing satisfactorily in the writing. Some will be more formally scheduled as problems arise or when the student has finished and has had a peer evaluation of a first draft. Such conferences may be for five or ten minutes as you try to identify a major problem with that writing and, in the process, help the student to verbalize the difficulty and its possible solution.

Students must retain ownership of their papers and must keep the responsibility. Hence, any marks on the draft should be made by the student. Once you begin writing on the draft, you are taking over the responsibility, and it isn't—or shouldn't be—your paper!

Notice the assumption: The first draft is not the final draft. Few, if any, experienced writers can sit down and produce a final copy in one draft. Yet, according to the evidence, even most high school students seem to think that a recopied first draft is all that needs to be done. Help your students realize that this is not so.

This is not to say that every piece of writing needs to be recopied. Recopying is not revising, and at the elementary level especially it is more likely to produce new "errors" over what were in the original draft. Have your students write on every other line of their papers so that they can revise on that same draft. Encourage them to draw arrows, insert, cross out sentences or whole paragraphs, and so on as they attempt to clarify the message they are attempting to communicate.

EDITING AND PUBLISHING

Editing consists of two entirely different operations: revising and proofreading. These are discussed in detail in Chapter 11. "Publishing" is used in the broadest sense as meaning that someone will receive the communication—and will read it. This topic is discussed in Chapter 12. Nevertheless, some pertinent comments need to be made here.

Revision is not a separate endeavor. Some prewriting activities will undoubtedly take place as the writer reconsiders the piece, seeks additional information on the topic, or thinks of other methods of handling some part of that topic. It is, however, an activity focusing on the content, not on the mechanics of the writing; it is part of the composing process rather than of the transcribing process.

In order to do a good job of revising, students must have some criteria. At this stage, involved lists do not seem appropriate. You might want to discuss with your youngsters the major goals in any writing: clarity and interest appeal. Further, in content writing in particular, another major concern is with accuracy.

Two techniques that assist in accomplishing these goals are quiet oral reading by the writer and reading by a peer. The former will aid in style and clarity, and the latter will also assist in accuracy.

Another technique for teaching pupils how to revise and what to revise for is group revision. Put a relatively *good* piece of writing on a transparency for class discussion. Then pick a major concern from your group as the focus and discuss that piece from that standpoint. Perhaps you are working on organization. Discuss how this particular piece is organized and developed. Are there other methods that could have been used? What are they? Which are most effective for this particular topic?

If your objective is to discuss ways of developing a topic, you might want to use several pieces from the class that demonstrate different methods, such as cause/effect, comparison/contrast, example, or even narrative.

Publication is a matter of seeing to it that someone—not always the teacher—reads the piece of writing. If students are writing often enough, it should be impossible for you as teacher to read everything. Therefore, small-group sharing, with some total group sharing, is appropriate. If content papers are done regularly, they should be placed in the logs so that you can review the composite collection of a few of your students each week, rather than face a flood of papers all at once.

Why should more formal publication be limited to language arts? Most schools have a school paper or magazine, and many classrooms publish their own class papers as well as books of stories for younger pupils. These are usually exclusively narrative and poetic writing. Why not have a science paper or magazine, with intriguing factual articles? A physical education book could present directions for enjoyable games or activities. An industrial arts or home economics newsletter might offer interesting "how to" articles. These same kinds of ideas can be used to write different types of books for younger children in the school.

An important final point here: Don't you be the editor! You certainly don't need the practice as much as your students. Let them get the experience. In fact, you might want to have a rotating set of editors so that many of your pupils might have a turn at the job.

EVALUATION

First, there is no excuse for evaluating a paper, within or outside the content areas, strictly on the mechanical "correctness." In fact, although additional and more involved means of evaulating are suggested in Chapter 13, I would be satisfied to evaluate content writing with just two of the criteria: clarity and accuracy. If the writer is accurate in handling the content of the paper and if that information is presented so that it can be readily understood, that is a good paper as compared with one that is mechanically perfect but unclear and inaccurate.

Second, remember that evaluation is used for many different purposes: appraisal of students' understanding of the content, diagnosis of needs, appraisal of program effectiveness, and "grading" of students. Most of our evaluative activities ought to be devoted to the first three if we are to be developing learners instead of merely assigning and sorting them.

Even when evaluation is used to grade the students, it is inappropriate to assign two grades to a paper, as so often happens in content areas: one grade for content and one for mechanics. What does a B for content and an F for mechanics mean? Is it a $C-$ or a $D+$ paper? The two should not be separated in writing. If the mechanics are so poor that they truly interfere with the clarity or accuracy of the paper, it is a poor paper. On the other hand, if they are matters of convention—minor misspellings, failure to capitalize a proper noun, and so on—while the content is clear and accurate, these are matters to be worked on, but the paper itself is not a poor paper.

SUMMARY

Although the major topics of this chapter are discussed fully in other chapters, some comments specific to writing in the content areas were made. Content writing was seen as important for a number of reasons: to provide material to write about, as an aid to learning the content itself, as a means of further developing skill in writing, to promote thinking skills, and to increase interest in the content itself.

Teachers were encouraged to remove the distinction of writing as an "English" skill and to recognize its role in all areas. The emphasis in writing, whether in content *or* "English," should be on the message rather than merely on the mechanics, and this emphasis should also be reflected in elimination of the "dual" grade for content writing. Staffs were advised to join together on a common writing objective for each grading period, so that objective would be reinforced by all. Lightening of the paper load was suggested through use of peer evaluation, short papers instead of one "term" paper, and evaluation of a sampling from each student.

Among prewriting activities suggested were additional techniques for vocabulary development, including specific affixes to be taught. The writing itself should encourage higher levels of thinking, such as analysis, synthesis, and evaluation, as opposed to the usual listing or summarization. Integration of subject areas was also suggested, to get youngsters to cross over the disciplinary lines.

Conferencing during writing and the expectation of revision were seen as important points. Suggestions for the latter included group revision, oral reading of a draft, and peer assistance.

Publication in the broad sense was suggested through sharing activities as well as through actual produciton of class books, magazines, or newspapers dealing with content material. That material should be evaluated primarily for its clarity and accuracy, with editing done by peers.

SUGGESTIONS FOR ACTION

1. Since you are most likely to be a language arts teacher reading this book, share this chapter with a colleague in one of the content areas. What kind of reaction do you get?

2. If you are a primary teacher, to what extent have you used science or social studies matter as a jumping-off point for writing? If you haven't done so, try it.

3. At upper levels, do you believe in the one long term paper? If so, try weekly "short subjects" for a while. See if you and your students don't benefit more.

4. If you work in a departmentalized school, talk with other staff members about a cooperative effort to improve writing, using one objective as a common goal over a period of weeks.

5. Do your youngsters understand the difference in style between narrative and expository writing? If you work with upper grades, take some examples of each and discuss them with the class. This kind of effort with "text grammar" will not only help in writing, it will also contribute to greater skill in reading that material.

6. To what extent have you gotten your pupils away from mere summarization in factual writing? Try some of the ideas suggested to get them to higher levels of thinking, such as analysis, synthesis, or evaluation.

7. At upper levels, evaluate the list of affixes suggested in this chapter. In fact, you might want to post the list and have your students check a chapter in social studies or science to find out how much some of these would help them.

8. Take one of the topics you are dealing with in content areas and see how far you can go in developing an interdisciplinary approach with your students' writing.

9. Are your students aware of the helpfulness of webbing or mapping? Demonstrate this to them as an alternative to outlining. They will probably like it better and, in the process of using mapping, will further understand what outlining is all about.

10. Have your students keep a daily log in one of the content areas for three or four weeks. Periodically check with them on the log and evaluate with them the effectiveness of this technique.

11. To what extent do your pupils take the initiative in revising their papers? This must be taught. If they are not revising, try some group techniques first, then shift to assisting them in revising through short conferences.

12. Do you have pupil editors in your class? If not, now is the time to begin.

13. What criteria for evaluation have you *shared* with your students? They need to know what to look for as much as—or more than—you do if they are to improve their writing.

14. Try publishing a content-area newspaper or magazine. Your pupils might even like to try their hands at "how to do it" books for others to read.

15. If your school is developing courses of study in the various areas, *cross-reference* them, referring that subject to the other subject areas.

REFERENCES

BECK, JAMES P., "Theory and Practice of Interdisciplinary English," *The English Journal,* 69 (February, 1980), 28–32. Presents justification and some examples of interdisciplinary writing, aimed at middle school and secondary.

OHIO DEPARTMENT OF EDUCATION, "Intervention," *Minimum Standard Series.* Columbus: Ohio Department of Education, 1983. Chapter V offers specific strategies for developing skill in writing, including suggestions for webbing and mapping.

TCHUDI, STEPHEN N., and SUSAN J. TCHUDI, *Teaching Writing in the Content Areas: Elementary School.* Washington, D.C.: National Education Association, 1983. Presents model units for teaching writing in the content areas.

ADDITIONAL RESOURCE

DEIGHTON, LEE C., *Vocabulary Development in the Classroom.* New York: Teachers College, Columbia University, 1959. Presents additional affixes that are frequently used and invariant in meaning.

7

Dealing with Grammar: Flexibility of Expression

For all a rhetorician's rules
Teach nothing but to name his tools.
SAMUEL BUTLER

THIS CHAPTER DEALS with *grammar,* a word sometimes substituted for *English* and one that is almost certain to bring thrills to the dedicated English teacher and chills to most students. More important, this chapter is an attempt to clarify "grammar" and to present some activities that will more likely accomplish the goal of the teacher by showing students how they can use the language to express their ideas in more flexible ways.

THIS THING CALLED GRAMMAR

Perhaps we had best begin by clarifying what it is we want to teach under the heading of "English." Traditionally, this subject has included everything from learning to name the parts of speech and correct word usage to making introductions and using the telephone. As a result of a survey he once did to determine what English teachers saw as the aims of English, Harold Allen collected 1,481 objectives. He quite justly concluded that any subject with so many purposes has *no* clear purpose.

To the general public, the purpose of teaching English is to teach "grammar." Grammar is *"Basic!"* Of course, we'd have to agree with the last sentence: One cannot communicate in a language without having control of the grammar of that language. The point is, however, that the five-year-old English-speaking child already knows the grammar of the language. Grammar has to do with the way words are strung together in order to make intelligible (or "legal") sentences in the language. "I brung the pencil" is grammatical; "I the brung pencil" is not.

Much of what is considered "grammar" by the lay public—and by some teachers—is nothing more than drill on word usage. As the linguist Bostain (1981) said, it is "other world English." In his words, "Grammarians don't tell it like it is, they tell it as if it were."

Unfortunately, the "back to basics" cries of the early 1980s have driven publishers back twenty-five years in terms of the English books published. The traditional grammar and word usage found in books prior to the late 1950s has risen again. About the only difference in the books today is inclusion of some writing activities—in many books only token efforts.

As this chapter—and the book itself—might indicate, we can be even more critical. We concur wholeheartedly with Thurber's statement made more than ninety years ago:

> The rules of good writing that have any proper place in the school may be printed on a single page. It is not knowledge of rules that is fundamental to the business of acquiring a mastery of English expression. To learn the rules by heart, to recite them daily, to hear lectures on their importance, will avail nothing. It is pitiful to see the trust in textbooks, in books of exercises in English, shown by the practice of schools that adopt bulky volumes, and try to labor through them against all reason and in defiance of human nature.
>
> It is useless to argue that the *average* teacher needs a book of exercises. The textbook is simply an obstacle to every teacher, whether superior, average, or inferior [Thurber, 1894].

Word Usage and Grammar

Word choice or usage is a matter of language habit. The criterion here is a social one and falls more into the realm of etiquette than into English. Any expression from "I don't have a pencil" to "I ain't got no pencil" communicates the lack of a pencil. However, the former is more socially acceptable *in school* than is the latter. Word usage must be evaluated in terms of its appropriateness to the given situation.

Other elements of usage are the result of a particular dialect community. As such, they are correct in the given dialect and are to be expected there. The individual who speaks with a group of another dialect may find his or her usage inappropriate to that group, whether the person happens to be a Black Dialect speaker talking with a group of "standard" English speakers, or vice-versa.

Some elements of usage in young children are a matter of overgeneralization. These creative analogies, such as "feets" for *feet* or "bringed" for *brought,* easily take care of themselves in time. In fact, some are almost poetic, such as the first-grader's remark that his dog was *barkative,* or another who said that, with the addition of more children, the classroom would be noisier and "crowdier."

How does one learn usage? It is learned through experience with the language in natural communicative situations. It is not learned nor changed through isolated drills. In fact, the teacher who would change one simple element must provide hundreds of experiences with that element in a variety of contexts before any change will be effected. For example, if you want to convince Fred to say "I have gone" instead of "I have went," you must provide hundreds of such experiences in a variety of contexts until "I have went" sounds strange to Fred. Meanwhile, however, Fred is going home and practicing—in *more* meaningful situations—"I have went." All of your effort is canceled!

When a particular usage is common to a language community, it is "correct" there. Some time ago, in a graduate class, my students and I were discussing a survey Pooley did of Wisconsin English teachers. I remarked at his surprise to find those English teachers most critical of one particular element, use of the double negative, because he had found that to be idiomatic among adults in Wisconsin. A very sophisticated and mature graduate student came up to me after class and said, "Dr. Hillerich, when you were quoting Pooley to the effect that the double negative was idiomatic in Wisconsin, I almost interrupted you to say that I was from Wisconsin and *I couldn't hardly* believe that!"

The comments made in Chapter 3 about changing dialect apply just as well to efforts directed at changing word usage. Both factors are matters of social appropriateness, and both will be adjusted—or not—in terms of the individual's social goals, providing the model has been available.

Moffett and Wagner (1983) suggested additional kinds of experiences with real language as a means of acquainting speakers with "standard" dialect. These included conversations with speakers of the "standard," role playing as such a speaker, listening to a text being read while following along visually, and choral reading of standard texts—in other words, again, an immersion in the language from as many vantage points as possible.

Furthermore, some of the elements of word usage formerly taught have—and had—no basis in reality in terms of the English language. They were arbitrarily determined or borrowed from Latin. Twenty-five years ago, Pooley (1960) suggested dropping the following, among others:

1. The distinction between *shall* and *will,* a dichotomy invented by John Wallis in 1674.
2. Concern for the split infinitive, one of the many carryovers from Latin, where the infinitive was one word.
3. Objection to *like* as a conjunction (replacing *as*).
4. Objection to the use of "different than," as opposed to "different from."
5. Insistence on the possessive form before a gerund.

We might even add some of the changes that seem apparent at present. Possibly it was Winston Churchill's statement that finally buried the rule about never ending a sentence with a preposition: "This is the sort of nonsense up with which I will not put." And is the distinction between *who* and *whom* being lost through utter confusion?

This same confusion of case is apparent with the pronoun *I.* It would seem that the English teacher's drill on use of the nominative in a compound subject (*She and I ran*) is overgeneralized to its misuse in a compound object (*Sally gave her and I a pen*). Now some grammarians are expressing concern for this hypercorrection, which wouldn't exist if the former had not been overly drilled.

These varied uses of case, carried from the Latin, offer little practical help in communication. For example, when you answer the phone and the caller asks for you, do you say "It is I" (or "This is she")? Or do you throw appearances to the wind and merely reply "It's me"? Many of us dodge the issue by answering "Speaking."

English: Content or Skill?

Much of what is called "grammar" in English classrooms has to do with learning the parts of speech. Students are taught to identify noun, pronoun, verb, adjective, adverb, preposition, conjunction, and interjection. These are taught too often as a content to be learned, abstract labels to be applied. Is it any wonder that studies asking pupils to rank, in order of preference, the subjects they study in school reveal that English consistently falls at the bottom of the list? Since there is nothing inherently distasteful about the language—certainly preschoolers don't avoid it or dread it—this low esteem must have something to do with what we, in school, have done to youngsters in the name of "English."

Besides, it should be obvious that most words cannot be labeled as particular parts of speech. What is *down?* That depends upon its use in a sentence:

> The *down* was soft (noun).
>
> They *downed* the aircraft with a missile (verb).
>
> She walked *down* the stairs (preposition).
>
> The *down* pillow is new (adjective).
>
> We live up but they live *down* (adverb).

More important, the learning of labels contributes nothing to one's skill in using the language. Most educated adults—unless they happen to be English teachers—do not remember the difference between a gerund and a participle. Yet, they consistently use both in regular speech and writing. Not only do they use them, they use them correctly (possibly dangling a participle once in a while).

Bostain (1981) quoted a letter in the *Washington Post* in which the writer insisted at great length that *adamant* was a noun and was not, is not, and could not be an adjective. Apparently this was a person well *drilled* on the parts of speech. How might he interpret our meaning if we said to him, "You are adamant"?

All this is to suggest that "English" is not a body of terms or content to be taught. It is not a science; it is an art. It is not a collection of facts to be learned; it is a skill to be used. One does not learn to use a language by talking about it or by learning its parts, any more than one learns to play the piano or paint a picture by learning to name keys or colors or the different styles used.

The Role of Grammar

First, we might clarify that there is no *one* grammar. There are grammars: traditional, structural, and transformational. Each of these has played a role in the English classroom.

Traditional grammar arose in the eighteenth century and represented an effort to transplant the rules and characteristics of Latin to the English language. It was a prescriptive grammar, telling users what they should and should not do, ignoring the facts that English was quite different from Latin and that a living language constantly changes.

Structural grammar, born in the twentieth century, broke from the Latin prescription. It was a descriptive grammar, attempting to tell what the language is like, not what it should be like. Another important contribution of the structuralists was their separation of syntax, the structure of sentences, from semantics or meaning. Parts of speech were classified according to function in the sentence rather than by "meaning."

Transformational grammar, attributed to Noam Chomsky, arose in the middle of this century and is also referred to as "generative" grammar. It too is descriptive of the real language, and it went beyond structural grammar to investigate how sentences are contructed ("generated"), combining the use of meaning along with structure.

Both transformational and structural grammar continue to have an influence on instruction in English by helping us better understand the nature of the language. And this is probably the major contribution of grammar to English classes: It is a body of knowledge that teachers should understand so they can further guide their students in developing skill in using the language. The evidence is clear that any formal grammar, as material to be taught to students, is of little or no value in increasing skill in the use of the language, either in speech or in writing.

This position is probably best stated and most often quoted in the research summary by Braddock and others (1963):

> In view of the widespread agreement of research studies based upon many types of students and teachers, the conclusion can be stated in strong and unqualified terms: the teaching of formal grammar has a negligible or, because it usually displaces some instruction and practice in actual composition, even a harmful effect on the improvement of writing [pp. 37–38].

Grammatical concepts are abstract. Even supporters of grammar instruction usually suggest that it be delayed until at least junior-high level. However, there is adequate research to question its use even in the secondary school.

One of the most thorough and carefully controlled studies was done by Elley and others (1976). Their three-year study included eight high school classes with three teachers who alternated classes. They compared the effectiveness of three treatments: Oregon curriculum (based on literary models), transformational grammar, and traditional grammar. Students were tested on twelve language variables. After two years, there was no difference in language or writing skill. After three years, some minor conventions of usage favored the transformational groups, but they also developed more negative attitudes toward language study. In a follow-up one year later, there were no significant differences among the groups.

A secondary English teacher in the Northwest Ohio Writing Project did a summary paper on the effectiveness of formal grammar instruction. Her concluding statement probably sums it up best:

> With research in this area [grammar] nearly fifty years old, why do grammar books intended to improve writing—complete with diagramming, parts of speech identified and defined, correct usage, punctuation, and spelling—sell and make publishers millionaires, researchers paupers, and teachers frustrated? [Cathi Neifer, 1982]

WHAT CAN BE TAUGHT ABOUT GRAMMAR

Children enter school with a wealth of language experience. The average five-year-old has mastered all of the sentence patterns of English and has thousands of words in the expressive vocabulary, not to mention additional words in the receptive vocabulary. The job of the school is not to teach that child English as if it were a foreign language. The job, in terms of "English instruction," is to raise to a conscious level this intuitive knowledge already possessed.

We'll break the task into two categories for instruction: first, those activities that develop greater awareness of what the language is like, "grammar," if you prefer to call it that; second, those that can contribute to greater skill in the use of the language, flexibility in sentence construction.

Understanding the Nature of the Language

For those teachers who simply *must* teach grammar by third or fourth grade, there are some linguistically honest understandings to which children can be led. In fact, it is not so much a matter of leading them as it is a case of opening their eyes to what they already know.

You might begin with the most basic fact of English: It is a word-order language. Your children know that! In Latin, for example, whether one said, "Paulus videt puellam" or "Puellam videt Paulus," the meaning is unchanged. In English, however, "Paul sees the girl" and "The girl sees Paul" express two entirely different meanings.

This understanding of word order might be so obvious as to be a waste of time, even at third grade. However, you can be certain of pupils' awareness by using a few scrambled sentences for them to rearrange in the appropriate word order to accomplish the intended meaning.

A second characteristic of the language is that all of our words can be sorted into two categories. Investigations of the language of young children report that, by age two, they have also established a grammar, with the two categories clearly defined in use. Linguists refer to the categories of adult language by various terms, such as "form class" and "structure" (or "function") words. So that we don't fall into the trap of traditional grammar, let me remind you that the terms themselves are not important to teach children! The conscious understanding is the important instructional item here.

You may begin experience in this area by putting on the board a sentence in which nonsense words have been substituted for all of the "content" or form class words, such as *The zop zupped on a zip.* Have youngsters read the sentence to discover that it sounds like English, but the words don't make sense. Have them identify and you underline the nonsense words. What real words could be substituted for the nonsense words to make sense? They'll easily arrive at form class words for appropriate slots, indicating a (singular) noun for *zop,* a (past form) verb of *zupped,* and a (singular) noun for *zip.*

Whether you call these substitutions "form class words," "square words," or "circle words" is immaterial. The important point is that youngsters are using their knowledge of the structure of the sentence to determine the kinds of words that fit into certain slots. Note that they are not using the "meaning" of the nonsense words in order to make that determination.

Change the sentence, putting nonsense words for the real words and leaving suggested replacement words for the original nonsense words: *Nam frog sat num nim rock.* Now have pupils read the sentence. They will find that, although they recognize the topic, the sentence doesn't sound much like English.

Some repeated experience with these kinds of examples will help youngsters realize that there is one group of words that carries semantic meanings—the form class words that you and I might refer to as nouns, verbs, adjectives, and adverbs. Another group, that of the structure words, serves as the glue to hold the language together. These latter words don't carry semantic meaning, but they are the foundation of the language. In fact, they also represent a closed class, consisting of fewer than 500 words. In contrast, the form class words are an open class, constantly changing as we add and drop members: *family room* has replaced *parlor,* and *crewel* has about replaced *embroidery,* but we'll no longer speak English when *the* and *a* are replaced.

The Parts of Speech

By fourth grade, *if you must* teach parts of speech, teach them honestly. No one recognizes a noun because it "names a person, place, or thing." In the example given earlier, did you or your children know that *zop* was a noun from that definition? You knew it was a noun because of other clues.

Put the sentence on the board again. Ask children how they knew that *girl, frog,* or similar words could be substituted there instead of *ran, sat,* or *the.* They can be helped to identify the criteria used to recognize a noun. In that nonsense sentence, *the* is a determiner or noun marker, signalling that a noun is coming. Further, if there can be a *zop,* there can certainly be more than one. Hence the ability to take a plural is another indication that the word is a noun type. By this same token, if there is a *zop,* it certainly could own something, so the ability to show possession is another characteristic of a noun.

To summarize their learning, you might chart the foregoing and, with your pupils, develop a test sentence that can be used in the future to check words to discover if they are used as nouns. The test sentence should contain a blank into which trial words are to be inserted to see if they are meaningful and if they retain the meaning of the original sentence. Your chart might look something like this:

A noun is a word that

1. can be preceded by a noun marker,
2. can take a plural,
3. can show possession,
4. makes sense in the sentence: Did you ever hear of (a/an) _____?

Did you notice that already we're getting involved in a lot of terminology and abstract considerations? In the above, we've assumed that children know what a "noun marker" is, that they understand "plural" and "possession," and that they recognize the three options in the test sentence: use of the marker *a,* use of the marker *an,* or absence of a marker. To add to the problem of checking, only the test sentence itself is functional when it comes to abstract nouns such as *peace* or *happiness.*

Traditionally, a verb has been defined as a word that expresses action or state of being. Which, if either, was expressed by *zupped*? Using that sentence or a similar one, have pupils identify how they knew what kind of word substituted for *zupped.* They should point out the ending *-ed,* which is one characteristic of a verb, as well as the position in the sentence following an already identified noun. With additional examples, they can also discover that such words might be preceded by verb markers such as *will* and *be.*

These clues, along with a test sentence—in this case, two to allow for *be*—can be charted for reference:

A verb is a word that

1. can have the endings *-es, -ed, -ing,*
2. can be preceded by verb markers such as *will, be, are, is,...,*
3. often follows a noun in a sentence,
4. makes sense in one of these sentences:
    a. The thing(s) ———.
    b. The thing(s) ——— happy.

In order to deal with adverbs and adjectives, you will need to expand the nonsense sentence or make up a number of real sentences that are short enough to avoid confusion. Even then, youngsters will not find it easy to distinguish some of these.

As an example, we'll use: *The rimmy zop zupped zamly on the zip.* Ask pupils what kinds of words make sense for *zamly.* They will probably suggest words such as *happily, lazily, quietly,* and so on. Shift *zamly* about in the sentence, or shift the suggested real words. Do they still make sense? Youngsters will have discovered one characteristic of the adverb, its mobility in a sentence. Further, if the zop could zup zamly, might it even zup *more zamly?* The ability to take comparatives or intensifiers is another characteristic of the adverb.

In addition to its position, the fact that *zamly* ends in *ly* will probably lead pupils to name adverbs that end so. If they do, have them identify this ending as another characteristic of many adverbs.

Following a great deal of experience with real and nonsense sentences, youngsters might develop a chart of clues for the adverb:

An adverb is a word that

1. often has the *-ly* ending,
2. is movable in the sentence,
3. can take an intensifier: *more, most,*
4. may have comparative forms: *-er, -est,*
5. makes sense in the sentence: She played very ———.

As you will note, the test sentence leaves a lot to be desired. It does not allow for adverbs of place or time. *Here, yesterday,* or *immediately* will not make sense in the test sentence. On the other hand, to delete *very* from that sentence leaves it open for nouns.

Adjectives are not any easier. There is just no substitute for lots of experience with the language to find out the kinds of words that can be used in certain positions in a sentence. And, again, what they are called is not the important fact.

Using the sentence *The rimmy zop zupped zamly on the zip*, pupils can examine *rimmy* to determine the kinds of words that can substitute for it. Again, because of the ending, they might be inclined to substitute *dusty, hungry, dirty,* and so on. While the suffix *-y* is commonly used to convert nouns to adjectives, it is not a major characteristic of adjectives, so use other examples as well. Students should discover that the adjective's possible position before a noun is one characteristic of this kind of word. Further, if something or someone is rimmy, could it be *more rimmy* than something else? These clues, plus a test sentence, will help to distinguish adjectives from adverbs.

A chart of this information might look like this:

An adjective is a word that

1. often precedes a noun,
2. may take an intensifier: *more, most,*
3. can have comparative forms: *-er, -est,*
4. makes sense in both blanks of the sentence: The _____ thing is very _____.

Structure words are members of a very limited class. They include noun markers, prepositions, conjunctions, and interjections.

The noun markers precede or signal nouns and include the articles (*the, a*) as well as number words, both indefinite (*some, many*) and definite (*two, three*).

Prepositions are best dealt with in natural settings as well. The definition that a preposition "shows a relationship" is not very helpful. In the sentence "John loves Mary," *loves,* a verb, certainly shows a relationship. The forty or so prepositions are best learned in phrases, where youngsters get the feel of the typical three-word rhythm: *on* the fence, *over* the hill, *in* the box.

Conjunctions are even more limited in number. The coordinating conjunctions are "connectors" of equivalent items: *and, but, or, nor, for.* Then there are the pairs, such as *neither/nor, either/or,* and so on. Finally, there are about two dozen subordinating conjunctions that can be used to begin subordinate clauses. These include *although, since, because, that, though, unless, while,* and so on.

Interjections are those isolated words thrown into a sentence to express some emotion: *Yeah! Oh! Ha! Good!*

Whether or not youngsters learn to name any of these groups of words has little if anything to do with skill in using English. They were using words from every category before they ever began in school. However, if exploration of the nature of the language is done in an enjoyable fashion, as opposed to dull drill on someone else's sentences, that experience might help to further interest in the language itself. If so, it is worthwhile.

Sentence Patterns

Back to a more basic stage, another factor to consider is the nature of the sentence itself. No one is helped to identify what is a sentence through the often-heard definition: "A sentence is a complete thought." The first step is to avoid attempting an abstract definition of such an elusive form as a "sentence." Of course, we can all identify examples of what are and what are not sentences. Further, we can make some general statements, such as the mechanical marks of a sentence are a group of words beginning with a capital letter and ending with end punctuation. We can also say that most sentences contain a "noun phrase and a verb phrase" or a "subject and a predicate," depending upon the terminology preferred. Any such definition is clear to one who already knows what sentences are like, but none is helpful to the uninitiated.

In clarifying what a sentence is, there is no substitute for lots of experience with a great variety of sentences. By the second or third grade, you might begin by helping youngsters become aware of the bipartite nature of English sentences. Our world is replete with things we talk about (subjects) and the things we say about them (predicates). With several examples, you can begin discussion of the two parts. Call them "subject" and "predicate" or "noun phrase" and "verb phrase," as you prefer. Then provide some partial sentences, both noun phrases and verb phrases, such as "A girl…," "The monkey…," "…ran," "…rode down the street," and so on. Let pupils add words to complete the sentences. Also have them take such fragments and put them together, just for the fun of it.

You might further acquaint pupils with this bipolar nature of English sentences by having one group write noun phrases and another write verb phrases. Agree beforehand that all noun phrases will be either all singular or all plural, and that all verbs will be in the past tense. Then randomly put a noun phrase with a verb phrase to form unusual sentences.

This same technique was used in *Shufflebook* by Hefter and Moskof (Golden Press). The "book" is actually a large deck of cards. On one side of each card is a noun phrase beginning with *And,* while the other side has a verb phrase in past tense. To make the cards more interesting, both noun and verb phrases are illustrated. The book is used by shuffling the cards and then reading through in order: "And two cows ... And six wagons ... And a farmer ... kissed." Once a verb phrase is read, that card is turned over to begin again with the noun phrase on the back. Perhaps your students would like to make a shufflebook for themselves or for a younger group.

Once pupils are clear about the two parts of a sentence, try expanding each of the parts. Have them expand on a noun phrase such as "The rabbit..." with various adjectives and prepositional phrases, so that the noun phrase might become "The tiny white rabbit with the fluffy tail and pink nose..." Older students might even add clauses such as "...that nibbled on every head of lettuce we planted."

Of course, the same kind of expansion can be done with the verb phrase, which might have been "...hopped away." Students may expand this to "...hopped quickly away across the grass to find a safer part of the yard because he saw a cat stalking along in the bushes."

The reverse, contracting sentences, is not always worthless academic drill. There are times when a writer may produce a more involved sentence and perhaps get fouled up on tense or number. It helps, in such a case, to be able to reduce the sentence to its simple subject and predicate. Such a process, however, is not very meaningful if students are presented with concocted textbook sentences. They should examine their own productions.

By about the fourth grade or so, you might want to make your students consciously aware of the kinds of sentences they produce. Once they are aware of the four form classes, various patterns can be demonstrated, reproduced with different ideas or content, and also expanded and contracted.

Most basic is the noun–verb (N–V) pattern: *Birds sing.* Perhaps you want to have pupils convert this basic sentence through the different tenses: *Birds sang, Birds will sing, Birds are singing.* They can also expand each of the basic forms to observe that the basic sentence pattern remains unchanged, regardless of the number of auxiliary verbs, phrases, or clauses that are added: *The tiny little birds on the back fence were singing sweetly as the dawn broke over the horizon.* Of course, this same point is true—and practice should be given in a similar manner—with all of the following patterns.

A most common sentence pattern is the noun–verb–noun (N–V–N): *Sherri hit the ball.* Have pupils write and manipulate additional sentences in this pattern.

Other patterns to be demonstrated and manipulated are shown in the following list, with *Vl, Adj,* and *Adv* representing linking verb, adjective, and adverb, respectively.

N–Vl–Adj:	My kitten is contented.
N–Vl–Adv:	My kitten is here.
N–Vl–N:	My kitten is Siamese.
N–V–N–N:	My kitten gave the dog a slap.
N–V–N–Adj:	My kitten made the dog's nose sore.

You might prefer to use a subscript to the nouns to indicate which refer to identities and which signify different referents. For example, the N–V–N pattern might be designated N_1–V–N_2 to show that the second noun has a different referent. In contrast, N_1–Vl–N_1 indicates that both nouns always have the same referent. Such labels also lead to two forms of the N–V–N–N pattern: N_1–V–N_2–N_3, as in *My kitten gave the dog a slap;* and N_1–V–N_2–N_2, as in *Mary calls the cat Boxer.*

You may also want to point out that any noun substitute is considered the *N* in these patterns, whether it is a noun or pronoun or—later—a gerund or infinitive, such as *To swim is my greatest pleasure* (N_1–Vl–N_2) or *Swimming is easy* (N–Vl–Adj). Furthermore, the addition or omission of adverbs does not change any pattern.

The foregoing suggestions are offered as a positive substitute for the "grammar" lessons that many teachers feel compelled to use. There is no evidence that even these will produce greater skill in writing. On the other hand, they do offer another way for youngsters to consciously manipulate their language. If approached with this attitude, not as a drill—and certainly not as a means of processing someones else's sentences—but as a way to have fun in playing with the language, they should be helpful.

SENTENCE COMBINING

Research does support the use of sentence-combining activities as a means of developing flexibility in sentence structure, with the resulting improvement in writing skill. Most of that research has been done at upper elementary levels, grades four through eight. However, many of the simple activities can be used orally as low as first grade, and all are more effective if there is discussion of the possibilities so that they become part of the oral repertoire.

Research in the mid-1960s (Bateman and Zidonis, 1966; Mellon, 1967) credited instruction in transformational grammar as the factor leading to success with sentence combining. O'Hare (1973), however, demonstrated that sentence combining was effective in producing greater skill in written language with seventh graders who had *no* formal grammar instruction. He found that the sentence combining itself, not the transformational grammar, contributed to the gains, and his findings have been verified in numerous studies since. However, as Crowhurst (1983) pointed out, sentence combining does not produce any involuntary syntactic operations: "Linguistic resources which were already within the student's competence are raised to conscious control."

Structured Exercises

O'Hare's lessons were very structured. Students were given a statement "problem" and were to solve it according to the direction given with the problem. The following examples are modeled after the O'Hare work, presenting the direction in parentheses after the problem (PROB), which is then followed by the possible solution (SOL).

A. Transforming single sentences

PROB: Sue went to the movies yesterday (*Negative*)

SOL: Sue did not go to the movies yesterday.

PROB: Someone called me on the phone. (*Who-question*)

SOL: Who called me on the phone?

PROB: A mouse is in my room. (*There-insert*).

SOL: There is a mouse in my room.

B. Combining two sentences (Note: *Something* is used as a place holder.)

PROB: Jenny shouted *something*.
        She caught a fish. (*That*)

SOL: Jenny shouted that she caught a fish.

PROB: *Something* is a fact.
        Ben is a good friend. (*It-That*)

SOL: It is a fact that Ben is a good friend.

PROB: Our class wondered *something*.
        Teachers manage to see everything. (*How*)

SOL: Our class wondered how teachers manage to see everything.
        (Note: Similar combinations can be made with *Who, What, When, Where,* and *Why.*)

O'Hare also introduced deletions (where students were to retain only italicized words) and clauses as part of the sentence-combining practice. Using the pattern of the solution to the following, additional problem statements can be made to practice use of *When, Where,* and *Why.*

PROB: We saw a strange mutt outside the classroom door.
        The dog's *fur was matted with mud.* (*Whose*)

SOL: We saw a strange mutt, whose fur was matted with mud, outside the classroom door.

To older students who have had progressively more complex practice with these kinds of combining activities, you might present a culminating problem such as the following:

PROB: You might present *something.*
        It is *a problem.*
        The problem is *culminating.*
        It is *such as the following.*
        Present it *to students.*
        The students should be *older.*
        The students should *have had practice.* (*Who*).
        The practice should be *progressively more complex.*
        It should be *with combining activities.*
        The activities should be *these kinds.* (*Of*)

Did you recognize the solution to be the sentence that preceded this problem?

Unstructured Exercises

Although O'Hare's work popularized sentence combining, subsequent research has demonstrated that his highly structured lessons were not necessarily the key to students' success. None has discredited his work, but Henderson (1980), for example, found that more "open" kinds of activities produced even greater improvement in the overall quality of students' writing. Hence, another—and possibly even better—method is to provide sentences to be combined and to ask for the "ways" in which this can be done. Then discuss the effect on meaning of the different solutions. In fact, we can agree with Crowhurst (1983) that the success of sentence combining in more recent studies may rest less in the exercises themselves than in their open patterns and especially in the amount of time spent in discussing the various options.

One technique is merely to present a portion of a sentence and let youngsters invent various methods of completing it. For example, imagine how many "fillers" your students could compose for the following verb phrase: "...is fun." A few examples might include *baseball, playing baseball in the Spring, swimming, to go on a camping trip, whatever we do in class,* and even *writing* (we hope!).

A noun phrase, such as "We like..." can be completed with just as great a variety of language structures, resulting not only in pupils' awareness of how much they already know but also leading to increased flexibility by learning additional options from one another.

Regardless of which method is used, structured or open, students need to be made aware of the possible ways of combining sentences. Again, as with O'Hare's technique, none of these requires knowledge of formal grammar, although some terms are used here as a matter of classification for you, the teacher.

Simple Compounding. This is an early stage and can be demonstrated with sentences or with any form class words, as shown in the following examples.

PROB: The boys played ball.
        The girls played ball too.

SOL: The boys played ball and the girls played ball too.
        The boys and girls played ball.

PROB: The horse ran across the field.
        The horse jumped the fence.

SOL: The horse ran across the field and jumped the fence.

Adjective Strings. With these and most others, a number of combinations is possible. Only a few examples of solutions are given here. In all cases, the follow-up discussion is most important.

PROB: Kari has a horse.
        The horse is old.
        The horse is tired.

SOL: Kari has a tired old horse.
        Kari's horse is old and tired. (Compounding)
        Kari's old horse is tired.
        Kari's tired horse is old.

Students should examine their suggested solutions to determine differences in emphasis. The first solution above focuses on the fact that Kari has something, whereas the other three stress the horse itself.

In the last two solutions, stress shifts from *tired* to *old*. Youngsters should be able to recognize such shifts without verbalization, or even knowledge, that a predicate adjective is more forceful than an adjective that merely precedes the noun it modifies.

Of course, adjective strings can be used with both subject and predicate nouns and can continue indefinitely:

> PROB: The girl has a horse.
> The girl is little.
> The girl is happy.
> The horse is old.
> The horse is tired.
>
> SOL: The happy little girl has a tired old horse.
> The happy little girl's horse..., and so on.

Possibly another point is in order here to illustrate how much children already know intuitively about their grammar. In the preceding example, you would not expect even a first-grader to order the first two adjectives in reverse: "The little happy girl.." Nor would you expect any difficulty in ordering adjectives of number and color: Even a kindergartener will say "two blue cars" rather than "blue two cars."

Subordinate Clauses: Introduce students to subordinate clauses as a means of combining sentences by giving them a few examples and letting them try their hands at producing others. Clauses may begin with *although, since, because,* and so on, as well as with *who, which,* and *that.*

> PROB: Ted likes to swim.
> Ted gets tired easily.
> Ted would rather play hockey.
>
> SOL: Although Ted likes to swim, he gets tired easily and would rather play hockey.
>
> PROB: Chess is a war game.
> It becomes more enjoyable with practice.
>
> SOL: Chess is a war game that becomes more enjoyable with practice.

Adverbial Phrases.

PROB: Tim met Susan.
        They met at the airport.

SOL: Tim met Susan at the airport.

Appositive Phrases.

PROB: The little puppy crept through the door.
        It was a nondescript mutt.

SOL: The little puppy, a nondescript mutt, crept through the door.

Participial Phrases.

PROB: That horse was determined to win the race.
        It ran like the wind.

SOL: Running like the wind, that horse was determined to win the race.

Possessive and Gerund.

PROB: Dottie sails in the summer.
        This keeps her busy all summer.

SOL: Dottie's sailing keeps her busy all summer.

After exposing students to the variety of combining techniques, have them try different solutions with the same problem. Following is a problem set and only a sampling of the possible solutions. After writing their own suggestions, students should compare and discuss the shifts in meaning that result from different choices.

PROB: The Manx cat is unusual.
        It is the only domestic cat born without a tail.
        It is husky.
        It has short hair.

SOL: The short-haired, husky Manx cat is unusual because it is the only domestic cat born without a tail.
        The Manx cat, short-haired and husky, is unusual because it is the only domestic cat born without a tail.
        The unusual Manx cat, the only domestic cat born without a tail, is short-haired and husky.
        The only domestic cat born without a tail, the short-haired, husky Manx cat is unusual.

Noun Substitutes. Preschoolers already know and use one noun substitute, the pronoun. Greater flexibility in sentence structure is gained if students also become aware of the other forms they may use in place of the subject or object noun. Let's assume that your student wants to express the idea that her cat likes food. Following are various noun substitutes that might be used:

Pronoun:	*It* is Simon Cat's major concern. (Presumes a referent for *it*.)
Gerund:	*Eating* is Simon Cat's major concern.
Possessive and Gerund:	*Simon Cat's eating* is his major concern.
Infinitive:	*To eat* is Simon Cat's major concern.
Noun Clause:	*What he will eat* is Simon Cat's major concern.

In the preceding cases, determination of a noun substitute can be made by deciding what can replace "it" at the beginning of the sentence. Of course, in the case of humans, the substitution will be for "he," "she," or "they." Furthermore, there is no need to use the formal grammatical labels shown in the list in order to be able to form the different kinds of sentences.

Instruction in all of the different forms discussed in this section on sentence combining is a matter of making students aware of the options and providing practice in their use. Although this experience may contribute to some intuitive use during composing, most of the application will take place in the revision stage of writing, a stage discussed in Chapter 11. Let's remember that, in the process of composing, the writer cannot attend to everything at once. However, a greater intuitive sense of language will make the revising process less traumatic.

A word of caution might also be in order here. Some critics of sentence combining have suggested that it leads students to believe that longer sentences are always better. This danger is avoided if there is discussion of the various ways of combining sentences and comparing their effectiveness, and if students continue to contract as well as expand sentences, as discussed early in this chapter.

Finally, I have made no effort to suggest a sequence for sentence combining. Teachers are advised to determine what processes their students already use and to continue from there. At the beginning levels, youngsters seem most inclined to expand on their ideas by using full clauses in the predicate. Beyond that, sequences vary and probably should differ with the background of the pupils. Teachers who are interested in a sequence might examine Lawlor's work (1983), in which he presented a sequence that makes sense in terms of what we know about children's language development. For example, single adjectives and adverbs precede use of phrases, phrases precede clauses, and gerunds and appositives are not used until more mature levels.

SUMMARY

This chapter has attempted to separate *grammar* from "correct usage" and has presented both as dangerous consumers of valuable instructional time, offering little if any positive results in terms of increasing skill in language, oral or written.

     In lieu of the former, the typical grammar instruction focusing on labels for parts of speech, suggestions were made to help youngsters raise to a conscious level that intuitive knowledge they already possess about the language. This knowledge includes understanding of the word-order nature of English, the bipolar nature of sentences, and even the way in which different words function in sentences. Sentence patterns were included not only to teach parts of speech but as a means of further understanding the many ways in which the language can be used.

     The foregoing were all offered with some reservation and with full knowledge that not even this kind of instruction has been demonstrated to contribute to skill in writing; they were offered with the thought that—if pursued with enjoyment, using children's own language instead of textbook sentences—they provide still another method of manipulating the language.

     Sentence combining is supported by research. Two types of activities were suggested, structured and open, with the latter appearing to be the more effective. Regardless of the type used, instruction and practice should be with the children's own sentences and with the intent of helping them discover that it can be fun to play with language.

SUGGESTIONS FOR ACTION

   1. Reevaluate your time if it is spent dealing with word usage. At the primary level, are you concerned with those creative analogies that will take care of themselves? At the middle grades, are you spending time in items that don't matter, such as split infinitives, *like* substituted for *as, different than* vs. *different from?*

2. At the upper grades, if you want to make students more aware of word usage, have them listen critically to the radio or television announcers for their "goofs."

3. How do your students rank "English"? Have them (anonymously) rank the subjects they study in school. Follow up with discussion of the reasons for the rankings.

4. By third grade or above—if you believe in teaching formal grammar—find out if your students are aware of the basic facts about English. Do they realize that it is a word-order language? Do they know that there are two classes of words? If not, try some of the "jabberwocky" sentences with them to demonstrate their intuitive knowledge.

5. At the upper grades, how are you teaching the parts of speech—assuming that you are? Do your students know how they *really* identify a noun or a verb? Try using the criteria they have with a sentence containing a nonsense word for the part of speech in question.

6. Have students make a "Shufflebook," or play a combining game to demonstrate the bipolar nature of English sentences. Have them expand on the noun phrase or verb phrase of some of these skeletal sentences to see how far they can go. You might use *when, where, how,* and *why* questions to help in the expansion.

7. At the primary grades, help your youngsters gain some flexibility in their use of sentences by taking one of *their* examples and having them suggest other ways of saying the same thing. They might also explore ways of combining sentences to avoid the repetition of the subject when they want to add adjectives. (Usually these children need no help in learning to string sentences together with *and*!)

8. At the upper grades—third and above—begin acquainting your students with some of the sentence-combining methods described in the latter part of this chapter. My own preference is for the more open-ended types of exercises.

9. At the upper grades you might also want to have students experiment with the different noun substitutes they can use for sentence subjects.

REFERENCES

BATEMAN, D. R., and F. J. ZIDONIS, *The Effect of a Study of Transformational Grammar on the Writing of Ninth and Tenth Graders,*

Research Report No. 6. Urbana: National Council of Teachers of English, 1966. Reports research on sentence combining in conjunction with transformational grammar.

BOSTAIN, JAMES C., "Wishing Will Not Make It So: A Linguist Takes on the Grammarians," *Today's Education,* 70 (April–May, 1981), 34–39. Criticizes conventional instruction on grammar and word usage.

BRADDOCK, RICHARD, RICHARD LLOYD-JONES, and LOWEL SCHOER, *Research in Written Composition.* Urbana: National Council of Teachers of English, 1963. Summarizes research on the relation between grammar instruction and skill in writing.

CROWHURST, MARION, "Sentence Combining: Maintaining Realistic Expectations," *College Composition and Communication,* 34 (February, 1983), 62–72. Points up the importance of discussing the effect of various sentence combinations on meaning.

ELLEY, W. B., I. H. BARHAM, H. LAMB, and M. WYLLIE, "The Role of Grammar in a Secondary School English Curriculum," *Research in the Teaching of English,* 10 (Spring, 1976), 5–21. Compares the effectiveness of three approaches at the secondary level: transformational grammar, traditional grammar, and a reading–writing emphasis.

HENDERSON, H. K., "A Comparison of the Effects of Practice with Signaled or Open Sentence Combining Exercises within Varying Instructional Frames." Unpublished doctoral dissertation, University of Houston, 1980 (*Dissertation Abstracts International,* 1981, 41, 55009A). Compares signaled and open types of sentence combining, with the latter revealing higher overall improvement in writing.

LAWLOR, JOSEPH, "Sentence Combining: A Sequence for Instruction," *Elementary School Journal,* 84 (September, 1983), 53–62. Describes a specific sequence of instruction for sentence-combining activities.

MELLON, J. C., *Transformational Sentence-Combining: A Method for Enhancing the Development of Syntactic Fluency in English Composition.* Cambridge: Harvard University, 1967.

MOFFETT, JAMES, and BETTY JANE WAGNER, *Student-Centered Language Arts and Reading, K–13.* Boston: Houghton Mifflin, 1983. A professional text on theory and practice in the language arts.

NEIFER, CATHI, "The Role of Grammar in Writing." Final position paper for the Northwest Ohio Writing Project, Bowling Green, Ohio, July, 1982. Summarizes research on the effect of grammar instruction on writing skill.

O'HARE, FRANK, *Sentence Combining: Improving Student Writing without Formal Grammar Instruction.* Urbana: National Council of Teachers of English, 1973. Demonstrates that the effectiveness of sentence combining does not rely on knowledge of formal grammar.

POOLEY, ROBERT C., "Dare Schools Set a Standard in English Usage?" *The English Journal,* 49 (March, 1960), 176–81. Suggests points for inclusion and exclusion in the teaching of English usage.

THURBER, SAMUEL, "The Conditions Needed for the Successful Teaching of English Composition," *The School Review,* 2 (January, 1894), 12–21. An early criticism of the teaching of English.

8

Conferencing
During Writing

Correction does much, but encouragement does more.
GOETHE

CHAPTER 2 DEALT with classroom management in broad terms, through a comparison of three kinds of organization. Whereas that chapter might be considered an overview, this one will present specifics on conferencing, which many of us see as the heart of the writing classroom. In fact, "heart" is an appropriate analogy here, since conferencing serves much the same functions in a writing class as the heart does in the body: It distributes nourishment, carries away impurities, and stimulates other organs.

First of all, this chapter presumes that writing will take place daily in your classroom—or at least nearly so. Not much will be accomplished through conferencing—or writing, for that matter—if writing is a part-time or sometime activity. At least thirty minutes per day must be set aside for writing if students are to become effective in this language art. This chapter is based on that premise.

Even more time could be justified. After all, what does "language arts" or "English" consist of? It is reading, writing, speaking, and listening. Every one of these is used (practiced) and, we hope, taught in the writing class. That teaching is through demonstration and discussion of specific elements and problem areas. Writing is "English" in the best sense. Not only does it involve the four components, but it does so in a much more personal sense than any textbook, since students are writing, reading, talking, and listening about topics of concern to them, expressed in language used by them.

VALUES OF CONFERENCING

As mentioned previously, the value of personal conferences is undisputed. While not encouraging such, we can point to evidence from the practice of Individualized Reading to show that even the most superficial conference in reading sparked increased interest on the part of pupils; an adult (their teacher) showed a personal interest in what they were reading. The same has been demonstrated in relation to writing (Graves, 1983; Silver, 1983; Turbill, 1982).

Of course, more specific conferences accomplish considerably more than increased interest. For example, skill development is not based on the preplanned sequence from an "English" book. It is a matter of specific instruction on an identified problem at the time of need and in application to a personal concern on the part of the student.

Second, in the process of conferencing, you get to know your students as individuals. You discover their interests and concerns. You help them express their ideas on paper, thereby clarifying their ideas for themselves.

Further, in the process, you discover the elements of writing as no textbook could clarify them for you. You will become much more aware of the specific problems presented by a topic, problems well beyond the mere mechanics. Difficulties such as "organization," "sequence," "transitions," "audience," and so on will become fleshed out, will be much more than mere words in an English text.

From the standpoint of pupils you will become a guide and helper rather than a wielder of the red pencil. In the process, they will become more open, more able to identify and admit their concerns about particular pieces of writing. Further, peer conferencing will help them to help one another and will weld them into a more cohesive and cooperative group. The competition that continues will be with self, not with others.

All children, from slow learners to gifted, need this kind of conferencing. You are giving your personal attention to them as individuals. Further, you are talking to them rather than merely jotting down a few shorthand notes—or worse, corrections—on their papers. The personal voice is attended to; the corrections are skimmed, at best, and discarded.

GETTING STARTED

Teachers of kindergarten or first grade have an easier job of establishing procedures than do most teachers; they can begin from scratch. In contrast, most teachers at other levels have a great retraining task, unless they are in a very unusual school. In most schools writing is a once-a-week, one-period, total-group activity, as described in the first example in Chapter 2. Retraining from that procedure to a workshop plan is more difficult than starting with the unspoiled.

Regardless of the level and previous experience, the goal is to establish writing as a daily activity in a workshop setting. This implies the teacher as a guide and model, children as writers and assistants to peers, and everyone at different stages as they work independently as well as cooperatively. This approach will require individual help, small group work, and total group experiences.

The first steps should be small ones, as any teacher knows. It is better to move slowly and consistently than to experience failure and have to retreat to the beginning. Too large a step results in frustration for children and teacher. Furthermore, a good workshop class requires planning; it is not a matter of just letting children do as they please. That is chaos.

As a teacher, you know the proper procedure for teaching a skill: initial teaching or demonstration, practice, reteaching if necessary, more practice, and application. So too, classroom procedures must be *taught*. And they cannot be taught all at once nor through mere admonishment. Begin with your most important, get it established, add another, and so on.

Obviously, procedures should be kept as simple as possible so that they don't interfere with the process. In fact, that is the purpose of establishing procedures—to facilitate the process.

Plan and discuss proposed procedures with your students. Often they have good suggestions, and whatever the decisions, they will be better understood and accepted if students are in on the planning. Furthermore, initial discussion will not ensure success. Review and possible revision of procedures must take place periodically. When a major procedural problem arises, again involve the group in its solution.

Your initial procedures will probably deal with materials: assurance of an abundance and variety of paper, pencils, and other implements, understanding of pencil sharpening, picking up and depositing paper and folders, and so on. If locations of materials are clearly established, as well as procedures for handling finished and partly finished copy, you will have eliminated a great source of interruption.

Although teachers differ in how they prefer to handle some of these mechanics, I believe that each child should have a writing log in which to keep all writing. This could be a manila folder with a decorated cover in first grade; however, as soon as possible I prefer a three-ring binder with dividers for different types of materials: a section for interesting words; another for scraps of ideas, jokes, puns, unusual sentences; another for initial drafts; and a final section for finished materials.

With younger children, you may prefer that the logs be kept in a box or special location in the room. This is merely to avoid the loss or damage so likely if they are kept in the children's possession.

Regardless of the format chosen, these logs or folders should be kept at school. Of course, for some special purpose you might allow a log to be checked out by a parent overnight. This is not suggested in order to limit communication with parents. That communication is important; however, it is best done with your guidance and over a collection of writings rather than on a piecemeal basis with each draft. The composite of writings in the log serves as an excellent basis for a parent conference.

In effect, the logs or folders are the students' "textbook" on writing. They are also your cumulative record of progress for each youngster. Although you will not be reading every paper as it is produced, you will examine each log periodically to note progress, needs, and accomplishments, as well as interests.

Ideally you could have writing at various times throughout the day, but that may be prohibited. In most schools there is a specified time for language arts. Further, children often feel more comfortable if they have a routine established and followed.

Regardless of your time restrictions, another step toward a writing workshop is taken when pupils understand that they will not all be at the same point in their writing at any given time. Break the lockstep. Let them know that you will be moving about to examine their papers, that everything they write will be read by someone at some stage—including, of course, the final stage—and that you will not be collecting papers at the end of the period.

CONFERENCES

Conferences are invaluable as early as the first grade. These children are spontaneous and interested in expressing themselves. In contrast, with older students you must surmount the traditional view of the teacher as the final passer of judgment on "finished" writing. You will need to convince, through initial experiences, that your role is one of assisting rather than merely evaluating. Your initial conferences will be short and will be more like training sessions for your students—and for you as well.

These first conferences will be informal, even superficial perhaps, as you move about the class during the writing. Many might last less than a minute. Your comments may be on what the child is writing about, an encouraging response to a specific idea in the paper, or a direct reply to a concern or problem expressed by the student.

The important point at this stage is to get youngsters to feel comfortable with your moving about the room, looking over their shoulders, and showing a personal interest in *what* they are writing about. Through this interaction, you need to demonstrate your role: You are an aide in the process rather than an evaluator after the fact; you are an interested party in what they have to say and how clearly they say it rather than a tabulator of mechanical errors.

You might conclude some of these initial periods with a few general comments to the class about some of the good ideas you saw. You may even ask one or two children to share some portion of their writing that demonstrates a particular point, or that is just well stated—even if it is just a sentence. You may even choose to share a problem you faced in your own writing before you began moving about that classroom. (Did you remember to do some of that writing too?)

Expanded Conferences

Once you and your students begin to feel comfortable with your movement and brief conferences, acquaint them with the next step— some initial record keeping. This might be introduced with a comment such as "I've noticed that some of you have all kinds of ideas to write about. Sometimes we get a good idea and then forget it when it comes time to write. Let's begin a list of topics (thoughts, ideas, words) that we can refer to when we want to write. Use the back cover of your folder (divider, section, etc.) to keep a running list of ideas. As I come around, you can show me some of the topics you've put down to write about."

Such a start might be furthered with some total group discussion of ideas and topics for writing. You might contribute techniques from Chapter 4 as well. In sharing, all will benefit from the exchange, as one idea triggers another.

Instead of beginning with this list of ideas to write about—or at another time—you will undoubtedly want to have each student begin another chart that will serve as a record of mechanics mastered in application. Since improvement in writing is often intangible, with so many elements involved, a chart of some kind on which to record accomplishments will help your students to see that they are making progress.

In comments to the group, similar to the preceding, you can introduce this chart: "Many of you have learned a lot about writing. You probably don't even realize how much. Inside the front cover of your folder, let's keep a chart so I can mark down each thing you learn as I see you using it correctly in your writing. For example, today I saw that Tim was capitalizing all the proper nouns in his paper, and Sally put the commas in series of words she used."

That chart may take many forms. In fact, you may prefer to duplicate a chart for each pupil to keep in the log. Primarily, it will have a column for the date of entry and another for the skill mastered or merely for comments, depending upon its purpose. Ultimately the log or folder may include several charts or records. In addition to one for skills, you might suggest another to record "What I Have Written" and possibly "Ideas to Write About" or "Things I'm Interested In." These are helpful not only for the student but also for you as you proceed with conferencing.

Now conferences can become a little more organized. Children already understand that you talk with each of them. At this point, they should be ready to understand your explanation that you will be taking a little more time with some, but you will see everyone within the week.

Remember again that what you focus on in the conferences is what you are reinforcing in children. If your initial focus is on mechanics, that will be their overriding concern. Yet, as Elbow (1973) said, "Writing badly...is a crucial part of learning to write well....Schools tend to emphasize success and thereby undermine learning. When the price of failure is very high, a learner tends to close himself off from improvement in this sort of complex, global skill [p. 136]."

Graves (1983) made essentially the same point in connection with the differences between learning to write in school and learning to speak at home: "Now [in school] there is a concern for early correctness and proper etiquette, with little attention given to content. In speech it was the other way around—content was primary, conventions secondary. Children have more ownership of their speech; they rent their writing [p. 162]."

Hence, your focus—and students need to be helped to understand this—will be on the content of the writing. In the brief conferences, comments will be very specific. Perhaps it is a matter of word choice: "You used *walked* several times here. Isn't there a more specific word you can choose? How did the character walk?" Or you may find that an idea needs elaboration: "Can you give an example or two here? Would that help the reader to understand your point?" Possibly an idea is unclear: "Please read this section to me. Does it make sense to you? What is your point here?" There are unlimited possibilities for specific concerns identified in a paper: the need for elaboration, variety of sentence structure, sequence, transitions, and so on.

It is a good idea at about this point, after you have completed two or three rounds of these brief conferences, to begin discussing peer conferencing with the group. You have established a model for conferences, pointing out interesting ideas, well-phrased sentences, clear organization, good word choice, and so on. Share this positive approach to writing with the group and encourage sharing of ideas and problems with a buddy.

Recognize that just as you are learning to use the conference approach, children have so much more to learn about it. Begin small. You might even demonstrate a conference to the group by having one student volunteer with a (good) piece of writing. In front of the group, possibly with the piece of writing on the overhead projector, proceed to discuss the example with the child. "What do you think is the best part?" "Why were you excited?" "How did you feel?"

As the conference routine becomes established, you might want to provide students with a brief outline of the kinds of questions or concerns they should attend to in their own conferences with peers. At the lower grades, this might consist of only a few points:

What is your favorite part?

Are you having trouble with any part? Which was the hard part?

What can you do to make this piece of writing even better?

At the upper grades, you might clarify the general criteria previously discussed and have students use those: clarity and interest appeal. These two criteria include word choice, sentence structure, and organization, as well as any mechanics that interfere with the communication. As students become more proficient at conferencing, you can also develop with them a guide to the more common problems and concerns, using items from the list suggested for you later in this chapter.

After the demonstration conference, discuss the kinds of questions you asked and why you asked those kinds. Point out that the purpose is to help the writer discover where ideas are unclear to the reader or disorganized to the point that they didn't make sense, as well as to call attention to what was particularly good about that piece of writing.

If possible, you might want to set aside a student conference center in the room, one other than where you sit for conferences. Further, you might decide to pick only one or two pupils as capable of holding conferences until others demonstrate ability. Regardless, your students should see that conferencing is a privilege that they will lose if they fail to demonstrate their own ability to handle such conferences properly.

Some teachers prefer conferencing teams instead of the one-to-one of a buddy system. This approach has the value of providing several views on the piece of writing. For example, you might have two peers read the paper, each offering at least one specific positive comment. Have the readers initial the paper to signify that it is, in their opinion, ready for a formal conference. Some teachers have even found it helpful, when they get to the point of grading a paper, also to grade the evaluators on their handling of that paper. Incidentally, regardless of the structure preferred, it is advisable that no student have the same evaluator(s) for more than one or two pieces of writing.

You may want to sit in on early peer conferences to provide initial guidance, either officially or by roaming about and dropping in on those in progress. The major point your youngsters need to realize is that they are there to read the paper and to offer help on ideas or content. Their primary questions as they read a classmate's paper should be: "Do I understand it? Is it clear?" If not, they need to point out where they have a problem so that the writer can make adjustments.

Tape recording of some peer evaluations can be a helpful means of improving those peer conferences. Play the tape for the group and discuss the procedures used. Encourage students in their conferences to share techniques such as various heuristics used in the development of their drafts.

Meanwhile, you can now begin to spend a little more time with some students who might be at a stage in their writing where they are bogged down or have a problem they can't seem to handle, whether at the prewriting stage, in the first draft, or in revision.

It is at this point too that you may want to begin some record keeping of your own as a result of conferences. Once again, format is a personal matter, whether it be a notebook with a page or two for each child, or a folder with just a listing of all the pupils. I much prefer the notebook with separate pages for each child, with a narrow column for the date of conference and a wider space for comments. Especially at the upper levels, this record can be made from the student's own summary statements resulting from the conference. That record should be presented to and reviewed with the student at subsequent conferences. Some teachers find their own record of more interest to the student than any that student might keep.

Regardless of the format you choose, keep the written comments specific and diagnostic and to a minimum. Focus on major points. If you begin to write too much, you will find yourself buried in a mass of unintelligible notes and your role changed from that of teacher to that of bookkeeper.

As a follow-up to these brief conferences, you may recognize that a number of your students have similar problems. That provides a goal for a temporary small group lesson in which you teach that skill to the identified students. You may even find a common deficiency that is worth reviewing with the total group.

Whether small group or total, the next step after the instruction is to have students pull a finished paper from their logs and check it for the particular item taught. No doubt many will be surprised to find how many errors they had and how they can do their own correcting with this kind of background.

Content of the Conferences

In these brief conferences you obviously cannot read everything any pupil has written. Of course, some may have written little or nothing, so you will need to begin there. Raise questions with that child about what he or she wanted to write. What is this youngster interested in? One of the major tools of the teacher in a conference is silence. Allow plenty of time, ten to fifteen seconds at least, for that youngster to answer. There is something about silence that requires a response.

Regardless of the writing, your comments should be supportive of the writer and the writing. This is not to say that blanket praise is the order of the day; however, you can always find something specific that is positive. The focus needs to be on the content and its clarity. If there is a point where you do not understand what the writer was trying to say, that is the question to ask: "What did you mean here? I don't understand." Get the writer to state orally what was meant, and then have the writer readjust the written statement on the basis of the oral.

No matter what the problem, it is absolutely essential that you never put a mark on the writer's paper in the process of your conferencing about that paper. The minute you do so it becomes *your* paper. You may—and should—offer help and make suggestions, but the writer must retain ownership of the paper; that piece of writing is the student's responsibility, not yours. Therefore any suggestions recorded on the paper should always be written by the student, not by you.

A large part of the task in these early stages is to develop the understanding that any first draft is to be revised. Although specifics for this instruction are discussed in Chapter 11, we need to develop the idea in conferences as well. Even high school students in traditional settings believe that the first draft is the final draft and—at best—that revision is recopying, possibly after some proofreading for mechanics.

Get your pupils, from first grade on, into the habit of writing on every other line so that they have space for some revision. Further, let them know that "messy" is better for the first draft! To emphasize the fact that a first draft is tentative, one school district has pupils use cheap yellow paper for the first draft, so that even the paper implies that another version is forthcoming. A fourth-grade teacher has her pupils refer to the first draft as a "sloppy copy."

As Graves (1983) pointed out, first-graders can learn to use arrows or numbers for inserts, can feel comfortable with cross-outs, and in other ways can learn to make changes on that first draft. Once this understanding is achieved, your class is ready for more formal, intensive conferences.

Scheduled Conferences

Pupils now understand that they will all have a turn with the teacher and that they can have helpful conferences with one another, whether with assigned buddies or with helpmates of their choice. They further understand that a first draft is not a final draft. They are now ready for more formal conferences based on "finished" first drafts, that is, on first drafts that are legible enough for them to read to the teacher.

Most youngsters will have written a number of pieces between their formal conferences. Hence, at the conference they should bring a conference draft of their *best* piece since the last conference. If they do this, they will be presenting writing that has been more carefully considered by them personally and by a peer evaluator. Thus you will more likely be able to focus on important problems rather than become bogged down with trivia.

You may even move to more detailed conference planning in the case of older students. For example, you might want them to come to the conference with doubtful spellings circled or questionable language underlined in preparation for the discussion with you. Again, it is important to shift that responsibility to the student. Also, you may need to reemphasize to the group the importance of class etiquette: These conferences should not be interrupted. Everyone will get a turn.

Plan that these scheduled first-draft conferences will last five to ten minutes. In fact, especially with older students, inform them of the time limitations. Admittedly, such a limit is arbitrary, and early conferences may run longer as you and students are learning. However, if you take too long in each conference you will limit your availability or extend the space between a given child's conferences. Furthermore, having a time limit will help both you and the student to remain task-oriented.

Have a portion of time, in addition to your own writing and moving about the class, allocated to these formal conferences. That time, incidentally, doesn't always have to be during the "writing period" if there are other times of the day when most youngsters are profitably occupied independently.

You will need a sign-up sheet that students can use when they are ready for a more formal conference. Of course, in the early stages there will be some students who don't sign up for conferences. As you move about in the informal sessions, make a note of the needs of such an individual. Then invite that person to a conference at a specified time on a given date in order to discuss a major item of concern.

In order to protect yourself from being swamped, you may want to include the stipulation that sign-ups are to be made only after the first draft has been reviewed with a peer. That reviewer should sign the paper as having agreed that it is ready for a conference with the teacher. Further, you are reminded again that the peer conference at this point is not a proofreading task; it is not concerned with the mechanics except to the extent that they may interfere with communication of the idea.

Locate the conference in a corner of the room, a little removed from the bustle of the group. A table is much preferred to the teacher's desk, since the former makes for a less threatening setting. Sit beside the conferee so you both can see the paper and so that you are a supporter rather than an adversary. Even the size of the chair can make a difference: Pupil chairs might not be as comfortable for you, but they keep you from towering over the student in a threatening posture.

A good conference requires planning on your part too. Based on your knowledge of this student, you may want to focus on clarity of expression, or this might be one who has problems in sequence or sentence structure. In any event, be certain that your conference is clearly focused on a major point and is not merely another shotgun attempt to resolve everything at once. As already stated, this focus should be on organization, clarity, and completeness of ideas rather than on mechanics.

This last statement suggests that questions you ask will be open-ended ones to which the student, not you, has the answer. Don't try to turn the piece into what you would have written. Not only must you provide considerable silence so that the student will speak, but practice the Rogerian art of questioning: "Are you saying...?" "Did I understand you to say...?"

After the student reads the conference draft orally while seated beside you, the conference might open with a general positive comment, such as "What do you think is the best part of your paper? Why do you like it?" Or you might use Elbow's (1973) technique: Ask for one word from the paper that best summarizes that piece, followed by one word not in the paper that summarizes it.

There are innumerable kinds of specific questions or comments one might make about the different pieces of writing that could be presented in just one classroom. It is impossible to list every kind. Following is just a sampling of concerns, any one of which might be spoken to in the discussion of a student's paper. For older students these items might be incorporated into a guide for their personal use or for use with peers. The major problem of the paper might relate to:

Focus: What is the main idea? What point did you want to get across?

Clarity: What did you mean by…?

Audience: Whom is this for? Is it clear to…?

Sequence: Did you tell things in the order the reader should read them?

Organization: You began with this point; later you came back to it. Will this be clear to the reader? Is there some way you might discuss everything you want to say on a point at one time?

Elaboration: What else does the reader need to know? Why did…? Instead of talking about your feelings, how can you show them? What else is likely to happen? What are some examples to demonstrate this?

Opening: Will this beginning really grab the reader? What other openings did you consider? How do they compare?

Ending: Does this ending drive your point home? What other endings did you consider? How do they compare?

Sentence Structure: Did you check this by oral reading to hear how the sentences sound? Do you have enough variety? Are there some choppy sentences that should be combined?

Vocabulary: Did you check for variety and precision? What words did you change? Why? What is your favorite word in this paper? Why? Are there any overused words remaining, such as *good, pretty, said, walked*?

One way to begin the conference is by having the pupil read the piece to you. With older students who have longer papers, you may prefer to receive the ready-for-conference draft the day before the scheduled conference in order to have time to read it over yourself, although most teachers find it better if the student does the reading. Regardless of your handling here, the next step is to raise questions. Perhaps the organization is not clear: "What is your main point here? Tell me in one sentence." "Where did you make that clear in the story?" Maybe it wasn't clear, or maybe it was only hinted at. Most often the student can easily and clearly state the point orally. Have the oral statement written down and compared with the initial copy as a means of providing insights for the revision.

"You seem to have departed from the main point about your favorite pet when you wrote this part about your vacation. Is there some way that the vacation related to the pet, or did you just get sidetracked?" This conversation might lead to the fact that the pupil has the potential for two stories here, or the relationship between the pet and the vacation might be real and need to be more clearly established.

Another pupil may have difficulty with sequence. After that story is read to you, raise questions about what happened first, and so on. Have the student identify proper sequence and use the oral explanation to write notes on the paper for revision. Sometimes it is even necessary to list and number the activities in order to clarify the sequence.

It is important in these conferences, as in any other, to avoid trying to teach or correct everything at once. Focus on a major concern, possibly from your notes from a previous conference. In the process, you will also want to point out some major accomplishment and possibly add it to the pupil's folder record of "Things I can do."

Keep the conference task-oriented. Your praise or criticism should be specific, never global or random. Further, both your positive comments and your guided questioning should relate to the writing, not to the child as a person. The student is not considered a good writer or a poor writer; it is the piece of writing that is well organized or may need work. It is the writing, not the student, that is being critically examined. It should also go without saying that any comparisons made must be of this piece of writing to previous ones by that same student, not to the writings of others.

Task-orientation also keeps the conference within time limits. Once the discussion strays to irrelevant topics, such as "what my little sister did yesterday," precious time is lost. On the other hand, what is or is not relevant will vary with the nature of the writing problem. Perhaps the student is having difficulty in getting a topic clearly in mind. "What my little sister did yesterday" might very well be pertinent to topic clarification.

Each formal conference should conclude with a clear summary statement by the teacher. This statement will identify the next course of action for the student in terms that can be implemented by that youngster. It will also lead to a mutually understood note in your record as to the progress made by that particular student.

Sometimes teachers find that completing too many versions of a paper becomes a chore for pupils. A happy compromise sequence seems to be (1) initial writing, (2) conference draft, (3) final copy. Between the conference draft and final copy, you and/or other students may have informal conferences (the roving kind, in your case) as you check on progress or answer a specific problem.

Of course, that formal conference could deal with the final draft of a piece of writing. However, such a conference seems less valuable. A final draft is *finished,* so constructive comments offer no guide to action; the evaluation is summative rather than formative. Such final drafts are better handled as matters for "publication."

SUMMARY

This chapter began with the values of conferencing, which include increased interest in writing on the part of the student, skill instruction tailored to the individual and taught in application, and increased understanding of students and of the writing act on the part of the teacher.

Suggestions for conferencing were discussed in some detail, from simple beginnings to the more formal scheduled conference. The careful beginning was seen as important for both student and teacher to learn procedures that would facilitate a workshop approach to writing. Further, procedures for conferencing itself were seen as instructional items so that students could become involved in peer conferences.

Record keeping (in simple form) and writing logs were both presented as means for teacher and students to see evidence of progress. Logs also provide a source of additional writing ideas as well as a record of progress for the individual pupil.

The conference itself must be a positive experience and should focus on one major point at a time. Initial, informal conferences may be of less than a minute in length, asking a simple question or providing a brief comment of assistance or encouragement. The scheduled conferences are more effective if devoted to discussion of a finished first draft that has been reviewed by a peer as well as by the original writer.

The chapter concluded with specific kinds of questions or items for focus in scheduled conferences. These were seen also as examples of items that might be incorporated into a guide for use by older students in their conferences with peers.

SUGGESTIONS FOR ACTION

(Unlike the suggestions in previous chapters, you might look upon the following as somewhat sequential. Begin at whatever point you think you and your class are ready and proceed from there.)

1. The most basic step is to begin circulating about the room during pupil writing, talking informally with youngsters while they write and about their writing.

2. Break the lockstep. Discuss with your pupils the fact that everyone isn't at the same stage in a piece of writing at the same time. Provide some simple procedures for classroom mechanics, including maintenance of a folder of writing. Continue the informal conferences.

3. Discuss with the group a few major points they should look for in writing. Demonstrate the use of these points with a volunteer so that the class can see how a brief evaluative conference is conducted. Let them try it with one another, either on a buddy system or in small groups. Follow up with a discussion of the kinds of questions and comments they were able to make.

4. Once your students understand that a finished first draft is not a final version, much less a final copy, begin scheduled conferences on first drafts that have been reviewed by a peer and revised.

5. Clarify procedures for log and record keeping. Maintain your own brief records on each child as well as the note of progress you enter in each student's log.

6. If you are here, you are most unusual! Continue your procedures and gradually refine points to look for in your own and in peer conferences. You might work with the group, in the case of older students, to develop some guidelines for peer conferencing.

REFERENCES

ELBOW, PETER, *Writing without Teachers.* New York: Oxford University Press, 1973. Addressed to mature writers, this little book contains some helpful ideas for any writing teacher.

GRAVES DONALD H. *Writing: Teachers and Children at Work.* Exeter, New Hampshire: Heinemann Educational Books, 1983. Based on work with first-graders over a two-year period, this book has implications for all levels.

SILVER, BILL, " 'Can You Read My Story?' Approaches to Conferencing with Children," *The Elementary School Journal,* 84 (September, 1983), 35–39. Discusses a three-part role of the teacher in conference: prodder, reflector, and collaborator.

TURBILL, JAN (ED.), *No Better Way to Teach Writing!* Rozelle, N.S.W., New Zealand: Primary English Teaching Association, 1982. Distributed by the National Council of Teachers of English. An excellent description of a conference–workshop approach to writing at the primary level.

9

Developing Skill
in Spelling

*When I read some of the rules for speaking and writing the English
language correctly, I think—*
Any fool can make a rule
And every fool will mind it.

THOREAU, 1860

CONSISTENTLY, WHEN I ASK groups of teachers why they believe we don't do
a better job of teaching writing, the first reply is "lack of time." How does
one gain time in the crowded school curriculum? One way to gain time is
to increase efficiency—to eliminate ineffective activities. The usual
method of teaching spelling is a prime target for this kind of
housecleaning.

Typically, teachers spend—if not squander—one half hour per day,
two-and-one-half hours per week, on the subject of spelling. Yet, Ernest
Horn (1960) pointed out that spelling could be taught effectively in little
more than one hour per week, providing teachers followed what research
suggested.

The research of spelling instruction is in more agreement than in
any other area of the curriculum. Not only that, but it has existed for the
better part of this century and has been virtually ignored by most
commercial spelling programs. Of course, the reason publishers haven't
followed the research is that they would have no excuse for publishing a
workbook merely for spelling. The book, if it existed, would have to focus
on something besides mere spelling; it would have to deal with writing,
language, or "English."

Not only have we wasted time with the traditional approach to
spelling, we have not taught children to spell correctly. In comparing the
third national assessment in writing with previous assessments, the
National Assessment of Educational Progress (1980–81) reported that

157

nine-year-olds were poorer in spelling and thirteen- and seventeen-year-olds were *significantly* poorer in their spelling. Hence, the extravagant time allotment has not contributed to skill in spelling.

PROBLEMS WITH TRADITIONAL SPELLING

The traditional spelling book is divided into weekly lessons. Each begins with a word list, usually organized in order to teach some generalization. For example, the lesson for the week may focus on the /ē/ sound, so the word list includes *bean, meat, seat,* and so on. It doesn't take a very bright child to figure out that any word on the test this week that has that sound is going to be spelled *ea.*

Often enrichment or "bonus" words are included in the lesson for children who already know how to spell the list words. Is this an attempt to make certain that *all* children will experience at least some failure in spelling? If a word is important enough for automatic spelling, it should be on the *regular* list; if it is not that important, why spend time on it at all?

The remainder of the lesson is usually devoted to manipulating the list words: adding endings, dividing the words into syllables, and so on. At least by the 1970s, most programs eliminated the context exercises, activities found useless in the research as far back as 1916.

Clearly, the spelling book dictates the way teachers handle spelling. Otherwise they would do a better job of using research, since a survey by Fitzsimmons and Loomer (1974) indicated that teachers *know* more than they use of the research in spelling.

Let's examine what I consider to be the major handicaps we must overcome if we are to do a better job in spelling. They include a lack of "teaching," failure to recognize—and help youngsters recognize—the role of spelling, and the traditional spelling-book emphasis on rules about spelling. This last point is the greatest fallacy we must overcome because it seems ingrained with many teachers. "Sound" spelling is *unsound.* It has enabled many youngsters to become proficient phonetic misspellers.

Lack of Teaching

Typically the week begins with "Okay, boys and girls. It's Monday morning. Take out your spelling books and study your spelling."

Usually there has been no review of the study method that should be used—and children *do* resist going through the study method. It needs to be reinforced regularly. More significant, such an admonition undermines any justification for studying anyhow. Manolakes (1975) reported that the average child knows how to spell 75 percent of the words at his or her grade level before study. That is comfortable, but it also means that there is no reason to study the words already known. Those should be identified and eliminated from the study list.

More telling was the report by Hillerich (May, 1982). For this study, Kovacs observed six elementary teachers for five to eight consecutive visits each. She recorded, minute by minute, what teachers and children were doing during the spelling period. An average of 46 percent of the time—and as much as 82 percent in the case of one teacher—was spent on administration and irrelevant activities. Much of the balance was devoted to oral correcting of the workbook pages. Meanwhile, 32 percent of the children's time was spent in activities that were not justified by the research on spelling instruction.

Too often the spelling book is used as busywork to keep pupils occupied while the teacher grades papers or engages in some other activity. Few teachers seem to *teach* spelling.

Failure to Recognize the Role of Spelling

Correct spelling should not be considered an academic topic; it is not to be classed with science, math, or reading instruction. It belongs in the class with etiquette. Correct spelling, as opposed to phonetic misspelling, is a courtesy to the reader.

Hence, students should be helped to realize that they need not be concerned about spelling with everything they write. Just as you or I certainly don't check on a doubtful spelling—perhaps of *avocado* or *mayonnaise*—when we make out a grocery list, there are times when children write that their writing is not "going anywhere." Only when we do a finished piece of writing that is leaving the confines of our close group do we, as adults, concern ourselves with correcting the final copy.

Although I have no solid research to back this view, it has been my experience with elementary school children that they have become immune to the constant reminder to spell correctly. In one school district, when teachers agreed to eliminate the corrections in primary grades and to "minimize" them in upper grades, we found significantly *fewer* misspellings from pretest to posttest after a period of one year.

Teaching Phonic Generalizations

Undoubtedly the greatest difficulty to surmount in improving spelling is to overcome the belief, reinforced by traditional spelling programs, that we can teach generalizations to children that will enable them to spell words they haven't memorized for spelling. Neither research with children nor research on the nature of the English language supports this generalization theory.

The largest study of the relationship between symbol and sound in English was reported by Hanna and others (1966). They programmed a computer with more than 300 rules—many more rules than any child can be programmed for. Then they tested the computer's ability to spell 17,000 English words. One finding of the study was that the computer was able to spell with 84 percent accuracy, so teachers can teach rules about spelling; they can build "spelling power."

However, the 84 percent accuracy was achieved as a result of several other manipulations. First, the *schwa* sound (as at the beginning of *about*) was certainly going to present a problem. That sound is the most frequent vowel sound in English, accounting for about 25 percent of all vowel occurrences in running speech, and it is spelled in about twenty-two different ways. Hence, the computer was set up to spell correctly the eight most frequent spellings: *schwa* spelled *a* will be spelled *a, o* will be spelled *o,* and so on. Then too, the computer was not asked to spell whole words; it was asked to spell phoneme by phoneme: It was not asked to spell *mat;* it was asked to spell /m/ in initial position, /a/ in medial position, and /t/ in final position. Since two out of three phonemes in English are consonants, which tend to be fairly regularly spelled, this manipulation also encouraged greater accuracy. As a result of all this, the computer was 84 percent accurate in spelling the phonemes in the 17,000 words.

Yet a closer inspection of this study reveals that, when the 17,000 words were fed into the computer as whole words, the computer was able to spell those words with only 49 percent accuracy. And children are expected to spell whole words! The child who spells *groups* as *groops* is not likely to be praised for being 80 percent correct—for being correct with four phonemes out of five! The word is still misspelled.

As a final point here, we might consider the study by Simon and Simon (1973). They used the Hanna program and, in effect, had a spelling contest between the computer and students in grades two through five who were working at the fourth-grade level. The computer made three times as many errors as the children on the list of new words and four times as many errors on the review words. The reason, of course, was that the computer was locked into the rules while the children could use their memory for words.

Numerous studies, including two by this author, have compared spelling success of children in a rule-oriented workbook approach with the success of children who merely studied a word list. Consistently, those youngsters who do not learn phonic rules for spelling are better spellers. In only one study was there no difference, and in no study that I have found did children who learned phonic rules spell better.

Common sense verifies this approach. There is no way one can be assured of the correct spelling of a word not specifically studied for its spelling. For example, consider the simple word *seek*. If you had not learned that spelling, you would recognize the following sounds: /s/, /ē/, and /k/. With no knowledge of the actual spelling, only of possible spellings of the sounds, you could spell that word 1,584 different ways, as follows:

/s/	/ē/	/k/
s (sun)	*ae (archaeology)*	*c (chic)*
c (cent)	*ea (each)*	*cc (account)*
ss (miss)	*ea-e (peace)*	*cch (saccharine)*
sc (science)	*e (be)*	*ck (black)*
st (listen)	*e-e (complete)*	*ch (chasm)*
psy (psychology)	*eo (people)*	*k (key)*
sw (sword)	*ee (tree)*	*kh (khaki)*
sch (schism)	*ee-e (sneeze)*	*lk (chalk)*
	ei (conceit)	*qu (liquor)*
	ei-e (conceive)	*que (antique)*
	ey (key)	*x (except)*
	i (liter)	
	i-e (gasoline)	
	ie (grief)	
	ie-e (believe)	
	oe (amoeba)	
	uay (quay)	
	y (any)	
8	$\times$ 18 $\times$	11 = 1,584

Of course, some followers of traditional spelling methods suggest teaching about the possible positions in which certain sounds can be spelled in a given way. If you were well enough acquainted with the positions in which various spellings could be used, you could cut the possibilities for the spelling of *seek* to 480 likely spellings ($6 \times 16 \times 5$), still a formidable number. As Sloboda (1980) stated, "One might say that whilst average spellers spell by rule, good spellers spell by rote." Or use the dictionary, we might add.

Are There Generalizable Patterns?

You might like to engage in a little research in your own class as I have done in others (Hillerich, November, 1982). Collect misspelled words of your pupils and classify them according to the type of error demonstrated. See if you can find some guidance for instruction.

Based on a variety of classes at different grade levels, I find very little that will lead to generalizable instruction, that is, to instruction that will carry over beyond the specific word misspelled. For example, what does one teach about omitted letters? It doesn't help much to tell children not to omit letters when they spell a word. Or what generalization would you teach one group of fourth-graders who collectively managed to spell *neighbor* twenty-two different ways?

Of course, a large group of misspellings in any class will be phonetic. In one fifth-grade class, *troop* and *stupid* were misspelled *troup* and *stoupid.* One might teach those children the *oo* spelling of that sound, only to get *groop* and *stoopid.* Even the classifications of misspellings are difficult, since no one can see inside the child's head. The spelling of *alon* for *alone* might be classed as one of a missing letter, but it could also be a phonetic misspelling of that sound from the analogy of *both.*

Examination of the efforts of others to classify errors in order to provide a basis for instruction has consistently failed. A summary of such research (Hillerich, November, 1982) concluded: "The search for 'hard spots' in words has identified a number of them: middle, right-of-middle, endings, and vowels. However, unless teachers plan to teach words made up of only beginnings—and with no vowels—these findings offer no positive direction for instruction."

Following studies in a number of classrooms, I found very few spelling errors which could be identified for instruction that leads to generalizations beyond the misspelled word. Three categories of errors can be diagnosed and followed with instruction: use of the apostrophe, homophone substitutions, and problems with adding endings to base words.

After pupils have been introduced to the use of apostrophes, every teacher knows what happens: They put apostrophes where they don't belong and leave them out where they should be. Generalizations that should be taught here deal with contractions and possessives.

The former are relatively easy to teach. Children need to understand that there are some words that are made from combinations and that the apostrophe shows the omission of a letter or letters.

Sometimes the teaching of possessives is made overly complex. Never give three rules when one will do. One method is to tell your youngsters to write the word they intend in its regular singular or plural form before they concern themselves with showing possession. After the intended form of the word is written, they should add an apostrophe and *s* unless the word is a plural that was made plural by the addition of *s.* In this case they add only the apostrophe. One fourth-grade teacher had a technique that also seemed to work well. She told her children to think of the apostrophe as a line dividing the word from the *s* marker. Then they could check to see if the word before that line was the intended form, singular or plural.

Homophone substitutions still exist at the graduate school level. Although instruction on the proper use of *there* and *their* will not generalize to *knew* and *new,* children need a great deal of experience with homophones. Mnemonic devices can be helpful in this instance. *There* has *here* in it (a place), whereas *their* has *heir* (a person); a *principal,* as opposed to a *principle,* is a *pal.* Give your pupils a few examples of these memory devices and let them make up their own for other homophones.

Misspellings involving endings fall into the categories of doubling or not doubling the final consonant, dropping or not dropping the final *e,* and changing or not changing final *y* to *i* when adding an ending. Horn (1960) pointed out generalizations that can be taught about these three problems:

1. Words accented on the last syllable (including one-syllable words) ending in a single consonant preceded by a single vowel, double the final consonant when the suffix begins with a vowel. *(nap–napped, infer–inferred,* but *nap–naps, troop–trooped)*

2. Words ending in "silent" *e* usually drop the final *e* before adding suffixes beginning with a vowel *(grade–grading)* but keep the final *e* before suffixes beginning with a consonant *(late–lately).*

3. Words ending in consonant and *y* change *y* to *i* before a suffix *(baby–babied)* unless the suffix begins with *i (baby–babying).* Do not change *y* to *i* in words ending in vowel and *y (toy–toying).*

Horn also added two other generalizations that have only modest application: The letter *q* is always followed by *u* in English, and English words do not end in *v.* He further pointed out that phonics instruction was not a substitute for the direct study of specific words for spelling.

These generalizations should be taught to students through a few examples, after which they should search for other examples of their own. For many of us, these rules are clumsy to remember: A few model words may be more practical. You might even want to post a chart showing the application of the three generalizations so that your pupils can refer to it as a reminder.

All of the foregoing, pointing out the fallacy of trying to teach generalizations that will enable the spelling of most English words, is not to imply that the English language has no pattern. We might say, in terms of spelling, that it has *too many* patterns. One must know a lot about a word before being able to understand its spelling: The spelling generalizations are after-the-fact reasoning. Following are just a few of the explanations for English spelling:

1. Simple sound spelling: *bat* might be considered a phonetic spelling.

2. Deeper sound spelling: *lake, change, chance,* where the final *e* changes the vowel sound or softens the *g* and *c,* respectively.

3. Historical sound spelling: *daughter,* where the *gh* was originally a guttural sound in the word. Also, *of,* where *f* was used for both /f/ and /v/ in Old English.

4. Reversal: *who,* which was *hwa* in Old English. Is this a matter of false analogy with *th, ch, sh, wh?*

5. Borrowing: *biscuit, khaki,* where the native spelling is retained.

6. False etymology by analogy: *isle* (from Old French) led to *island,* even though there was no *s* in Old English *iegland.*

7. Morphophonemic alternation: *athlete/athletic* or *angel/angelic* do not change spelling even though the pronunciation of the vowel sound changes.

8. Webster's mistakes: *honor* came from the French *honneur,* not from the Latin *honor* and should have been spelled *honour.*

9. Johnson's mistakes: *ache* came from the Old English *aece,* not from the Greek *akhos.*

10. Early printers' idiosyncrasies: *distill,* as compared with the British *distil,* where early printers often justified columns by doubling a final letter to fill space.

11. Plain confusion: the distinction between the *-er* and *-re* ending in American and British English *(center/centre, meager/meagre),* while both agree on *ogre.*

If you work with older students, you might want to acquaint them with some of this information and get them started on some etymology. This is still another way to get them interested in language.

TEACHING CORRECT SPELLING

Teachers who want to be assured of teaching their students to spell correctly need only follow the pattern consistently laid out in the research. If you want to teach correct spelling instead of phonetic misspelling, you need to (1) use a good word list, (2) introduce words with a pretest and immediate correction by the pupil, (3) teach pupils how to study a word for spelling, and (4) have them keep a record of progress so that they can measure their success.

The Word List

The unabridged dictionary has more than 500,000 entries. No one suggests attempting to teach even a major portion of that lexicon. In fact, only about 3,000 words need to be taught specifically for spelling, if the words are chosen in terms of their frequency of use.

Many words will never be written by an individual, so they need not be learned for spelling. On the other hand, some are so frequently used that their spelling must be automatic if the individual is to be at all fluent in writing. And that is the point of the word list in spelling. It is not a list that is used—like the material in the basal reader—to develop a skill that generalizes beyond that list. The word list in spelling is a security blanket that enables fluency in writing—that is all!

We know, for example, that just three words—*I, and, the*—account for 10 percent of all the words anyone writes. The ten most frequently used words account for 25 percent of all written words, whether by children or adults. In fact, there is about a 75 percent overlap between the writing vocabularies of children and adults.

Table 9.1 contains a list, in order of frequency of use, of the hundred most frequently used words, based on a count of 380,342 words from the writing of children in grades two through six (Hillerich, 1978). Beside each word is the frequency with which that word was used.

The one hundred words in Table 9.1 account for 60 percent of all the words used by these elementary school children. This being true, how many more words do we need for spelling? One clue lies in the fact that the frequency of use rapidly diminished from the first word to the one-hundredth word, from 16,178 occurrences to only 565.

A possible word list for spelling is offered in the appendix. It was developed through reference to four major sources: Rinsland's (1945) count of words in children's writing, Hillerich's (1978) count of modern children's writing, Kucera and Francis's (1967) count of words in adult printed material, and Carroll and others' (1971) count of words in school materials from grades three through nine.

Although the list in the appendix contains only the base forms, addition of the major regularly inflected forms will result in about 2,460 words. In checking back against the original sources, that number of

TABLE 9.1. Inflected count, in order of frequency of use, of the one hundred words used most frequently by children in writing.

I	16,178	went	1,756	know	793
and	15,273	them	1,727	your	783
the	13,556	she	1,722	home	777
a	12,327	out	1,719	house	777
to	12,075	at	1,630	an	764
was	7,162	are	1,605	around	755
in	6,929	just	1,594	see	750
it	5,882	because	1,587	think	750
of	5,405	what	1,511	down	749
my	4,539	if	1,457	over	744
he	4,499	day	1,428	by	742
is	4,229	his	1,338	did	734
you	3,867	this	1,246	mother	731
that	3,623	not	1,217	our	714
we	3,352	very	1,186	don't	709
when	3,251	go	1,176	school	702
they	3,050	do	1,151	little	698
on	3,022	about	1,122	into	696
would	2,703	some	1,121	who	679
me	2,421	her	1,112	after	678
for	2,399	him	1,112	no	662
but	2,359	could	1,061	am	645
have	2,333	as	1,049	well	640
up	2,187	get	1,014	two	610
had	2,146	got	1,009	put	602
there	2,102	came	992	man	588
with	2,098	time	967	didn't	580
one	2,095	back	946	us	569
be	2,084	will	915	things	566
so	2,083	can	913	too	565
all	2,018	people	884		
said	2,014	from	869		
were	1,924	saw	839		
then	1,854	now	815		
like	1,792	or	812		

From Hillerich, Robert L., *A Writing Vocabulary of Elementary Children,* 1978. Courtesy of Charles C Thomas, Publisher, Springfield, Illinois. Reprinted by permission.

words, which can be taught by the end of sixth grade, accounts for more than 96 percent of all the words anyone—child or adult—will write in a lifetime. The addition of another thousand words will increase the coverage by only 2 percent and is therefore questionable.

These facts about words raise two important points. First, why then do teachers want to "enrich" the word list for brighter youngsters who can spell the words at their grade level? Usually the added words are ones for which the youngster has no use at present, or only a passing use in the case of words from the content areas. Those in the latter instance can be checked against the glossary or the dictionary after writing is completed, since the child will probably never again write the word *igneous* after that science unit on rocks is completed.

Second, since words rapidly diminish in their importance, the word list should be organized in order of their frequency of use: The most frequently used words should be taught first. This also has implications for the older student who is a very poor speller. Move that child down to an appropriate list, even that of grade two, if he or she can't spell those words. After all, that word list is the security blanket for writing, and one is certainly more handicapped if unable to spell *the, was, home,* and so on, than if unable to spell *organization, definite,* or even *carburetor.*

Within a grade level, once the decision has been made about which words are most frequently used and should be taught first, the word lists should be equal in difficulty. This often comes as a surprise to teachers. Yet, an unknown word is an unknown word, and it doesn't make much sense to have a list of twenty words in September where the child knows how to spell them all, and a list of twenty words in May where all are unknown for spelling.

Other than this balance for difficulty, the words can be grouped randomly. No generalization is going to be taught with that list. You may, however, want to have some groupings contain a variety of spellings of the same sound if you are going to include dictionary instruction as suggested in a later section of this chapter.

Another question also arises about the words on the spelling list: What if children don't know the meaning of the word? Such a situation suggests one of two problems: Either the word is inappropriate for the grade or the child needs additional language development before being concerned with its spelling. No one should learn to spell a word for which that individual has no meaning. We never write words that we don't "know."

Once the word list has been selected, children need to be properly placed in that list. The appendix also contains a placement test, nothing more than a sampling of the words from each list. If you are using a commercial spelling program, sample word lists from the grade level books can be used as well. A child ought to be able to spell, before study, at least 50 percent of the words on the weekly list. If not, that youngster needs to be placed in a lower-level list.

Pretest with Immediate Correction

Thomas Horn (1947) reported that the pretest with immediate correction by the pupil accounts for 90 to 95 percent of all the learning that takes place in spelling. Others have verified the importance of this powerful tool.

The pretest should be administered like any spelling test, but before children have had an opportunity to see the word list. Usually we teach before we test, but in this case the test is not of the child; it is the child's testing of the word list.

In the process of immediate correction after the pretest, that youngster discovers which words need to be studied. Furthermore, in correcting their own tests, children discover where they made a mistake in each misspelled word. It doesn't help to point out hard spots in words, since individuals have different hard spots in the same word. Nor does it help to have lists of "demon" spelling words. A composite of four "demon" lists, totaling 398 words, indicated agreement on only ten words. Individuals have their own "demons" too. However, it does help to discover where one's own misspelling occurred in a given word.

Years ago, while working to develop a spelling program, teachers helped me see the importance of a pretest sheet. This is nothing more than a lined page on which the list words form the first column, with a middle column for writing the pretest and a third column for corrections, as shown in Figure 9.1.

The sheet should be given to youngsters with the words folded under so they don't see them until after the pretest. Dictate the words in typical spelling-test fashion: say the word, use it in a sentence, repeat the word. After the entire test has been administered, pupils are to fold open the word list so they can see as well as hear the correct spellings.

Each student is to correct his or her own paper, writing the correction for any misspelled word in the third column. That column then becomes the list for study. Furthermore, comparison with the misspelled word serves to identify where that individual made a mistake.

A few teachers have claimed that they must cut the word list off the pretest sheet in order to keep children from peeking at the words during the pretest. They distribute that portion of the sheet after the test is completed. This is certainly an alternative that preserves the value of seeing the correct spellings after pretest, but I prefer to work with such youngsters to help them realize the importance of taking the pretest as it is intended. They should know that it is really a short-cut to help them learn words they will need in their writing.

The Study Method

Once students have completed the pretest, it is time to review the study method. Each pupil should have a copy. Initial experiences and some

Date_____ Name_____

Directions
1. Fold column 1 along dotted line.
2. Write the spelling test words in column 2.
3. Unfold column 1 to check your spelling.
4. In column 3, write the correct spelling for any words you missed.

Lesson 4 Words	Pretest	Corrections
1. end	1. _____	_____
2. bone	2. _____	_____
3. never	3. _____	_____
4. shop	4. _____	_____
5. head	5. _____	_____
6. I'll	6. _____	_____
7. spell	7. _____	_____
8. left	8. _____	_____
9. that's	9. _____	_____
10. met	10. _____	_____
11. bet		
12. late		
13		

FIGURE 9.1. Example of a Pretest Sheet.
Reprinted by permission from *Spelling for Writing* by Hillerich, Robert L., and Sharon Gould, Level 3, Charles E. Merrill Publishing Company. © 1981 Bell & Howell.

review can be with the total group, where you put a difficult word on the chalkboard or on the overhead projector and go through the steps with your students.

The study method itself was developed by Ernest Horn. Although no one has improved on it, he himself made one revision from his original version. Initially, he had suggested that the word to be studied be pronounced by syllable. He later found that this didn't help in learning to spell the word.

Following is a simplified version of the study method that can be easily taught to pupils:

1. Look at the word. Say it.
2. Close your eyes and spell the word. Check to see if you are correct. If not, start over.
3. Cover the word and write it. Check to see you are correct. If not, start over. (Repeat #3 two more times.)

Although this study method can be easily "taught" to pupils, they often resist going through the process. It is important to convince them that it is really a time saver. Constant review and reminding are necessary. However, the fact that they don't use the method with twenty words on a list should be some encouragement; they need to study only words they didn't know how to spell.

You will note that the study method itself implies that learning to spell a word correctly is a matter of memorization. Consistently, research on the factors that make for good spelling brings out the importance of visual memory. Correct spelling is a visual memory, kinesthetic operation. Check yourself. When someone asks you to spell a very difficult word, what do you do? If you are like most of us, you will probably begin to spell the word, close your eyes or look at the ceiling, then ask for a pencil so you can write that word in order to *see* if it looks right.

Although writing the word is a part of the study method, the mechanical writing of each word "ten times" is worthless. It is a mindless task; attention may be on anything but the word being written. In fact, many youngsters, given that assignment, will write the first letter ten times, then the next letter, and so on, or find some other creative method to thwart their learning.

Also, this visual memory must be focused on the *spelling* of a word. There is a low relationship between spelling and reading ability. Reading certainly contributes to an enlarged vocabulary, but it does not necessarily contribute to spelling skill. The good reader uses context and focuses on meaning: The good reader reads ideas, not words. In contrast, the good speller must note every letter in a word, and in proper sequence.

The importance of visual memory brings up another point. Its opposite, oral spelling, contributes *nothing* to spelling skill. This fact has implications for the typical "spelling bee," as well as for the manner in which most children "study" spelling. When they ask Mother to "help me with my spelling," they really mean "give me an oral spelling test." If your students study spelling at home, be certain that an explanation and copy of the study method go home to parents so they can truly help their children to study spelling.

Additional Checks on Spelling

Two additional checks or tests are needed on the list: a check test to determine how the study is going and a final test to assess mastery. The pretest, check test, and mastery test must each be on separate days so that there is time for study between each test. Other than that, they may be on consecutive days in the week or on alternate days, such as Monday, Wednesday, and Friday. Whatever the days, the check test and mastery test should be given on the words missed on pretest.

The Record of Progress

Most teachers are familiar with the record of progress. This is included in most spelling programs in order to provide the student with a sense of accomplishment. It is nothing more than a provision, by week, for developing a bar graph indicating the number of words spelled correctly. Usually there is a column for each week with the vertical axis indicating the number of words spelled correctly.

In using a pretest approach, that record of progress must serve two functions. First, the student records the number of words spelled correctly on pretest. This is the number of "Words I already knew without studying." No great point should be made of this or you will encourage children to peek at next week's words prior to pretest. In such a case, short-term memory could get them through the pretest without their really knowing how to spell the word.

A second entry on the record is the result of the mastery test. This should be entered in a different color to indicate the "Words I learned by studying." Likewise, this final entry indicates the total number of words known from that weekly list.

Individualizing the Spelling Program

A first—and minimum—step toward individualizing spelling is to be certain that students are in the appropriate word list. Those who cannot spell at least half of the words correctly on pretest should be in a lower-level list for at least two reasons: (1) They probably cannot spell many of the words at the lower level—words that are more important because they are more frequently used; (2) if they are misspelling most of the words on the pretest, the pretest is not a learning experience—it is a confusing jumble.

A compromise between the ideal and the practical suggests no more than three lists in use in any given classroom. Each group can be given its pretest, either by the teacher or by a student from another group. Even though each pupil in the group may have different words for the check test and mastery test, the entire group can be administered the list once, and each pupil can write only his or her own words. They know which are their words, since they corrected their own pretests and studied those words.

Of course, complete individualization can be accomplished by pairing students on a buddy system or by putting the list words on tape.

At the upper end of the scale, what does the teacher do with the student who spells all words correctly on the pretest? I suggest that that youngster has better things to do than spend time on spelling that week. Acceleration in the word list seems pointless, since some children will be encouraged to do a superficial job by racing to see how far they can get. Even the conscientious will find themselves studying words at higher levels for which they have no current use. It seems far better to have such students work on their writing activities, library books, or some other more fruitful and interesting activity.

BEYOND THE WORD LIST

As you can see, the research-based approach to the spelling list can be accomplished in an hour or so per week. Unfortunately, the word list is not enough. As stated, mastery of that security list ensures correct spelling of 96 percent of all the words anyone will write. Approximately 3,500 words will ensure correct spelling of about 98 percent. Even so, one is not considered a good speller if even 2 percent of words are misspelled. How can correct spelling of this 2 percent be assured, when no one can guess which of the 500,000 words will make up that 2 percent?

It is here that a properly focused book or good teacher direction becomes essential. In addition to the security list, three other factors are necessary if an individual is to become a perfect speller in application. Those factors are: ability to use a dictionary *for spelling,* development of a spelling "conscience," and lots of writing.

Use of a Dictionary for Spelling

Most spelling programs, reading programs, and English programs teach pupils how to use a dictionary. However, that use is limited to pronunciation and meaning. You will be hard pressed to find a book that teaches students how to use a dictionary *for spelling.* In fact, I can go into most eighth-grade classrooms in which a child asks for a spelling. Of course the teacher says, "You know how to use a dictionary. Look it up." The child's response usually is, "How'm I gonna find it if I don't know how to spell it?"

We have to teach children how to "find it when they don't know how to spell it." What do you do when you want to look up the spelling of some strange word? You begin your educated guessing. If you wanted to find the spelling of /kam ə ′rad ə rē/, you might begin with the analogy of *comrade* and try looking for it under *com-.* When you didn't find the word there, would you conclude that it wasn't in your dictionary (as many uninstructed students do) or would you try another spelling? Naturally, you'd pursue the latter direction and eventually find the word spelled *camaraderie.*

Our job is to provide the "education" and then take students by the hand and show them how it applies to using the dictionary for spelling. That "education" is a matter of guiding students to explore the *possible* spellings of sounds. The experience can begin easily at second grade and should continue, constantly expanding, through eighth grade. It should include the fifteen vowel sounds as well as the variety of initial spellings of consonant sounds. Think of the problem a student would have in finding the spelling of *gnu* or *mnemonic* if that person knew only the *n* and *kn* spellings of /n/ in initial position.

You might begin by presenting any vowel sound at second or third grade. Have children identify the sound you are talking about through a few examples: /ē/, the vowel sound you hear at the beginning of *eel* and *easy.* Then have them reexamine a page of printed material that they have already read to find as many words as they can that contain that vowel sound. Put their list on the board and have them sort the words according to the spellings. You might have a list such as the following:

The Spellings of /ē/

ea	ee	e	ey	eo
eat	meet	be	key	people
easy	seen	we		
east				
meat				

As pupils become more familiar with this technique, you might want them to keep a chart in their language logs for each of the vowel sounds, adding to it as they find additional words in their reading. Periodically, make a composite on the board or overhead projector to discuss the findings. Obviously, you will draw no generalization from these findings, other than the fact that a given vowel sound can be spelled in many ways.

At each grade level, students will find even more spellings and a greater variety of words. They will need to make charts for the consonant sounds in initial position as well.

In several studies, I have found this "exploration" approach more effective for spelling skill than teaching rules. Incidentally, this is true not only of spelling; studies in reading resulted in the same conclusion: Pupils who learned phonic rules about vowels did not score as high in reading as did those who merely explored "possible" spellings of vowel sounds.

These experiences will provide the "education" for using a dictionary, but application is still necessary. Once pupils have learned the locational skills for using a dictionary, give them orally a word that you are fairly certain they don't know how to spell. Step by step, demonstrate with them how they can find that word in a dictionary. It's best to begin this instruction with a regularly spelled initial consonant so that pupils aren't all over the dictionary.

Perhaps you would begin with a word like /māt/ *(mate)*. Children should guess that it will begin with *m,* so they enter the dictionary in that section. "How might the /ā/ sound be spelled?" Someone might suggest *ai,* as in *mail.* When they check, they find nothing spelled *mait.* Perhaps someone will suggest *ay* or *a* spellings. Repeated checking should lead them to the *a–e* spelling of *mate.*

Interesting practice, once children have learned to use a pronunciation key, can be provided by putting a word or two on the board in pronunciation spelling. If a homophone is used, be certain to include context or a definition. During their free time, students can use the dictionary key to decide on the pronunciation and then attempt to find the correct spelling in the dictionary. Soon you should have some of your students suggesting challenge words for the class. Let the students take over that section of the chalkboard or bulletin board.

Developing a Spelling Conscience

All that has gone before is still not sufficient to guarantee correct spelling in application. Every teacher has had the experience with children who get 100 percent on the spelling test on Friday morning, then misspell some of the very same words in a piece of writing that afternoon. You and I excuse this in our own writing as a "typographical error," but we don't let youngsters get by with that.

It is a fact that children *can* spell better than they do in their writing. Goss (1959) had fifth-graders write, allowed them time to proof their papers, then collected the writing and made a list of misspelled words for each pupil. He went back to the individual students and gave them a test of the words they misspelled on their papers. Those students knew how to spell 55 percent of the words they misspelled in their writing.

I've had a number of teachers replicate this study. A fifth-grade teacher found that her students knew how to spell 57 percent of the words they misspelled; a third-grade teacher, 75 percent. You might like to check your own class on this.

Although research has not provided a definite guide to the means for developing a spelling conscience, there are several techniques that, I've found, will considerably reduce the number of errors in application.

The first is to acquaint youngsters with the role of spelling as a courtesy to the reader. This has been previously discussed as a need to let them know that we don't worry about spelling unless a paper is going somewhere important.

A second technique is to have youngsters not interrupt their writing in order to check on a word. Have them circle or underline that doubtful word and continue. This habit is important to develop from first grade on, and not because first-graders have such great trains of thought that we don't want to derail them. It is important because the other habit—putting down a phonetic spelling—often misleads the conscientious older student who goes back to proofread and forgets the original uncertainty about that word. (It looks okay now.) In contrast, if the word has been marked, that word can be checked after the writing, either by using a dictionary or, in the case of younger pupils, by asking the teacher.

A third technique is to teach children specifically how to proofread for mechanics. It is not enough to teach them how to use the mechanics; they must learn how to proofread for each one. This topic is discussed in Chapter 10.

Write! Write! Write!

The final factor in the making of good spellers is lots of writing. After all, that is the only reason we teach spelling. One can read, speak, and listen very effectively without being able to spell a single word. Spelling is needed only for writing.

Secondly, that security list represents a mechanical skill, and, like any mechanical skill, it gets "rusty" if it is not used. However, if children do a lot of writing, they are constantly practicing the spellings of words they have studied because those words are frequently used. In fact, I contend that, if students write every day, they do not need review tests in spelling. If the words studied in the lists are appropriate—that is, frequently used—they will be repeatedly used in that writing.

Three Routes to Spelling a Word

From what has been discussed in this chapter, we might summarize by indicating that there are three routes to the spelling of any word. Only two of these will ensure *correct* spelling, as indicated in Figure 9.2.

The first route, as shown in Figure 9.2, is through recall of the correct spelling of the word from the security list or automatic spelling vocabulary. The second is through use of the dictionary, presupposed by the awareness of uncertainty and knowledge of possible spellings. The third route, spelling by sound, will lead to a phonetic spelling that may or may not be correct.

BEGINNING AND ENDING OF SPELLING INSTRUCTION

As already indicated, learning to spell the security list is a finite activity; it deals with a limited number of words. Formal spelling instruction should probably not begin until second grade and should end before secondary school, except as a remedial program.

Spelling in Grade One

Summaries of research usually indicate that formal spelling instruction should begin at "high first grade or beginning second grade." This same

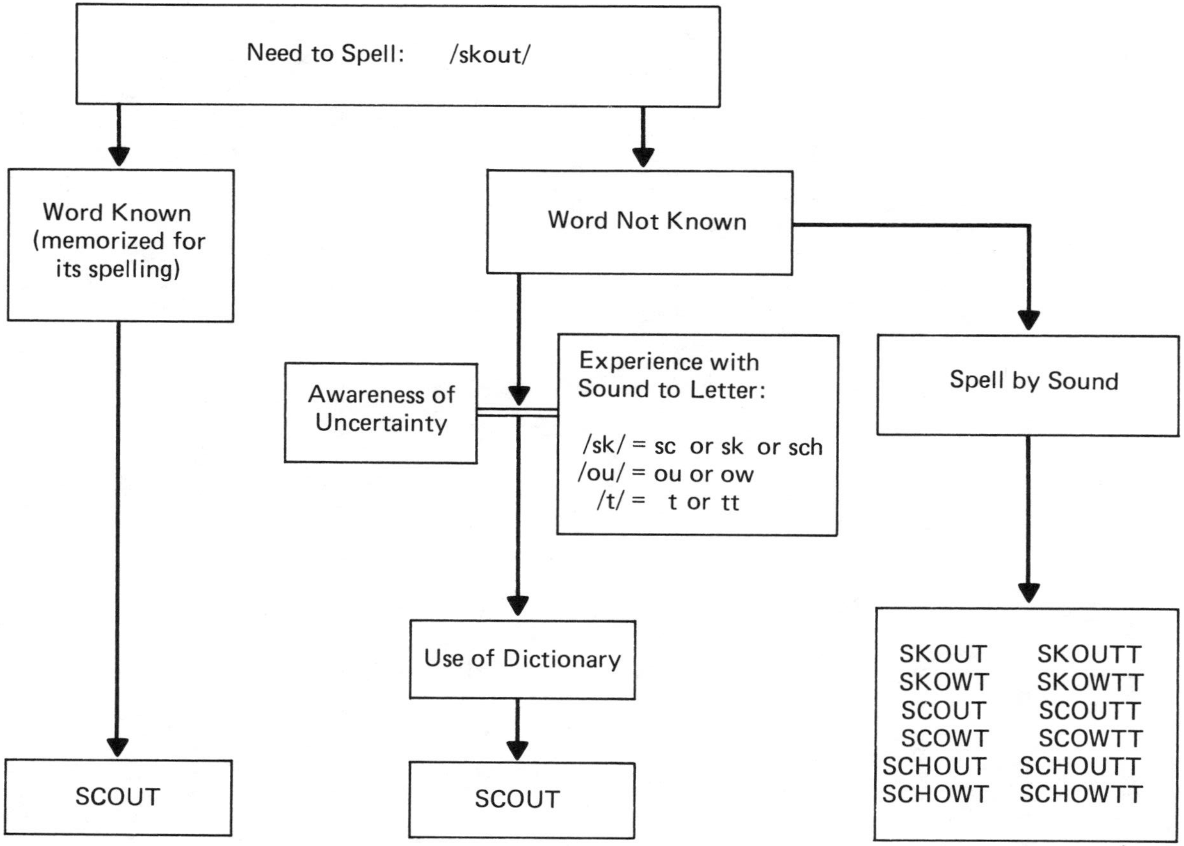

FIGURE 9.2. Three Routes to the Spelling of a Word.

From: Hillerich, Robert L., "Spelling: What Can Be Diagnosed?" The Elementary School Journal 83 (November 1982), 138–47. Reprinted by permission.

equivocal position is implied by commercial spelling series, where a book is available for the second half of first grade, but the words in that book are repeated at the second grade level.

In an effort to resolve the question, Battenberg and Hillerich (1968) randomly assigned ten first-grade teachers to teach a spelling list of one hundred words while another ten taught no formal spelling. Upon entry to second grade, those pupils who had devoted half the year to studying one hundred words spelled only two words better on a twenty-five-word test. Hence, it appears more efficient to wait until second grade for a formal list.

This is not to say that nothing should be done toward spelling in the first grade. The teachers in the study just cited who did not teach formal spelling had their children writing daily. In fact, the children began with rebus sentences when they knew how to spell only a few structure words such as *the, was,* and *in.*

Furthermore, most first-grade teachers know they can convert the reading phonics for consonants to spelling by reversing the thinking. Once children know in reading that *t* represents the sound they hear at the beginning of *tent* or *turtle,* they should also be led to realize that the sound they hear at the beginning of any word beginning like *tent* will likely be spelled *t.* Then, for unknown spellings, those youngsters can at least write some of the consonants and mark that word for help from the teacher later, when the writing is completed.

In recent years there has been some interest in invented spellings of young children. Read (1975) was one of the early investigators of this phenomonon; others have followed and verified his findings. Young children begin with random scribbling to represent writing. Then they begin to use some consonant letters appropriately to represent those sounds. As vowels enter the spelling effort, the long vowel sounds tend to be spelled by the letter name: *bake* is spelled *bak.* Short vowel sounds are usually spelled, at this early stage, with the letter whose name most closely resembles the sound. For example, *ship* may be spelled *sep,* and *him* may be spelled *hem,* since the letter name and the vowel sound /i/ are both articulated as high, forward sounds. Both are formed in that position in the mouth.

From this point, children may develop some unique spellings of the vowel sounds as they become familiar with the existence of digraphs *(rain, head, meat)* and the *e* marker *(gate, ice, note).* As a result of false analogy they might spell *meat* as *mete,* or *rain* as *rane.* Ultimately, most children will arrive at conventional spelling.

From this research, teachers can establish the level at which their children perform. Further than that, it seems to me the practical implication of such research is that teachers should be tolerant of the spelling efforts of young children. Stress too early on correctness will only discourage writing or encourage use of a limited number of words whose spellings are known.

Spelling in Middle and High School

As indicated previously, fewer than 3,000 words account for 96 percent of all the words anyone will write. Such a list can be mastered by the average student by the end of the sixth grade. The addition of another thousand words, usually taught at grades seven and eight, adds only about 2 percent more coverage. Hence, it is a judgment call whether or not formal spelling should be taught to the majority of students in junior high or middle school. Certainly there is no excuse for studying a more exotic list at the secondary level.

Conversely, the fact that the "average" child can master this list by the end of the sixth grade also indicates that about half of the pupil population in a typical school will not master it. Therefore, there is need for the study of words on the elementary list by older students who cannot spell the majority of those words.

This need—call it "remedial spelling" if you wish—extends through the high school level in the case of some students. However, the task of the teacher is to establish and monitor the program, not to be involved daily in its conduct. Suggestions for individualizing were made previously, and some provision should be made for their use. Meanwhile, instruction should continue as needed on the use of the dictionary for spelling.

SUMMARY

This chapter suggested that spelling instruction is a place where additional time can be gained through following the research. It began with a discussion of some of the problems in the teaching of spelling, including failure to teach and the failure to recognize the proper role of spelling itself. A major problem lies in the traditional approach to spelling as one of building skill in phonics that will enable the spelling of a word not studied for spelling. This fallacy was discussed along with a presentation of the few structural rules that will generalize to other words for spelling.

Most of the chapter dealt with the research-based approach to teaching the basic word list. This begins with a word list of about 3,000 words, organized in terms of frequency of use. Each weekly list is introduced through a pretest with immediate correction by the student so that the student can identify the words needing study and can also discover where a mistake was made in the spelling of that word. The study method for spelling was outlined, a method based on visual memory and kinesthetic practice. After a check test and mastery test, a record of progress is to be kept by students to show their progress.

Although this procedure will lead to skill with the basic word list, additional measures are necessary if correct spelling is to be consistently achieved in writing. These additional requirements include skill in using a dictionary for spelling, the development of a spelling conscience, and lots of practice in writing itself.

Evidence suggests that formal spelling instruction, using a word list, should not begin until the second grade. Further, it should be completed by most children by sixth grade, or by eighth grade at the outside. Nevertheless, there are some students, even at the secondary level, who still need to learn the spellings of words in the elementary list. For them, an individualized approach was suggested, using the elementary list.

In brief, if students are to spell correctly in writing, they need: (1) *fluency,* gained through the automatic security list; (2) the *knowledge* of the structural generalizations suggested; (3) a *desire* to spell correctly, the "spelling conscience"; and (4) the *ability* to use a dictionary to check the spelling of words that are not automatic.

SUGGESTIONS FOR ACTION

1. How many of your students are misplaced in spelling? Try a pretest of the list words and see how many students miss more than 50 percent of those words. If this error rate is consistent over two or three weeks, those pupils should be placed in a lower-level list.

2. With third grade or above, have pupils take one page of their writing and count the total words, total different words, and frequency of use of each word. They will become aware that very few words make up the largest proportion of all words they write. These are the most important for the automatic spelling vocabulary.

3. If you don't already use a pretest with immediate correction, try it for just six weeks, complete with a pretest sheet. You might be surprised at students' improvement in spelling the list words.

4. Engage your students in a little linguistic research. Take one of the phonic generalizations that might be taught in your spelling program. Have students find all of the words they can, from library books, readers, or other texts, that come under that generalization. Let them discover how often the generalization is true and how often it is not.

5. Engage in some research yourself. Collect the spelling errors you find in pupils' writing. Categorize the kinds of errors and examine them in an attempt to determine what can be taught that will generalize to other words. Do you find anything beyond what was suggested in this chapter?

6. Another tack for your research: Replicate the study by Goss in your classroom. Of their misspelled words in writing, what percentage can your pupils spell correctly when tested on those words?

7. How regularly do your students use the study method? You might want to give them a copy of the simplified version in this chapter and, after reviewing it with them, have them check its effectiveness for a few weeks.

8. If you haven't already done so, you might want to begin exploring the spellings of sounds with your pupils. Have them keep a chart for each of the vowel sounds. Periodically review their findings with them by making a composite on the chalkboard or overhead. You might also add a little fun by following the pattern used in this chapter with *seek.* Present a simple word and have students determine how many different ways that word could be spelled if they went only by sound.

9. Once pupils have some familiarity with the possible spellings of sounds, *teach* them how to use a dictionary for spelling as outlined in this chapter. Then you might want to begin putting a challenge word or two on the board in pronunciation spelling for them to find in the dictionary for its correct spelling.

10. Do your students realize the role of spelling as a courtesy to the reader? If not, it is important to work with them to delay concern about spelling until the final proofreading stage. Establish a procedure, underlining or circling, that will identify uncertainty about words in the initial writing.

11. Would your students benefit from seeing the "three routes to spelling"? Put them on the overhead projector for discussion.

12. If you don't have adopted spelling texts in your school, try developing your program from the lists in the appendix. That automatic spelling vocabulary is too important to be left to chance, and we know that incidental spelling instruction is accidental spelling instruction.

REFERENCES

BATTENBERG, DONALD, and ROBERT L. HILLERICH, "Effectiveness of Teaching Spelling in Grade One," unpublished study, Glenview, Illinois, 1968. Reports results of a comparison of twenty teachers, half of whom taught spelling in grade one and half who did not.

CARROLL, JOHN B., PETER DAVIES, and BARRY RICHMAN, *The American Heritage Word Frequency Book.* Boston: Houghton Mifflin Company, 1971. An alphabetical and frequency listing of more than 86,000 words based on analysis of vocabularies of school materials in grades three through nine.

FITZSIMMONS, ROBERT J., and BRADLEY M. LOOMER, *Improved Spelling Through Scientific Investigation.* Iowa City: Iowa State Department of Public Instruction and the University of Iowa, 1974. Reports results of a survey of Iowa teachers, indicating their knowledge of spelling research and the degree to which they use it in teaching.

GOSS, JAMES, "Analysis of Accuracy of Spelling in Written Compositions of Elementary School Children and the Effects of Proofreading Emphasis Upon Accuracy," doctoral dissertation, University of Oklahoma, 1959.

HANNA, PAUL R., JEAN S. HANNA, RICHARD E. HODGES, and EDWIN H. RUDORF JR., *Phoneme–Grapheme Correspondences as Cues to Spelling Improvement.* Washington, D.C.: U.S. Office of Education, 1966. A computer study of the sound–symbol correspondences in 17,000 English words.

HILLERICH, ROBERT L., *A Writing Vocabulary of Elementary Children.* Springfield: Charles C Thomas, Publishers, 1978. Reports alphabetically the frequency of use at each grade level of 380,342 words used in writing by elementary school children.

———, "That's Teaching Spelling???" *Educational Leadership,* 39 (May, 1982), 615–17, 633. Reports teacher and pupil behaviors during the time designated for "spelling" in six classrooms during the course of thirty-four observations.

———, "Spelling: What Can Be Diagnosed?" *The Elementary School Journal,* 83 (November, 1982), 138–47. Summarizes research on types of errors in spelling that can lead to generalizable instruction.

HORN, ERNEST, "Spelling," in Chester W. Harris (ed.), *Encyclopedia of Educational Research.* New York: The Macmillan Company, 1960, pp. 1337–54. A thorough summary of research on spelling, with its implications for instruction.

HORN, THOMAS, "The Effect of the Corrected Test on Learning to Spell," *The Elementary School Journal,* 47 (January, 1947), 277–85. Reports research supporting the pupil-corrected pretest as a significant contributor to spelling success.

KUCERA, HENRY, and W. NELSON FRANCIS, *Computational Analysis of Present-Day English.* Providence, Rhode Island: Brown University Press, 1967. An alphabetical and frequency ranking of more than 50,000 words from adult printed material.

MANOLAKES, GEORGE "The Teaching of Spelling: A Pilot Study," *Elementary English,* 52 (February, 1975), 243–47. Reports on percentages of words in spelling programs that are known before study by the pupils.

NATIONAL ASSESSMENT OF EDUCATIONAL PROGRESS, " 'No Major Changes' Seen in Writing Skills," *National Assessment of Educational Progress Newsletter,* 13 (Winter, 1980–81), 1–3. Compares writing and spelling achievements among the three national assessments.

READ, CHARLES, *Children's Categorization of Speech Sounds in English.* Urbana: National Council of Teachers of English, 1975. Reports on the invented spellings of young children.

RINSLAND, HENRY, *A Basic Vocabulary of Elementary School Children.* New York: The Macmillan Company, 1945. Reports more than 25,000 words used in writing by children in grades one through eight.

SIMON, DORTHEA P., and HERBERT A. SIMON, "Alternative Uses of Phonemic Information in Spelling," *Review of Educational Research,* 43 (Winter, 1973), 115–37. Reports results of comparing spelling by a computer, programmed for more than 300 rules, with the spelling skill of elementary children working at fourth-grade level.

SLOBODA, JOHN A., "Visual Imagery and Individual Differences in Spelling" in Uta Frith (ed.), *Cognitive Processes in Spelling.* New York: Academic Press, Inc., 1980, pp. 231–48. Presents results of two experiments on imagery, indicating that rules for spelling are not sufficient to ensure correct spelling.

ADDITIONAL RESOURCE

HILLERICH, ROBERT L., *Spelling: An Element in Written Expression.* Columbus: Charles Merrill, 1981. A thorough treatment of the history and research as well as methods of teaching spelling.

10

Developing Skill in Other Mechanics

True ease in writing comes from art, not chance,
As those move easiest who have learn'd to dance.

ALEXANDER POPE, 1711

THIS CHAPTER DEALS with the mechanics of writing—capitalization, punctuation, and format—with some remarks on handwriting as it affects communication. Many of these mechanical elements are matters of convention, courtesies to the reader; others affect the clarity of a piece of writing.

The precise use of some items of punctuation varies from style book to style book. As Gibaldi and Achtert (1980) pointed out, "Although there are many required uses, punctuation is, to some extent, a matter of personal preference. But, while certain practices are optional, consistency is mandatory."

Style manuals tend to change with changing times when reporting appropriate conventions. There was a total of forty-nine additions to the style manual between the 1973 and 1983 editions of the G. & C. Merriam Collegiate dictionaries. For example, commas are used more sparingly than they were in the past, and dashes more frequently. The apostrophe showing possession is usually eliminated in titles of organizations or businesses, such as "State Supervisors Association." Likewise, periods are no longer used after the abbreviations of state names, nor are capital letters used in any but the first word of article titles in some journals.

The computer is introducing a whole new era in the elimination of punctuation. Look at your mail. Have you noticed the omission of periods after abbreviations and initials, the omission of the comma between city and state? How will this affect style manuals in a few years?

185

Despite some options of personal choice and the lack of any definite sequence in which elements must be taught, we do have some teaching responsibility. Following is a list of the major elements that ought to be taught in the elementary school. More detailed listings, if required, are available in any style manual or in the "Handbook of Style" at the back of Webster's Ninth New Collegiate Dictionary (1983).

MECHANICS TO BE TAUGHT

The following list represents the major elements of mechanics to be taught in elementary schools. Notably absent are the semicolon and the dash, both of which can create more problems than they solve at this level.

Although there is no research to suggest a sequence for teaching, common sense dictates that capitalization of the first word in a sentence and end punctuation are first. Thereafter, elements should be taught as the need arises, but always one at a time.

Capitalize the first letter of:
    The first word in a sentence or fragment
    The pronoun *I*
    Proper nouns: The First National Bank
    Proper adjectives: American
    Titles when associated with a person's name: Uncle John, President Lincoln
    The first, last, and all other words in titles except for internal conjunctions, prepositions, and articles: *On the Meaning of Poetry.*
    The first word in each line of poetry

Use a period:
    To conclude a statement or fragment
    After most abbreviations: Mr., Ms. but not NY or DC
    After initials: John H. Smith

Use a question mark:
    To conclude a question

Use an exclamation mark:
    To conclude a statement showing strong feeling

Use an apostrophe:
    To indicate possession: the girl's parents, the girls' parents
    To mark omission in contractions: can't, isn't

Use a comma:

To separate items in a series: chocolate, cake, ice cream

To separate independent clauses joined by a coordinating conjunction: They went home after school, but we went to the library.

To set off a long introductory clause or phrase: As soon as the sun came up the next morning, the visitors left.

After the greeting in a friendly letter: Dear May,

After the close in a letter: Sincerely,

To set off words in direct address: Fred, I didn't know you were here.

To set off mild interjections: Oh, I didn't know that.

To separate city and state: Dunedin, Florida

To separate day from year in dates: June 22, 1986

To set off appositives and other nonrestrictive elements in a sentence: Shannon, a friendly little girl, is bright.

To avoid ambiguity: At daybreak and after, breakfast was served.

Use a colon:

After the greeting in a business letter: Dear Ms. Johnson:

To separate hour from minutes in time: 7:45 P.M.

To introduce a series: Terry carried her materials: books, pencils, etc.

Use quotation marks:

To enclose direct quotations: Josh asked, "Who are you?"

To enclose titles of poems, short stories, songs, etc.: "The Star Spangled Banner"

Use underlining:

To indicate book titles: <u>Teaching Children to Write, K–8</u>

When referring to a word rather than to its meaning: How do you spell <u>cat</u>?

Use a hyphen:

In some compound words: postage-due, but not postmark

To indicate an unfinished word at the end of a line

Use appropriate format for:

A paragraph

A friendly letter

A business letter

An envelope

An outline

SOME SUGGESTIONS FOR TEACHING

Most mechanics are taught through initial demonstration, practice, re-teaching as necessary, and finally in application. These elements should be taught when a need is identified in students' writing. Further, pupils can be referred back to reading material they have been exposed to in order to see the element modeled. Whenever possible, it seems advisable to relate the mechanic to its function as a representation of some speech behavior.

As a counterpoint, however, Smith (1982) has suggested that the mechanics are *all* conventions that have little or no relationship to speech. He includes commas, for example, as failing to indicate pauses or changes in pitch. Although we might agree in the majority of instances, there are some uses of punctuation that *do* signal in print certain oral behaviors. (Note in this last sentence the difference in pause—and meaning—if the comma had been placed after *agree* rather than after *instances*.) Probably everyone is familiar with the potential nonsense that arises from the alternate to each of the following sentences:

1a. What's in the road ahead?

  b. What's in the road, a head?

2a. As we walked, above our heads a jet appeared.

  b. As we walked above our heads, a jet appeared.

While the Greeks may have gotten by without punctuation, clarity of intent is certainly aided by its use in such instances. Admittedly, the punctuation might not offer the additional clarity that is included by the use of pitch in speech. For example, pitch may rise or fall on the word *saw* in the following sentence, depending upon the speaker's desire to emphasize that word:

When we got up, we saw that it was raining.

Nevertheless, there seem to be many items of punctuation that can be taught in a meaningful way, as signals to the reader that a pause is intended. Whenever this clarification is possible, it will assist the writer in proofreading aloud; that writer can check to see if the intended pauses are appropriately indicated.

It is also advisable to remember that mechanics are not taught for their own sake in writing any more than phonics is taught for its own sake in reading. Both are means toward improvement of the main objectives, writing for clarity and reading for meaning.

To demonstrate this point, I recall a fifth-grade teacher's asking how she should grade a particular theme. It was an excellent description of a character desperately searching for someone. The teacher's concern was with the conclusion, where the frustrated character ultimately was going from door to door, "Knocking. Knocking. Knocking." Fragments! How could anyone give an *A* to this beautiful paper that concluded with fragments? My conclusion was that the youngster in question showed considerable skill in recognizing the period as the longer kind of pause intended here. Of course, with a little more sophistication the writer could have used ellipses instead. However, I believe that child got the idea from deJong's *Hurry Home, Candy,* where one chapter concluded with "Running. Running. Running."

First of all, I believe it is helpful if students prepare and keep their own "handbooks" of the mechanics they have been taught. This may be no more than a page or two in their language logs. At lower grades it may consist of a chart posted at the front of the room for reference. This kind of aid should be used in addition to the individual entry in the log of "Things I have learned," since what has been taught and what an individual might have learned can be quite different.

Conventions

As stated, many mechanics are conventions that could as well take different forms if society agreed. These are matters of courtesy to the reader, just as correct spelling is necessary instead of phonetic misspelling. For example, there would be no difference in clarity if one used a colon after the greeting in a friendly letter and a comma after a greeting in a business letter.

Conventions can be taught by providing examples of use from printed materials. Many should require little if any extraneous practice, since they are matter-of-fact dictums that need only reminding, which can come via the chart or handbook at the proofreading stage.

All matters of capitalization are conventions, as are matters of format, such as paragraphing. Although rules for paragraphing are taught, one is hard pressed to find them followed precisely in print. In many cases what would be one long paragraph is broken arbitrarily to ease reading. Not that there is no pattern to paragraphing; only that a "paragraph" is about as nebulous to define as is a "sentence." It takes much experience to get the feel of paragraphing. (And perhaps some of us never do!)

Abbreviations are probably best taught as matters of spelling, complete with the period. Of course, names of states are now abbreviated without the period. Further, the tendency seems to be to eliminate periods in the use of A.M. and P.M.

Use of the hyphen in some compounds is also a matter for spelling and use of the dictionary. In a discussion, you might clarify with older students that we have three kinds of compounds: open, hyphenated, and closed. The historical progression seems to be in that order. Closely associated words may begin as open compounds *(coffee cake)*, become more closely associated as hyphenated *(cold-blooded)*, and finally become a closed compound *(coffeepot)*. You might have noticed this phenomenon occurring at present with *in-service* becoming *inservice*. The ultimate check on any of these is a good and current dictionary.

Even the use of the apostrophe in contractions has little if anything to do with clarity. These are words, just as their full equivalents are words. However, although the translation of a contraction such as *can't* to the words *can not* in reading is a waste of time, that translation for spelling can be helpful. The convention is to use the apostrophe to indicate missing letters. Because *cant* could be an intelligible spelling, discussion of the function of the apostrophe can be helpful to youngsters.

Of course, some of the conventions, while arbitrary, do signal distinctions in meaning once their use is understood. For example, although the reverse would serve as well, it is the custom to distinguish book titles in writing by underlining, as opposed to the use of quotations for story titles. Likewise, underlining (italics in print) is used to refer to a word itself as opposed to its referent or meaning.

Some uses of the comma are conventions: separation of main clauses in a compound sentence, where length often determines use or omission; setting off of mild interjections or words in direct address; as well as separation of city and state or day of the month and year. These are elements that must just be memorized.

None of this is meant to dismiss these items in a cavalier fashion as insignificant. They are just as important as correct spelling. The point is that there is no way to explain why we do this, we just must—until the convention changes—if we are to be respected as educated writers.

Mechanics for Clarity

End punctuation clearly signals a pause between expressions, a more definite pause than does the comma. The author's intended meaning determines whether that end punctuation will be a period, a question mark, or an exclamation mark. These items are easily taught, albeit not so readily used by young children.

To repeat from Chapter 9, use of apostrophe for possession can be taught more simply than it usually is. One technique is to have students write the word, singular or plural as intended, then add apostrophe and *s* unless the word is plural and so formed by adding *s,* in which case they merely add the apostrophe. The second suggestion, probably more helpful in proofreading, is to have students consider the apostrophe as an imaginary line dividing the word from its possessive marker. Then they can examine the word itself to see if it is in the intended form, singular or plural.

You may want to simplify use of the possessive even further. *Webster's New Ninth Collegiate Dictionary* (1983) recognizes omission of the *s* even in singular possessives that do not add an extra syllable in speech, for example, the *princess'* crown and the *prince's* crown. Such a sensible style enables writers to relate mechanics to spoken language instead of an arbitrary convention.

Most teachers do a good job of clarifying use of a comma in series. They demonstrate the ambiguity in a sentence that includes chocolate cake ice cream, and so on.

This avoidance of ambiguity, in fact, makes up the other uses of the comma. Appositives or other nonrestrictive elements in many cases need to be set off in order to ensure clarity. For example, there is quite a difference in the following two statements, and that difference is completely dependent upon the commas:

> Cats who bite and scratch are not good pets.
>
> Cats, who bite and scratch, are not good pets.

Notice also that, to differentiate the two sentences in speech, the reader uses the commas as signals for pauses, just as in the case with commas in series. Youngsters can be aided in their use of commas by learning to designate with a comma those pauses intended within sentences.

The use of quotation marks, while also conventional, does relate to meaning and is a most difficult mechanic to teach because it involves so many others. Teachers usually begin with the undivided quotation of one sentence. Most find use of the cartoon balloon an easy way to introduce quotation marks. Then the quotation marks merely substitute for the balloon and explanatory words are added outside the marks, as shown in Figure 10-1.

Without the balloons this becomes the following exchange:

Jack asked, "What animal is gray and has four legs and a trunk?"
"A mouse on vacation," replied Jill.

FIGURE 10.1.

Even here we see the complication of other mechanics. When the quotation follows the explanatory words it is separated from them by a comma, and all punctuation within the quotation is retained as in any other sentence. When the quotation precedes the explanatory words, the same is true with questions and exclamations. However, a comma replaces the period that would be at the end of the quote in order to separate it from the explanatory words.

Divided quotations follow the same principle when those explanatory words come between sentences, as in the following:

"I have a question for you," said Jack. "What animal is gray and has four legs and a trunk?"

Again, the comma sets off the first sentence from the explanatory words. However, *Jack* ends the first of the two sentences in the example above and must be followed by a period. Conversely, when the explanatory words come within the quoted sentence, commas set it off as they would any nonrestrictive or parenthetical elements within a sentence, as follows:

"What animal," asked Jack, "is gray and has four legs and a trunk?"

As any teacher knows, straightening out the mechanics of quotations is a difficult task. Posting an example of each of the types can help students by providing a reference for them at the point when they are proofreading.

Letter writing, both friendly and business, is amply provided for in many texts. The conventions are often a matter of personal taste, although the trend seems definitely toward keeping all items flush with the left margin. The important teaching part seems to me to be on the content of the letter, rather than to drop the matter once the format has been taught. For example, a business letter should be brief, to the point, and clear in its purpose and expected action. A friendly letter should reveal some of the writer as well as an interest in the activities of the recipient. And a thank-you letter should say "thank you," specify the reason for the thanks, and how the gift or favor is appreciated and will be used. Of course, letters that are actually mailed are by far the most meaningful.

Outlining is a difficult task at all levels. The teaching of this important skill seems best initiated through writing rather than through reading, since outlining is a matter of organizing thinking. It is much easier to identify one's own thinking on a topic than it is to ferret out the thinking of another writer.

This task also is best begun without the complications of outline form. Introduce a familiar topic for writing, one that lends itself to some natural division, such as "Games I Like." Ask students how they might break this into sections so they don't mix up all the different kinds of games. They might suggest "indoor and outdoor," "warm weather and cold weather," "at home and at school," and so on. Each of the two members of the pair selected becomes a major topic under which students can indent and list specific games—the subtopics.

After some experience with this kind of "outlining," students can be taught outline form. Here again, I'd post an example of format, after the teaching, so that it can serve as a reference. The important point about outlining is the organization of thinking, not the format.

HANDWRITING

Handwriting, along with spelling, makes up the major portion of the task of transcribing. Further, some problems in letter formation or poor handwriting can be confounded with errors in spelling. Therefore, until all children are using a typewriter or word processor, teachers will be plagued with the task of its teaching.

This section represents no attempt at outlining a complete program in handwriting. Such are available commercially and in use in most schools. However, a few basic principles do seem to be appropriate here.

First of all, Gage raised a question in a handwriting conference in 1961 that, to my knowledge, is still unanswered in the research: To what extent is handwriting amenable to instruction? Can teachers have a major impact or does the greater influence lie in the physiological and social heritage of the child? Regardless of the answer, we realize that teachers must make every effort to help youngsters improve their handwriting.

Left-handed students are more adequately provided for these days in handwriting programs. It appears that they too can write legibly, and without the backhand slant, if accommodations are made. Their papers must be slanted toward their left elbow, just as the right-handed writer has the paper slanted toward the right elbow. Also, most classrooms equipped with armchair desks should include some for left-handers.

Basic Principles for Handwriting

Most schools begin handwriting instruction with manuscript because this form is more closely related to the print used in reading and is, therefore, helpful in that respect. Transition to cursive writing is made in second or third grade, most often in second.

Is the early transition one part of the problem? Children have just begun to be comfortable with their learned letter formations and now must change to a different form. To carry this a step further, we might question the change at all. In her summary of the research, Hildreth (1960) pointed out that—given equal practice—manuscript is at least as fast as and is more legible than cursive.

Even though educators did not accept Hildreth's conclusion into practice, we can at least make a strong case for delaying the transition until children have had some time to enjoy mastery of manuscript. Most authorities further suggest that manuscript be maintained throughout the grades because of the need for "printing" on so many forms. Further, at least during the year of transition, pupils should have the option for use in their regular writing and in their spelling tests.

Various programs differ somewhat in their suggestions for letter formation. Nevertheless, the criteria for evaluating handwriting are straightforward and well agreed upon. They are legibility and fluency.

Fluency is translated to speed: the ability to write rapidly. Legibility includes several elements: correctness of letter formation; uniformity in size, spacing, slant, and pressure or darkness of letters; and alignment or placement within the lines. Legibility is included in the global concern for "neatness."

Such criteria do not prescribe any particular publisher's letter formation, only that there be forms recognizable by other readers. This position suggests allowance for individual preferences, once a basic form is learned. After that, consistency within the individual's writing becomes a more important factor.

Common Problems

Because of a variety of studies, we know that just a few problems account for the majority of illegibilities in handwriting. In fact, malformations of *a, e, r,* and *t* account for 45 percent of such difficulties.

Well over half of the illegibilities that occur in cursive writing can be accounted for in a class through correction of the following major problems:

Intended Letter	Written Like:
a	u, o, or ci
b	li
d	cl
e	i
i	e
h	li
k	u
m	w
n	u
o	a
r	i, n
t	l
w	m, ur

One small point can make a further cosmetic refinement to neatness of writing. In addition to the uniformity mentioned previously, students should learn to bring the tail of the final letter in each word up to the height of the lowercase letters instead of letting it die at the line.

Demonstrate this with a comparison of the two styles in just one line of writing. Have students experiment to see which is more attractive to them.

SUMMARY

This brief chapter has not been intended as a substitute for a handbook on style, since most schools have their own English books or access to a good dictionary for that purpose. It began with a listing of the major elements of mechanics to be taught in elementary school. These were divided into those that are purely conventions to be memorized and those that relate to clarity and can be related to oral behaviors. The latter discussion included suggestions for teaching such items as commas, outlining, and quotations. A major point is that instruction should focus on mechanics as another aid to clarity in writing.

The section on handwriting presented the usually agreed upon criteria for evaluating handwriting: fluency and legibility. The elements of legibility were clarified, and a listing of the most common obstructions to legibility was presented. Within the limits of accepted convention, students should be allowed—in fact, expected—to develop personal variations in handwriting style.

SUGGESTIONS FOR ACTION

1. Do you maintain a chart or some listing of the mechanics taught as a reference for your students? If not, you might want to begin one.

2. If they don't already do so, you might want your pupils to keep a record in their language logs of the mechanics they have been taught. In addition, you might record those mastered by each individual in that child's log.

3. Select a mechanic from children's writing that seems to be a common problem and teach that mechanic to the group. After their next writing, remind pupils of how to use that mechanic and have them check their papers for it. Then collect those papers and see how effectively they have learned that mechanic. Reteach as necessary.

4. If you teach fourth grade or above, try the proposed technique for teaching outlining. Begin that teaching with a topic that pupils are very familiar with. After some practice, introduce outline form and keep a chart of that form posted for reference.

5. Have you used cartoon balloons to clarify the use of quotation marks? If not, you might want to try it.

6. To what extent does your instruction on letter writing focus on the *content* of a "good" letter? The next time you are working on letter writing, develop with students criteria for the content of that type of letter. Also, make certain the letters are going somewhere.

7. If your students are not aware of the two major criteria for handwriting, discuss them as major goals in transcription.

8. If handwriting is a problem with your group, use the criteria in this chapter to determine which is the top priority: slant, letter formation, spacing, uniformity of size, or alignment. Work on the one that seems most serious.

9. What are the major problems in illegibility with your class? If you work with older students, present them with the list of the most frequently malformed letters included in this chapter. Have them analyze their own—or a partner's—paper to determine if those are the problems that exist. Then teaching can be more meaningful.

REFERENCES

GIBALDI, JOSEPH and WALTER S. ACHTERT, *Modern Language Association Handbook.* New York: Modern Language Association, 1980. One of a number of excellent handbooks on style for use in checking on mechanics.

HILDRETH, GERTRUDE, "Manuscript Writing after Sixty Years," *Elementary English,* 37 (January, 1960), 3–13. A summary of the research on manuscript writing.

SMITH, FRANK, *Writing and the Writer.* New York: Holt, Rinehart and Winston, 1982. A thorough discussion of the nature and process of writing.

Webster's Ninth New Collegiate Dictionary. Springfield: G. & C. Merriam Company, 1983. Accepted as the authority in abridged dictionaries; it includes a "Handbook of Style."

11

Editing: Revising and Proofreading

Blot out, correct, insert, refine,
Enlarge, diminish, interline;
Be mindful, when invention fails,
To scratch your head, and bite your nails.
JONATHAN SWIFT

As ANY WOODWORKER KNOWS, the most perfect measuring, sawing, clamping, and gluing will never provide a beautiful piece of furniture. Quality shows as a result of finishing: sanding, filling, sealing, and rubbing. So too the draft in writing is a rough piece that requires the same attention to finishing. We call this editing, and it consists of two distinct activities: revising and proofreading.

While some use the terms *editing* and *revising* interchangeably, everyone seems to retain the distinction from proofreading. Revising has to do with the content of the piece of writing, its clarity and interest appeal. Hence, concerns are with organization, word choice, sentence structure, and so on. Proofreading is a final act that deals with mechanics, the conventions or courtesy of written communication. Neither revision nor proofreading has been well taught in writing classes.

REVISING

Murray (1978) referred to three stages in the writing process: prevision, vision, and revision. First are the planning, researching, and other activities of prewriting. Vision represents the first draft, where the writer gets ideas on paper, and revision clarifies the ideas for more effective communication to the reader.

As reported in the national assessment of writing, even high school students admit to little or no experience in revision. At best, they may recopy a paper. However, recopying is not revision. As the term itself implies, *re-vision* is a matter of "viewing again," of examining a piece of writing anew, seeing it now from the eyes of a reader, and making appropriate adjustments.

The process of revision clearly demonstrates the recursive nature of writing. Some revision takes place in the planning stage, during prewriting, as the writer begins to deal with the subject. During drafting itself choices are made in terms of wording, sentence structure, and organization. In this stage also, it is likely that some changes will be made in the process of getting the initial ideas on paper. Ultimately, however, after the ideas are drafted, revision enables the writer to arrive at a polished piece.

As Murray (October, 1978) pointed out, revision is actually "the process of seeing what you've said to discover what you have to say." This is another way of stating E. M. Forster's comment: "How do I know what I think until I see what I say?"

Students need to be led to realize the joy of revision, rather than to be satisfied with anything that is put on paper. They need to understand that the first draft is just that. It is the collection of their ideas that can become a useful "sloppy copy," replete with arrows for insertions, crossouts, rewritten lines, and alternate word choices. Attention at this stage is always on clarity and organization, not on "correctness."

Furthermore, initial steps in revision must come *before* the teacher conference. Although additional revision will result from the conference, there is no point in expecting revision of any kind after the teacher's evaluation of a finished copy. The piece is done! In fact, a regular procedure can be established: personal revision, peer assistance with further revision, then teacher help followed by additional revising.

If revision is approached as a way of playing with the language, instead of a "lesson" on skills, children will enjoy the process. This enjoyment is made more accessible if they have gotten into the practice of writing on every other line of paper, so they have room to make revisions, and if they are not expected always to endure the chore of recopying. This latter is nothing more than a mechanical task of transcription that takes the fun out of writing for many children.

In working on revision, always allow students to choose the piece they want to revise. If a piece of writing is not important to that student, there is no point in going to the labor of revising it. Further, a current piece is usually not appropriate for a serious revision; when the writer is too close to the piece, it is difficult to take the kind of objective view that facilitates revision. If students keep their writings in a log, they can select a more distant piece, one that has "cooled."

Initial instruction in revision is best done on a group basis and can begin easily in second grade, if not in first. Use a good example from the class, one about which many positive comments can be made, and one with which you and the class are not likely to get sidetracked on mechanical errors that would detour you to proofreading comments. Place the example on the chalkboard or on a transparency so that everyone can see it. Begin by pointing out or asking classmates to point out some of the good features: word choice, organization, ideas, and so on. You and the class might then pick one major point that is common in the class as a suggestion for improvement. For example, consider the following from a second-grader:

> Saturday we went to the zoo. And we saw lots of animals. We liked the monkeys best because they were so silly. And we threw peanuts to them. And my little brother thought the monkeys were making faces. And he made faces at them. And then we went home.

After discussing the ideas, the interest appeal of the humor, and so on, the teacher asked the class if anyone could see how this "good story" could be made even better. Almost at once a number of the youngsters pointed out that most of the sentences began with *and.* Of course most of them wrote this way, but in an examination of the piece they were able to recognize that this was not the best way to write. They took out the *and*s. Although there were other elements that could be discussed—the ending, expansion of "animals," explanation of "we," and so on—the teacher resisted further discussion. A point had been made, and youngsters now had one more specific item to look for as they went about revising their writings.

This point is probably one of the most important to keep in mind: Youngsters can't learn or do everything at once. Develop one point at a time with the group, then remind them of what they have learned and follow up with individuals in the conference, noting in their logs when they seem to have mastered a particular point.

As youngsters mature, discussion of word choice is another important item. This is especially true of the overworked words: *said, walked, asked, pretty.* Of course, use of a thesaurus can also be overdone:

One teacher evaluated themes at upper grades more on the number of exotic words used than on the appropriateness of those words. The focus in word choice must be on precision and appropriateness of the word to convey the message intended.

Group revision, using a student example, is also an opportunity to apply the instruction and practice you may have provided in sentence combining. Can your students recognize when certain sentences are better combined and where the shorter sentence provides the variety or makes the point? Combining merely for the sake of longer sentences is certainly not a goal in writing.

Student examples are not always the best to use. Don't hesitate to share with students some examples of your own efforts, complete with your crossouts and insertions, amplified with your frustrations as you attempted to smooth out a section. Too often students believe that they are the only ones who suffer in writing. Let them know that everyone who hopes to produce anything worthwhile must go through much the same anguish in deciding on a word or on a sequence.

In addition to modeling your own early drafts, have youngsters offer before-and-after pieces for comparison. This also makes for a good group lesson on revision, providing opportunity for questions about reasons for change and further clarifying the process the writer went through. In fact, comparisons are probably more effective if they are of an initial draft with a subsequent draft, not a final one.

In peer or teacher conferences, you might encourage your students to follow the suggestion of Wiener (1981): Have the writer read the paper aloud twice to a listener, first to provide the general idea, second to allow attention to specifics. The listener might paraphrase the main idea, asking if this is what was meant. Conversely, the listener might ask: "What is your main point? What is this about?" Especially if the main point wasn't clear, such questions might lead to a verbal response that more precisely states it and can be used in the revision.

The highly complex task of revision is basically simple in terms of what it entails. The writer has essentially only four choices in revising: make additions, make deletions, make substitutions, or reorganize the information. Once initial instruction or demonstration has been presented to a class, the teacher might turn these four options into questions to serve as a guide for revision.

More helpful in making decisions about revision might be a more specific list, which should also be developed through discussion with the class. Such a listing would include items such as the following:

1. Is the topic clear? What is this piece about?
2. Is the information appropriately organized? (Outlining *after* the writing may be helpful on this point.)
3. Are the elements in proper sequence, logically or chronologically?
4. Are transitions made smoothly?
5. Do I need more detail or specifics to clarify or add interest?
6. Is there extraneous material that should be deleted?
7. Is the degree of formality appropriate for the intended audience?
8. Are the sentences varied? Is there a pleasant rhythm when I read the piece aloud?
9. Are there words that are not as precise or appropriate as they could be?
10. Do I have an effective beginning and ending?

Such a list can be used as a guide as each student evaluates his or her own piece of writing. It might also be used as a guide for the peer evaluator who can then raise questions or even attach questions to the piece of writing being reviewed.

Whatever the guidelines or methods used, revision must be made a part of writing and must become a habit with students. Many rough drafts enable students to continue practicing what they already know; thoughtful revision provides growth.

PROOFREADING

In contrast to revision, proofreading is a surface-level kind of editing. It is the cosmetic adjustment, the packaging, that ensures more ready acceptance by the reader. It is important because it is socially demanded and because its neglect leaves mechanical errors, "noise" that interferes with communication.

Skill in proofreading is also lacking among students. This is an element of writing that must be taught, not merely admonished, as it usually is. It involves all of the mechanics: capitalization, punctuation, spelling, and format. Further, it is the last action taken on the revised draft, and, if the paper is recopied, it must be repeated on the clean copy.

In the reminder to "proofread your papers," teachers too often imply that this is a once-over process. On the contrary, the proofreader must examine the paper several times for different purposes. No student can be expected to proofread a paper in one swoop for all of the elements of capitalization, punctuation, and spelling. Even adults fail at such an effort.

If you didn't find a typographical error in this book, it is probably the first perfectly proofed book to be published. Sydney Harris once reported an effort at Edinburgh University to produce an error-free publication. After exhaustive proofreading by experts, the manuscript was posted for two weeks with a reward offered for any error found. Upon publication, the volume still contained errors; in fact, one error was in the first line of the first page. And we expect students to do a perfect job!

Chapter 10, or any style manual for that matter, contains a list of mechanics required for writing. There is no need to repeat them. Here we'll merely point out some of the techniques for developing skill in proofreading for those elements.

First of all, students should not be expected to proofread for a mechanic not taught. Again, you are reminded that everything can't be accomplished at once. Teach the most important first. "Most important" may be what you consider most basic to writing, or it may be the problem most students in your class seem to have.

As each item of capitalization or punctuation is taught, post a list or have youngsters add it to the style manual you may have them developing in their logs. Then *teach* them how to proofread for that item. In many cases, you will find that using a mechanic and proofreading for it require two different procedures.

When proofreading for end punctuation, the reader must attend to sentences, must determine if there is a subject and predicate, and must indicate by the appropriate mark whether the statement is a declaration, an exclamation, or a question. In contrast, proofreading for a capital letter at the beginning of a sentence requires no reading at all. In this case, the proofreader merely skims to end punctuation and determines if the letter following that end mark is capitalized.

As pointed out in Chapter 10, some elements of punctuation can be determined by pauses in speech. Uses of commas within sentences—whether to separate items in a series or to mark off nonrestrictive phrases and clauses or other parenthetical items—are best identified by a soft oral reading of the selection.

Contrast the latter with most of the conventions: the colon after the greeting in a letter, capitalization of any kind, period after an abbreviation, and so on. Such items are best identified through use of a checklist, since they are arbitrary.

Proofreading for spelling is still another process. Although use of context is one of the essential skills for success in reading, context can often lead a proofreader into "reading" what was intended instead of what was actually written. One technique for the beginner is to proofread backwards for spelling, beginning with the last word on the paper, since recognition of spelling errors requires looking at each word specifically for its spelling. Of course, this technique won't help in identifying misused homophones, such as *there* for *their,* where use of context is necessary.

One preliminary step in helping youngsters to do a better job of proofreading for spelling is to help them develop an awareness of uncertainty. As suggested in Chapter 9, writers should develop the habit of identifying—by circling or underlining—any word whose spelling is uncertain. Then proofing for spelling is merely a matter of checking those words. To leave the word unmarked in the initial draft is to invite oversight in the proofreading, where the youngster may not remember the uncertainty that existed in the initial writing.

Reasonable Expectations

As stated, even educated adults often fail in attempts to perfectly proofread a manuscript. Children are not likely to do better. We must recognize that unreasonable expectations lead, at best, to superficial efforts and ultimately to less than that.

One technique that should be considered is to expect students to proofread a paper only for the item taught. Review the item as students are completing a draft and review the procedure for proofreading for that item. Then ask them to proof for it. Such papers should be examined by you to determine who has mastered the skill in proofreading and who needs further instruction. Even with these papers, you should not do the editing for your students.

Just as group revision can be helpful, so too you can use the group technique for proofreading instruction. In this case, the example you use on the board or on a transparency should be one that you construct. Don't embarrass students by using one of their mechanically poor drafts.

Using the example, have students identify mechanical errors. In the process, it is important to discuss how they identified the error, to clarify with them the procedures they can use to be more efficient in proofreading. Here again, the examples should be limited to items of mechanics that have been previously taught, and the fact that you have constructed the example further ensures such a limitation.

Beginning at third or fourth grade, a further step can be taken. Have students pick one of their pieces of writing to attempt a perfect proofreading. First review the elements they have been taught to proofread for and how they are to read for those items. A listing on the board or transparency will be needed if students have not developed a style manual in their logs. Then ask for a perfectly proofread first paragraph, noting that it must be read several times for the various purposes involved in editing.

If your students can do a perfect job of proofreading the first paragraph of a piece of writing, they have the skill you want to develop. It would seem to be busywork for them to continue on with the remainder of the piece of writing—*unless* that particular piece is to go somewhere important.

Taking such an approach will let students know the purpose of proofreading; it is to provide the polishing touches on a piece of writing that is important enough to go outside the confines of the close group. Proofreading is not a chore demanded of children merely to keep them busy.

Classroom Editors

As stated frequently in this book and others, you as teacher should not play editor. You don't need the practice, and students don't learn anything from your red pencil except a dislike for writing.

In contrast, it is always easier to see someone else's mistakes than it is to identify our own. Hence, you might like to establish editing teams in your class. A team of two or three students can serve as editors for a week. Then a new team is appointed or elected. In fact, it is sometimes helpful to use the technique of organizations, having only one member of the team replaced each week, so that there is carryover.

An editorial team does not relieve the responsibility individual writers have for proofreading. However, that team can be the ultimate check before writing is released for publication. They are the ones who can be free with the red pencil, sending material back to the writer when it is incomprehensible or even when it is not adequately revised to be ready for proofreading.

There are differences of opinion about whether or not the teacher should make final corrections on a child's paper that is to be published. Graves (1983) suggests that the teacher correct any mechanics that are beyond the child before a piece of writing goes public, although he also adds that some pupils need to learn through audience reaction to take more care in their editing. I am more inclined to take the position of the national publications of childrens' material: We need to teach and guide where we can, but the child should maintain ownership of the paper.

Recopying

Personally, I hesitate to encourage much recopying. For one thing, young children can take a perfectly proofread rough copy and, in the recopying, put in new errors. In fact, the preceding statement shouldn't be limited to "young children." Haven't you had the experience, as I have, of typing a final draft only to find new errors in the final copy? Again, our excuse is "typographical errors," but children can't get by with that.

Besides, recopying is a mechanical chore unless it has some purpose. I've seen some schools where instruction has been given on calligraphy. The ultimate finished copy is then reproduced in beautiful script for posting, thus providing a purpose for recopying. In any event, I suggest limiting recopying to pieces of writing that are "going some- where" important. That might include posting on the bulletin board for the world to see, or it might be a matter of "publication" in a class paper. However, to recopy merely for the teacher's pleasure is not a very good purpose.

Despite the preceding, a lot of recopying will take place in a writing classroom. Most of the pieces of writing will be "published" in some form. Then the recopying is purposeful. Children who have pieces of writing to be read will begin to take pride in the finished product and will want to have it appear in final form, even to the point of being concerned about the handwriting itself.

SUMMARY

This chapter clarified the distinction between revision and proofreading. The former has to do with style, word choice, organization, and other elements of clarity and interest; the latter deals with the mechanics of capitalization, punctuation, spelling, and format. Both are important and often neglected features of writing.

Students need instruction and practice in revision, and they need to discover that it can be an enjoyable, satisfying portion of writing. Best performed on a preferred piece of writing, one worth further thought, revision can be taught initially in group situations, focusing on one element at a time. A suggested list of considerations for revision was provided.

Proofreading must also be taught as a techinque for discovering problems with mechanics, after the mechanic itself has been presented to youngsters. Group instruction is also possible for initial work on this skill, which should deal with one item at a time. The use of classroom editors was suggested as one means of providing additional practice in proofreading.

Finally, recopying was seen as necessary only when a piece of writing is going public. This is the final polishing, a task not to be performed on every piece of writing.

SUGGESTIONS FOR ACTION

1. Try a lesson in group revision with your pupils. Use a good example on which the group can begin by pointing out positive features. Then ask if anyone can find areas where the writing can be made even more clear or interesting.

2. From some examples of classroom writing, you might like to work with your students to develop a guide to revision, listing some of the elements they are aware of and should be concerned with.

3. Do your students use oral reading to check their early drafts? You might like to have them try it.

4. Use a model of your own writing to demonstrate some of the reasons for change in a paper. You might also use a before-and-after version from the class.

5. If your students don't have a handbook of style, you might like to begin developing one with them that will be kept in their logs for reference. Have them add to it as a new mechanic is learned.

6. Try a group lesson in proofreading, making certain to discuss *how* one proofreads for that element.

7. Appoint or have the class elect a team of editors who will be responsible for final clearance of any paper. Each editor might even specialize for a few days on one mechanic before changing to another.

8. Consider the section on recopying. What is your position? Can you help your youngsters to develop a pride in recopied drafts by expecting such only when a piece of writing is being made public? What positive effect might this have even on handwriting?

REFERENCES

GRAVES, DONALD H., *Writing: Teachers and Children at Work.* Exeter, New Hampshire: Heinemann Educational Books, 1983. Reports on two years of work with first-graders in writing.

MURRAY, DONALD M., "Internal Revision: A Process of Discovery," in Cooper, Charles R., and Lee Odell, *Research on Composing.* Urbana: National Council of Teachers of English, 1978. Discusses the writing process and what Murray calls the two forms of revision: internal and external.

————, "Teach the Motivating Force of Revision," *The English Journal,* 67 (October, 1978), 56–60. Demonstrates how a student can be awakened to the joy of revision.

WIENER, HARVEY S. *The Writing Room.* New York: Oxford University Press, 1981. An excellent resource for a workshop approach to writing, aimed primarily at the secondary and college level.

12

Publishing

There is nothing more dreadful to an author than neglect, compared with which reproach, hatred and opposition are names of happiness.

SAMUEL JOHNSON

WRITERS WRITE FOR SOMEONE to read. A statement of the obvious? Yet how often do children write in school only to have the teacher check their papers and give them a grade, with possibly a remark on how well they wrote? The idea, the communication of information or feelings, is too often neglected.

This chapter deals with publishing in the broadest sense as the dissemination of a piece of writing to an audience who will read for and react to the content, an audience that truly receives the message. Such "publication" may range from a readership of a few peers in the classroom, to school-wide distribution, to national audiences. Any such consideration also entails recognition that, when one writes daily, not every piece of writing is worth publication.

IMMEDIATE AUDIENCES

In the kind of workshop approach to writing previously described in this book, youngsters always have access to peers for reactions. Further, in developing skill in revision, the writer will also develop some judgment about which pieces of writing are worthy of going beyond his or her own log.

Many avenues are open to readers within a classroom. Informal sharing with classmates individually or in small groups provides one kind of audience. Another is provided by the bulletin board, where finished pieces of writing can be posted for the entire class to examine. In some classes, groups maintain story folders, open to any reader, containing finished products of the class members and providing enjoyment as well as ideas for additional writing.

More extensive classroom publications can take many forms, from one page to full-fledged newspapers. Some classes prefer more of a magazine format, containing fiction, fact, and poetry, or even a purely factual "Science Magazine" or "History Journal," as suggested in Chapter 6. The possibilities are unlimited, from nonsense dictionaries to "how to do it" booklets.

Older students can also write stories, poems, or collections for younger classes. Some middle-grade teachers even provide a basic word list, such as suggested in Chapter 9, so that their students can write beginning-to-read material for first-graders. These products not only have the advantage of motivating the writer because that writing will be read by someone, they also motivate the reader—the younger pupil who knows the author or the brother or sister of the author.

Whether it is for use within the class or beyond, further importance can be placed on the writing by binding it into a book. In some schools, such books are catalogued and placed in the school library to be checked out in the same manner as any other book. Their popularity often exceeds that of the commercial library books. Furthermore, such real publication provides a true stimulus to do a good job of revision and proofreading.

BINDING CHILDREN'S BOOKS

Although simple books can be made merely by using an oaktag cover, with pages fastened in by staples or paper fasteners, such do not have the stature of a real binding. Bound books may include finished pages of a manuscript or blank pages bound to serve as the book into which final copy is written. The former is much preferred, since serious errors in the latter will require an entire new book.

Making the Cover

1. Cut two pieces of cardboard, each about ½ inch longer and ¼ inch wider than the size of the pages to be bound, thus allowing ¼ inch of cover beyond the page edges on all sides except the spine. For example, if you are folding or cutting 8½ × 11 paper, pages will be 8½ × 5½, so each of the two pieces of cardboard should be 9 × 5¾.

2. Place the two pieces of cardboard side by side about ⅛ inch apart (slightly more than the estimated thickness of the book). Tape them with a cloth tape, such as librarian's tape, as shown in Figure 12.1.

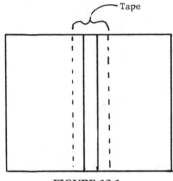

FIGURE 12.1.

3. Select your cover material. It may be cloth, wallpaper, or a child's drawing, although sturdy material is preferred. Cut it about 1½ inches longer and wider than the taped cardboard. Place it *face down* and put the taped cardboard on it with the taped side down, as shown in Figure 12.2.

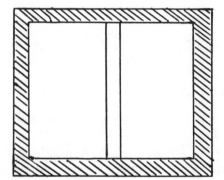

FIGURE 12.2 Shaded area is the back of the cover material, extending 3/4 inch beyond the cardboard on all four sides.

(If you use a child's drawing and want to make the cover more durable, cut the drawing to exactly the size of the taped cover. Then place it face down on clear ConTact paper that has been cut to allow folding over the cardboard and continue as directed in steps 3 and 4. Of course, since ConTact is preglued, glue is not needed in steps 5 and 6.)

4. Using white casein glue, glue the cover material to the cardboard.

5. Fold the corners over the cardboard and glue them as shown in Figure 12.3.

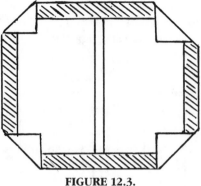

FIGURE 12.3.

6. Now fold the edges over and glue them as shown in Figure 12.4. This completes the cover.

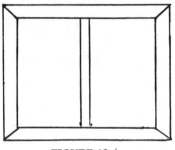

FIGURE 12.4.

Binding the Pages

There are several methods of binding pages besides using the unsightly paper fasteners. Pages may be stapled or sewn, depending upon your preference and time limitations. Furthermore, the pages may be separate sheets or they may consist of many sheets folded in half. The latter is usually used only when children are to be supplied with blank books, since it requires considerable planning: Half of the first page in the book is also the last page in that book, and so on.

   1. Assemble the pages to be bound. Get a piece of sturdy paper, such as butcher paper, and cut it to form a cover for the pages. This cover, which will serve as the end pages, should be the size of the book pages when they are opened flat.

   2. Place the book pages evenly and securely inside the end pages. Draw a line down the spine side of the booklet, about ¼ inch from the spine, as shown in Figure 12.5. (Note: If you are stapling, staple on the line and skip to step 6.)

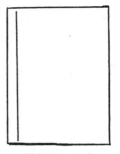

FIGURE 12.5.

3. On the line, mark a point 1 inch from the top of the book and 1 inch from the bottom. Then mark the midpoint between these two. Put an additional mark halfway between these, as shown in Figure 12.6. (Note: If your book pages are 11 inches high, space *two* marks evenly between each of the end marks and the mid mark.)

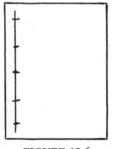

FIGURE 12.6.

4. Using a nail or a similar instrument, punch a hole through all the papers at each of the marks.

5. With a heavy thread or dental floss, begin sewing in the middle hole, leaving enough thread to enable you to tie the ends when you finish. Follow the procedure shown in Figure 12.7, tying the ends securely when you are finished.

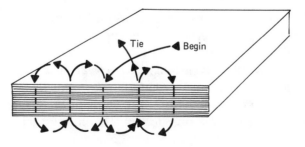

FIGURE 12.7.

6. Now glue the end pieces to the inside of your cardboard cover, and the book is finished. Your end pieces should be just short of coming to the edge of the cover, as shown in Figure 12.8.

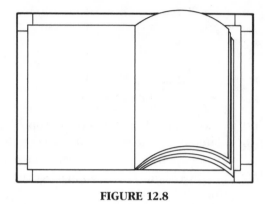

FIGURE 12.8

If your book pages consist of sheets that have been folded in half rather than cut, do not follow steps 2 and 3 as indicated. Instead, open the pages flat and use the fold line in the center to mark the points specified in step 3. Then continue with steps 4 through 6.

REACHING BEYOND THE SCHOOL

Purposeful writing can take many forms, depending upon the interests and maturity of students, and ranging from letters to literary and factual works. Some examples follow, along with sources for publication of the latter types.

Letters and Notes

Most basic is the kind of writing that we are all familiar with. Communiques to parents may be invitations to an open house, reports on some school activity, announcements, and so on. Writing a letter to a classmate who is ill is another purposeful kind of writing in which content is clearly identified: happenings at school, concern and best wishes for the peer, and so on.

Students may, however, become involved in a broader audience. As a result of interest in a book or author, they may write to that author about a point in the book, for additional information, or merely to express their delight with the work. If such letters are sent in care of the publisher, a reply will be forthcoming, often accompanied by a photograph, bookmark, or some other memento.

From a social studies topic, students might become interested in a social or political matter. They should be encouraged to express their concern, make their comments, or offer their suggestions in letters to their representative or senator, state or local. Likewise, requests for information about a state or locale can be addressed to the chamber of commerce in the capital or city of interest.

Publishing in National Magazines

Although publishing beyond the classroom is not the primary goal of writing, children should be made aware of submitting and encouraged to submit particularly good examples of their writing to various magazines. Nothing encourages more writing like publication.

Before making such submissions, several points should be kept in mind and discussed with students.

1. Teacher and pupil must become familiar with the potential magazine being considered.
2. Submit only to one publisher at a time and so state in your accompanying letter. However, youngsters should also realize that they shouldn't give up after a rejection. Part of getting published is having the right material in the right place at the right time.
3. Editors want original work. Neither teacher nor parent should tamper with the child's material. In fact, most often a statement to this effect must be included.
4. Always keep a copy of the material. Most often, if a stamped, self-addressed envelope is included with the manuscript, it will be returned, but play safe.
5. Identify the work clearly, including all information designated by the publisher.
6. Address the material specifically to the department intended in the magazine.
7. Finally, don't expect a reply overnight! It may take six months.

Following is a partial listing of current magazines that publish children's writing. Most are monthlies, but you should always examine current issues for more detail before submitting a manuscript for publication. A complete listing can be found in the "Juvenile" section of the current edition of *Writer's Market* (Cincinnati: Writer's Digest Books).

American Girl, 830 Third Avenue, New York, NY 10022. (For girls, 10–16) Accepts stories, poems, art, letters, and snapshots.

Boys Life, North Brunswick, NJ 08902. (For boys, 8–17, Scouts favored) Accepts hobby and "how to do it" ideas, jokes, unusual activities, and even photos and news clippings of activities.

Child Life, P.O. Box 567B, Indianapolis, IN 46206 (For ages 9–14) Publishes jokes, riddles, poems, letters, artwork, recipes, and short (500-word) articles.

Children's Playmate, P.O. Box 567B, Indianapolis, IN 46206. (For ages 5–8) Accepts poems, jokes, riddles, and colored or painted artwork.

Cricket, P.O. Box 100, LaSalle, IL 61301. (For ages 6–12) Offers prizes in monthly contests for stories, art, poems. Entries must be accompanied by teacher or parent note guaranteeing originality.

Current Events, 245 Long Hill Road, Middletown, CT 06457. (Middle school) Publishes jokes, letters, and puzzles.

Current Science, 245 Long Hill Road, Midddletown, CT 06457. (Middle school) Publishes science-related materials and often specifies topics.

Daisy, 830 Third Avenue, New York, NY 10022. (Primarily for Girl Scouts) "Daisy Art and Writing" publishes original art and writing. Girl Scouts should include their troop number.

Dynamite, 50 West 44th Street, New York, NY 10036. (For ages 8–12) Publishes gags, jokes, tricks, and funny ideas in "Hot Stuff," as well as gripes in "Bummers."

Ebony Jr.!, 820 South Michigan Avenue, Chicago, IL 60605. (For ages 6–12) Sponsors writing contests and publishes poems, jokes, riddles, short stories, artwork, and letters.

Electric Company Magazine, P.O. Box 2926, Boulder, CO 80322. Accepts jokes, riddles, drawings, and clever ideas.

Fun Publishing Company, P.O. Box 40283, Indianapolis, IN 46240. (For ages 6–15) Assembles stories, poems, and articles into annual book-length publications. Deadline for intermediate and junior high is March 30; for primary, April 30.

Highlights for Children, 803 Church Street, Honesdale, PA 18431. (For ages 2–11) Accepts artwork, poems, and stories. Contributions must be signed by teacher or parent indicating originality.

Jack and Jill, P.O. Box 567B, Indianapolis, IN 46206. (For ages 8–12) Accepts short stories (500 words), poems, letters, and artwork.

Kids, 747 Third Avenue, New York, NY 10017. (For ages 5–15) Publishes short stories and nonfiction, poems, art, puzzles, games, and comic strips.

Kids for Ecology, P.O. Box P-7126, Philadelphia, PA 19117. (For ages 5–14) Accepts any form of contribution related to ecology. Include T-shirt size, since authors of published material receive a "Kids for Ecology" T-shirt.

Know Your World, 245 Long Hill Road, Middletown, CT 06457. (For ages 10–16) A high-interest, low-vocabulary publication—includes jokes, riddles, short stories, poems, and letters.

National Geographic World, 17th and M Streets N.W., Washington, DC 20036. (For ages 8–14) Publishes letters, games, puzzles, and photojournalism.

Odyssey, 411 East Mason Street, P.O. Box 92788, Milwaukee, WI 53202. (For ages 8–12) Accepts letters, riddles, and art. Will send a free sample copy and information.

Ranger Rick's Nature Magazine, P.O. Box 2299, Philadelphia, PA 19103. (For ages 4–12) Publishes letters, poems, and artwork on nature topics.

Read, 245 Long Hill Road, Middletown, CT 06457. (For ages 11–13) Publishes jokes and poetry regularly; annually includes poems, short stories, plays, jokes, cartoons, puzzles, art, and nonfiction.

Stone Soup, P.O. Box 83, Santa Cruz, CA 95063. (For ages up to 14) Publishes stories, poems, plays, book reviews, and artwork. Children serve as guest editors, and published contributors receive a free copy of the magazine.

Wee Wisdom, Unity Village, MO 64065. (For ages 6–11) Publishes short stories and poems. Teacher or parent must guarantee originality.

Weewise Tree, American Indian Historical Society, 1451 Masonic Avenue, San Francisco, CA 94117. (For ages 6–11) Publishes stories, poems, and artwork related to native Americans.

Young World, 1100 Waterway Boulevard, P.O. Box 567B, Indianapolis, IN 46206. (For ages 10–14) Accepts poems, jokes, artwork, letters, and stories or articles under 1,000 words.

A YOUNG AUTHORS' CONFERENCE

An excellent method of promoting and publicizing children's writing is through a young authors' conference. Whether called a "Young Authors' Conference," "Young Writers' Conference," or "Young Writers' Workshop," such gatherings often involve the entire community or larger area. Not only do they stimulate young writers, but they are also an excellent public relations medium, inviting newspaper publicity as well as television coverage.

A large school district might sponsor such a conference. In smaller districts, usually several combine or sponsor the conference under the auspices of the county office of education, intermediate district, or area education agency. Furthermore, these latter agencies, as well as the staff in the state office of education, can often provide advice and guidance in planning such a conference.

The conference is usually a full-day affair, involving all students, parents, and teachers. An author—sometimes several—presents comments about writing, and often teachers or university faculty direct sessions with parents and children about writing.

Organizing the Conference

A Young Authors' Conference cannot be set up overnight. In fact, lead time is usually about a year, depending upon the number of participants expected and the geographic area involved. The first step is to establish a steering committee made up of representatives of the various districts, schools, or agencies participating. Each member of the steering committee can, in turn, become chair of one of the subcommittees that will be needed: guides, parking, lunch or refreshments, presenters, arrangements, book exhibit, and so on.

Most conferences are self-supporting or assisted by grants from service clubs and local merchants. Only a nominal fee, if any, should be charged, so that no child is excluded from participation.

Authors should be contacted early, since many are booked for at least a year in advance. You may have some good local authors, and they should be contacted first. Also, it is advisable, if at all possible, to get recommendations of authors that someone has heard speak to youngsters. Some good writers are not necessarily effective in speaking to children.

The author will expect to have an exhibit at the conference. In addition, fees for speaking vary greatly, so this should be investigated with the author or authors being considered. Sometimes the publisher of that author will help defray costs by at least paying transportation.

Although it is important to have a professional writer speak to students, many smaller sessions should also be planned. In these, whether workshop or lecture sessions, teachers, administrators, university faculty, and college students can be used. The committee can plan the kinds of sessions they want and then can usually find appropriate faculty to staff those sessions. Unless some travel is involved, most often there is no charge for this kind of service to the community. Nonetheless, such contributions should be recognized by the committee through a letter, certificate, corsage, or some other token of appreciation.

The subcommittee in charge of the book exhibit will need to staff that exhibit during the day, selling the books. The publisher should be willing to send books on consignment, usually at about a 20 percent discount, and you pay for the books not returned plus all transportation costs. Since the latter can mount up, it is wise to plan the quantity carefully. Unless you are in a very affluent area, most often paperback editions are ones that are purchased, so a minimum of hardcover books will be required.

Local newspapers are usually most happy to get information about authors and conference participants. Someone should work closely with the education reporter or editor of the local paper. Oftentimes these people are also appropriate as presenters to a group session about writing for the newspaper, how newspapers operate, and so on.

Most often Young Writers' (or Authors') Conferences are held on Saturday. Especially if a large number of children are involved, this is one of the few days when an adequate facility might be available. Such facilities to be considered are a large high school or university buildings if such are nearby.

Depending upon the kind of participation, the conference might be for all children in grades K–6, K–8, or K–12. Regardless of the grade-level designation, *all* students in the geographic area should be involved. Not all may attend, but if facilities allow, everyone should have the opportunity.

A snack or light lunch is often appropriate, with the conference ending early in the afternoon. However, this too can be flexible. If a snack is provided, a nominal fee can be charged to cover that lunch, or some local restaurants might volunteer to provide it. In fact, even though the conference might be supported by external funds, some schools have found it wise to charge a very nominal fee merely to have some count of the number of participants to be expected. Mere registration for sessions is often no guarantee of attendance on a Saturday, although youngsters are usually excited about such a conference.

The Big Day

Conferences vary in how writing is used during the day. In some, each child brings a piece of writing to read and share with a small group of others for comment and discussion. In others, more of a workshop atmosphere prevails. Children bring their writing implements and do the writing at the workshop, possibly under the direction of a visiting writing teacher.

In the latter case too, some prefer to have a given small group remain together for most of the day. There might be a presentation of 30 to 45 minutes on the topic they have chosen, then participants write, using that information, for about the same period of time. Finally, a third equal-time period is allowed for sharing of the writing and comments.

In any case, children should have options of sessions to attend. Some conferences are organized so that youngsters choose among types of writing: newspaper, poetry, mystery, biography, and so on. Others may merely divide the participants into small groups by age or grade level to share their writing.

Although busing of the youngsters to the site is always possible, many schools prefer to make transportation the responsibility of the parents. As a result, provision needs to be made for occupying the parents' time. Usually it is better if there are special sessions for these parents, rather than have them involved in the same sessions as their children, so youngsters are less intimidated by the adult presence. The parent sessions may be handled by the school or university faculty, who will present topics of interest to parents: what parents can do at home, current trends in teaching writing in the schools, and so on. Regardless of the topics or procedures, everyone should participate in the author's presentation, parents as well as pupils.

A few sponsors of conferences provide for awards to exceptional writers, and most give every youngster a certificate of participation. This latter is advisable because it recognizes the efforts of all, encourages all participants to continue writing, and avoids some of the hard feelings that can result when parents or others disagree with judges' decisions.

Follow-Up

Once the day is over, work begins anew for the committee. There are bills to pay, thank-you letters to send to all contributors, and suggestions to collect that will correct problems encountered as planning gets underway for next year's conference.

This is indeed the time to begin planning for next year's conference. Ideas and improvements are still fresh in mind. Small-group presenters can be evaluated to determine which groups and speakers were most effective. And, of course, it is not too soon to begin making contacts with authors for next year's conference.

The committee itself will be reorganized for a subsequent year. It is usually a good policy to carry some members over from year to year in order to maintain continuity, perhaps allowing for two-year terms, with only half of the members being new each year.

SUMMARY

This chapter presented ideas for publication in the broadest sense, that is, having the writing read by an audience, whether within the classroom, within the school, or beyond the confines of a local readership.

Suggestions were made for sharing, posting, or disseminating pieces of writing through letters, class-prepared newspapers and magazines, and books. Directions for binding books were included, with the suggestion that such books be made part of the school library collection.

In reaching beyond the school, students might write purposeful letters to adults, both within and outside the community. Such letters might be opinions to elected officials or inquiries to businesses or chambers of commerce, as well as reactions to favorite authors.

Specific suggestions were made about writing for publication in national magazines of interest to students, and a selected listing of such magazines was provided.

Finally, a Young Authors' Conference was recommended for its stimulating effects as well as for its positive public relations. Comments included tips on organizing the conference, suggestions for the content and activities to be included, and reminders about the follow-up requirements.

SUGGESTIONS FOR ACTION

1. What happens to finished pieces of writing in your class? Try some of the ideas presented that would be most helpful in your class: a bulletin board display, class newspaper, open folder of writings, class magazine, poetry collection, or a "how to do it" booklet.

2. If you work with middle- or upper-grade students, have them write stories or poems for younger children. You might even want to supply a basic word list, taken from Chapter 9 or from the first-grade basal, for them to use in writing the material.

3. Your students might be more interested in writing if their finished pieces were bound into books that could be used in other classes or in the library. Older students can be given directions to make their own bound books.

4. What topics from social studies or science, music or art, might lead to some purposeful letter writing, either for more information or to express some opinions about a topic?

5. Some of your youngsters might be interested in writing for a national publication. Share this possibility and some of the sources with them.

6. Does your school participate in a Young Authors' Conference? If not, you might want to get one started. Initiate discussions with other staff members and your principal. You could begin on a very limited basis with such a conference within your own school, inviting representatives from the local newspaper to talk about writing. Even your classroom, turned into a writing workshop with one outside speaker, can be an enjoyable first step in the right direction.

13

Evaluating

Whoever thinks a faultless piece to see,
Thinks what ne'er was, nor is, nor e'er shall be.
ALEXANDER POPE, 1709

THIS CHAPTER REPRESENTS an effort to deal with the broad area of evaluation in writing. It will attempt to clarify and provide direction on the who, what, when, why, and how of evaluation. Entire books have been written on the subject!

Before getting to specifics, however, I'd like to quote a passage that I use at the beginning of every workshop or class I do on writing. I believe it is not only the best statement on evaluation, it is the finest statement made on attitudes toward writing itself.

> Some criticism, no doubt, is constructive, but too much is a subtle poison. A friend of mine told me of a club he belonged to in his undergraduate days at the University of Wisconsin. The members were a group of brilliant boys, some with real literary talent. At each meeting one of them would read a story or essay he had written and submit it to the criticism of the others. No punches were pulled; each manuscript was mercilessly dissected. The sessions were so brutal that the club members dubbed themselves *The Stranglers.* This club was strictly a masculine affair, so naturally the coeds formed a comparable group of their own known as *The Wranglers.* They, too, read their manuscripts aloud. But the criticism was much gentler. In fact, there was almost none at all. The Wranglers hunted for kind things to say. All efforts, however feeble, were encouraged.
>
> The payoff came about twenty years later, when some alumnus made an analysis of his classmates' careers. Of all the bright

young talent in The Stranglers, not one had made a literary reputation of any kind. Out of The Wranglers had come half a dozen successful writers, some of national prominence, led by Marjorie Kinnan Rawlings, who wrote *The Yearling.* Coincidence? Hardly. The amount of basic talent in the two groups was much the same. But The Wranglers gave one another a lift. The Stranglers promoted self-criticism, self-disparagement, self-doubt. In choosing a name for themselves, they had been wiser than they knew [From *A Touch of Wonder* by Arthur Gordon. © 1974 by Fleming H. Revell Company. Published by Fleming H. Revell Company. Used by permission].

To begin with, the term *evaluation* is used advisedly. Some refer to the "assessment" of writing. The former term is a judgmental one, whereas the latter refers more to measurement. Although we might wish we could measure writing skill accurately, it seems that the most effective measures we know to date fall more into the category of judgment as opposed to precise measurement. This statement does not necessarily imply a lack of accuracy or even of reliability; more likely it is an indication that we are dealing with an "art" more than a "science."

The 1980s have seen a rapid expansion in competency assessment in writing. In 1981, McCready and Melton reported that already forty states were developing or using competency tests. Some might decry this direction, but it is not altogether regrettable. Teachers tend to teach that which is tested. Perhaps the current emphasis on competency that includes writing will lead to more instruction. On the other hand, if it merely leads to more testing, it can be a detriment: Every minute devoted to testing is a minute lost from instruction. One of the points in this chapter is that evaluation should be an integral part of instruction; there is no need for separate writing—or worse, separate testing—just for the assessment. Learning should be the focus, and writing done for that purpose can become part of the evaluation procedure.

Any evaluation must be in terms of the goals established as well as in line with the purposes of that evaluation. These two points will be discussed before presenting methods of evaluation.

GOALS OF A WRITING PROGRAM

Too often traditional approaches have begun with evaluation without ever establishing explicit goals. Nevertheless, there are goals, at least by implication. If evaluation is a matter of checking mechanical errors, the goals must be to have students write correctly spelled words with appropriate capitalization and punctuation.

Although specific objectives may vary among schools or from one year to the next within a school, educators—as well as the general public—would agree that the overriding goal of any writing program ought to be to develop students who can communicate clearly and effectively in writing to an intended audience. If this is true, then evaluative procedures ought to reflect this concern and be established to judge the degree to which the goal is accomplished by each individual and by the student body as a whole.

It is interesting to note the shift in emphasis between the writing objectives for the 1973–74 and the 1983–84 National Assessment of Educational Progress in Writing, as shown in Figures 13.1 and 13.2.

The major shift in the latest assessment was from an emphasis on the products of writing to an emphasis on the process. Objectives I and III in Figure 13.2 represent entirely new categories reflecting this change in emphasis, and Objective II has been broadened considerably. Concern for the quality of the process is most often ignored in evaluation, yet evidence suggests that it is a key to the quality of the product.

REVISED WRITING OBJECTIVES
An Outline

I. *Demonstrates ability in writing to reveal personal feelings and ideas.*
   A. Through free expression
   B. Through the use of conventional modes of discourse

II. *Demonstrates ability to write in response to a wide range of societal demands and obligations. Ability is defined to include correctness in usage, punctuation, spelling, and form or convention as appropriate to particular writing tasks, e.g., manuscripts, letters.*
   A. Social
      1. Personal
      2. Organizational
      3. Community
   B. Business/Vocational
   C. Scholastic

III. *Indicates the importance attached to writing skills.*
   A. Recognizes the necessity of writing for a variety of needs (as in I and II)
   B. Writes to fulfill those needs
   C. Gets satisfaction, even enjoyment, from having written something well

FIGURE 13.1. Writing Objectives for the the 1973–74 Assessment.

Outline of Writing Objectives

I. Students Use Writing as a Way of Thinking and Learning
   A. Subject Knowledge
   B. Self-Knowledge

II. Students Use Writing to Accomplish a Variety of Purposes
   A. Informative Writing
   B. Persuasive Writing
   C. Literary Writing

III. Students Manage the Writing Process
   A. Generate
   B. Draft
   C. Revise
   D. Edit

IV. Students Control the Forms of Written Language
   A. Organization and Elaboration
   B. Conventions (Usage and Mechanics)

V. Students Appreciate the Value of Writing
   A. Value for Interpersonal Communication
   B. Value for Society
   C. Value for Self

FIGURE 13.2. Writing Objectives for the 1983–84 Assessment.

One method of developing specific objectives to be evaluated within the school, for the entire school as well as for each level, might be to pull out from the course of study the major objectives listed there. One should be able to assume that some thought was given to that listing, and therefore these are objectives toward which the instructional program is directed. Of course, such an initial effort might also lead to some rethinking of those course objectives before their attainment becomes part of the evaluation procedure. Conversely, as reported in one school, identification of these objectives can bring about a realization that the standardized test adopted for the district does not fit the objectives so identified.

PURPOSES FOR EVALUATING

Just as in the case of writing instruction itself, the number of different purposes for which educators evaluate leads to confusion about methods used. Primarily, teachers evaluate for three major purposes: reporting to pupil and/or parent, diagnosis of pupil needs, and program evaluation.

Reporting

First, let's clarify that "grading" is neither evaluation nor reporting. The grade on a report card is a meaningless symbol, regardless of the number of letters or numerals in the grade book that average out to the final "report card grade." The National Council of Teachers of English has gone on record as being opposed to the grade in writing. Hence, there is no attempt here to discuss that particular aspect of reporting.

On the other hand, along with that required report card grade, it is important for teachers to communicate to both pupil and parent how that pupil is developing in written composition. That reporting should be in plain English, should deal with specific skills that have been accomplished and are in the process of being learned, should be documented with examples, should reflect degree of progress for that individual as compared with his or her previous status, and probably should include—at least at one point in the year—an indication of that individual's status as compared with the typical student at that grade level.

I believe that this limitation on the frequency of reporting a comparative status is an important one. The focus in reporting ought to be on the individual being reported on in terms of the other stated points if we believe that often-heard maxim that we develop each child to that child's potential. Very few individuals ever change appreciably in terms of their relative status in a group, so no parent or child needs to hear—at every grading period— "You are the best" or "You are the worst" writer in the class. On the other hand, at some time during the progress of the year, it is only fair that parents be given some indication of how their child is doing as compared with the typical youngster of that age, probably more to avoid misconceptions and false expectations than to avoid undue pressure, as might become the case of the brighter student. Besides, reporting on the other points keeps the focus where it should be, on the quality of the writing as opposed to having it become a commentary on the quality of the individual.

The basis for that reporting is the accumulation of writings the student has completed over the period of time. Here again, no one changes appreciably in writing skill from day to day; conversely, any writer can have a particularly "good" or "bad" day, whether in terms of mood, topic, or other circumstances. The collection of pieces will demonstrate the trend, smooth out the curve, and reveal true accomplishments.

Using such a collection of writings will also enable you, as teacher, to point out what you have been working on, specific skills mastered since the last writings, and even some needs. Pointing out the needs can be important to the parent who might believe you are unaware of those misspelled words you failed to circle or those commas you didn't fill in with a red pen. Often the teacher's identification of "errors" that the parent didn't even notice is proof enough that the teacher knows what is needed.

If the writings are kept in a folder along with a record of progress, as suggested in Chapter 8, both parent and child can see what achievements have been accomplished. With only report card grades as the measure, the development of skill in writing is an intangible accomplishment; examples of that writing bring it into the realm of concrete reality.

What you decide to report will vary with the age of the students and with your particular goals during that reporting period. With older students, you may provide a variety of information about their growth, and that information might be the same that you provide to their parents. With younger pupils, your reporting to them will undoubtedly be less detailed and will focus on major accomplishments made during the particular period. In all cases, however, remember that you are reporting on the writing done—on its quality and development—and not on the quality of the student.

Diagnosis

To some, *diagnosis* is a frightening, clinical term. However, it should not be. There will be times when a teacher will make use of some instrument or technique, such as those discussed under "Methods of Evaluating" later in this chapter, but most often that "diagnosis" will be nothing more than checking to see if Fred is now putting a capital letter at the beginning of a sentence, or if Erin has finally started telling things in proper sequence.

Individual diagnosis ought to be continuous; good teaching is diagnostic teaching. Hence, most of your diagnosis will be informal and day-to-day, as you teach, observe degree of mastery, and reteach as needed. Here, your conferencing enables more specific individual diagnosis, and your record keeping guarantees more accurate tracking of accomplishments and needs. Also, that folder of writings for each child, discussed previously, is an excellent fund of information on these specifics.

Program Evaluation

You, as an individual teacher, should want to evaluate the effectiveness of the program in your classroom periodically. Also, I hope that, as a staff, teachers in your school or district do a periodic evaluation of the total program in writing. It is here—in classroom, school, and school district—that both aspects of the writing program—process and product—should be examined.

The first, process, is often neglected in any kind of evaluation, where too often only the product is examined. Yet, without an appropriate process, products are unlikely to improve.

To my knowledge, there is no instrument to be used in order to evaluate the process of writing. Such evaluation is a matter of determining the extent to which procedures for a good writing program are followed by teachers and pupils. Your checklist, if you want such, might be made from the first chapter or from the Postscript in this book. It will consist of an examination of the extent to which pupils are engaged in prewriting, daily writing, conferencing, revising, publication, and so on.

It is important, in process evaluation, to look within these major divisions to observe how well pupils are using their time. In prewriting, are they actively contributing to a discussion; do they take time for preparation; and is that time profitably engaged? During the writing, is there also provision for alternation with reading, for using resources such as books or individual interviews; and are their pauses indications of some reconsideration of the writing or merely symptoms of confusion? Is revising practiced as a personal check on clarity; is peer assistance sought; and do these efforts result in some adjustment to the original draft?

Product evaluation is a matter of sampling the writings of students at each grade level—or at designated grade levels, if you prefer. This can be done once each year, preferably at each grade level, but alternate grades will serve the purpose providing the designated grade levels are consistent from year to year. If the writing to be evaluated is done at the same time of year, on essentially the same topic, and evaluated in the same manner each year, the district can establish its own "norms," in effect can have its own baseline data against which to check each year's progress in writing. More detailed information from school districts that have engaged in this kind of status evaluation can be found in Hillerich (1971a, 1971b) and McCaig (1981).

Of course, if desired, the school district—or classroom teacher—can go beyond this kind of status evaluation of the program by using a detailed analytic scale to evaluate the same papers for strengths and weaknesses. Such an approach will provide diagnostic information for improving the program. For example, perhaps most of the papers are strong on unity/coherence but present some weaknesses in terms of sentence structure, word choice, or even certain mechanics. Such findings offer clues to program revision.

Unfortunately, we have no perfect instrument to "assess" the quality of written products. Nevertheless, we have a number that offer a reasonable evaluation of those products. Furthermore, since evaluation of a subject area is more likely to encourage its teaching, we ought to use what we have until better instruments become available, and the device or devices we choose ought to be selected in terms of our goals or purposes in that subject area.

Table 13.1 provides a summary of the various procedures that can be used for the three purposes just discussed. It can serve as a guide to the following section, which discusses each of these procedures.

TABLE 13.1. Summary of information outcomes from the various methods of evaluating.

PROCEDURE	REPORTING (TO PUPIL/PARENT)	DIAGNOSIS (INDIVIDUAL)	PROGRAM EVALUATION (GROUP)
Process[a]	Inform on direction, past and present.	Clues to needed instruction.	Clues to needed changes in program.
Norm-Referenced	Status of individual.	No value.	Status of group.
Analytic	Instructional detail.	Information for specific needs.	Detail for specific needs.
Primary Trait	Information on the trait.	Information on the trait.	Information on the trait.
Holistic: Global	Status only.	No value.	Status only.
Holistic: Rubric	Detail on rubric items.	Detail on rubric items.	Detail on rubric items.
Words/T-Unit	Status; possible clues re: sentence construction.	Possible clues re: sentence construction.	Status of group; possible clues re: sentence construction.
Linguistic Analyses	Detail on linguistic patterns.	Clues of linguistic needs.	Clues to linguistic needs for group.

[a] "Process" is not a device or an instrument, but it is included here as a procedure not to be forgotten in the process of evaluation.

METHODS OF EVALUATING

Some educators might raise the question: Is evaluation of writing a threat to creativity? I believe it is more a threat to mediocrity if done properly. If we are to improve skill in writing, we *must* evaluate the degree to which we accomplish this goal. However, several points must be kept in mind.

First, the method of evaluation must be chosen to match the goals and purposes for writing, as well as the use to which results will be put and the audience to whom the results will be reported. An evaluation of status can be helpful in program evaluation, whereas more diagnostic information is needed for improving instruction and even for reporting accomplishments to parents or student.

Second, evaluation may be either short term or long term. The former may be important on a day-to-day basis as you attempt to improve one skill at a time with the individual. The latter must be a prime concern in program evaluation, whether in classroom or school district, as we look to the ultimate accomplishments of students. I recall the difficult position of allowing short-term goals to suffer for the long-term results in a school district where written expression was emphasized at the expense of mechanics in the primary grades. Naturally, results of standardized testing at the beginning of grade four were disastrous. The payoff came at grade seven with the first group of these students, where the writing and interest were not only improved, but scores for "correctness" of mechanics were higher than ever before.

A third factor to consider in choosing a method of evaluating is how evaluation is to be reported, and to whom. Again, there is an interrelationship with the previous points: If the goal is merely to report relative status of the individual to the parent, a status measure—even a standardized test—can be used. If the goal is to improve instruction, some more diagnostic device is essential. Furthermore, results must be in a different form for parents as opposed to educators, since the former are not likely to understand some of the educational jargon we frequently use.

Finally, any device chosen must be considered in terms of the limitations of time, and especially time that might be taken from instruction. Hence, it seems that a writing sample, which is in itself a learning process, can also be used as the basis for evaluation, as opposed to a standardized instrument that takes time from instruction and offers no substantive educational value to the student. In this frame of reference, there is also a likelihood that evaluation will be a continuous process; it will not be an unrelated activity arbitrarily inserted into the ongoing program.

Overview of Methods

One classification of evaluation procedures is their grouping as either "atomistic" or "holistic." The former group includes all procedures that rely on a *count* and summation of individual features of a piece of writing: checklists, norm-referenced tests, number of words used per T-unit, and so on. A commonly accepted definition of "holistic" evaluation is that of Cooper (1977): "I am using the term 'holistic' to mean any procedure which stops short of enumerating linguistic, rhetorical, or informational features of a piece of writing [p. 4]."

This neat dichotomy, although theoretically discrete, becomes a little blurred in practice. "Holistic" approaches include everything from an almost-pure holistic evaluation in the case of "general impression" scoring to the nearly atomistic use to which some raters put the "analytic scale" method. Nevertheless, the distinction is maintained by the fact that atomistic approaches are a matter of counting; holistic depend upon a sorting of quality in relation to certain "anchor" or example papers for each of the levels of quality.

Holdzkom and others (1980) separate several methods that Cooper classifies together as holistic methods. They refer to "holistic," "analytical," and "primary trait" scoring separately, and this seems best for our purposes here, since these three are quite different degrees of holistic evaluation. We'll begin with an explanation of the two major atomistic forms, norm-referenced tests and number of words used per T-unit, and continue with the holistic methods: Holdzkom's "holistic" or general impression, primary trait, and analytic scale.

Norm-Referenced Tests

There seems to be little question that many norm-referenced tests are reliable: A given test will consistently provide very similar results for the same student. On the other hand, many question these tests' validity: Do they truly measure skill in writing by merely measuring accuracy of mechanics and usage? Yet reports indicate that results of such tests do correlate well with measures of actual writing (Stiggins, 1982; Charney, 1984).

Of course, we could go into a tirade about our educational disease of correlation. Suffice it to say that mechanics, as well as IQ, age, experience, and so on, all *correlate* with writing skill, but do you want to use such measures to evaluate your writing program? Conversely, if the goal is merely to arrive at a status measure for the group, norm-referenced tests are one viable alternative.

Following are some examples of such norm-referenced tests. Anyone considering use of any of these is advised to consult the current edition of *Tests in Print* for additional information and evaluative comments.

1. The language section of any of the major achievement test batteries:

    California Test of Basic Skills
    Iowa Test of Basic Skills

Metropolitan Achievement Test
SRA Achievement Test
Stanford Achievement Test
The 3-R's Test

2. Language Arts: IOX Objectives-Based Tests (Grades K–6)
3. Language Arts Diagnostic Probes (Grades 3–9)
4. Sequential Tests of Educational Progress: English Expression (Grades 4–6, 7–9)
5. Sequential Tests of Educational Progress: Mechanics of Writing (Grades 4–6, 7–9)

Words per T-Unit

As stated in Chapter 3, the best single measure of sophistication in language use, oral or written, is the number of words used per T-unit (Hunt, 1965; Loban, 1976; O'Donnell, 1967). A T-unit is defined as any independent clause with all of its subordinate clauses and modifiers. Not only is this seemingly mechanical technique for determining sophistication of language supported by research, it is verified by common sense. Compare the following two ten-word sentences stating essentially the same idea:

> It started to rain, and we went into the house.
>
> When it started to rain, we went into the house.

The first sentence of ten words is a compound sentence and therefore consists of two T-units: "It started to rain" and "and we went into the house." Hence, this writer used an average of five words per T-unit. In contrast, the second sentence, a complex sentence, has only one independent clause and is therefore one T-unit of ten words. It is more sophisticated to subordinate ideas within the same sentence, and, conversely, more sophisticated thinking tends to be expressed in more complex sentences.

Of course, this means of evaluation is not appropriate to atypical writing, whether poetry, stream of consciousness, or the prose of a new Hemingway. Furthermore, it is not diagnostic, since it provides only a measure of relative status.

In its support, the T-unit measure is objective and reliable, for individuals or for groups, if the goal is to determine relative status or growth from one period to the next. Hence, this can be a useful and inexpensive device for assessing, on a random sampling basis, the effectiveness of the writing program in terms of improvement from year to year in the school district—or in the classroom—so long as the type of writing used is similar for each assessment period.

This latter caution is based on findings of Crowhurst and Piche (1979), who reported that the same student used more words per T-unit when writing persuasive or argumentative pieces than when writing narrative or descriptive ones. Once more, common sense verifies this point: Persuasive or argumentative writing will include sentences expanded with clauses such as "because..."

Table 13.2, although certainly not intended as a table of norms, provides some indication of the number of words per T-unit that one might expect at different grade levels.

TABLE 13.2. Words per T-unit written at various grade levels.

	CROWHURST AND PICHE (1979)	HILLERICH (1971)	HUNT (1965)	LOBAN (1976)[a]	O'DONNELL (1967)
Grade					
3				7.60	7.67
4		10.08	8.6	8.02	
5		10.44		8.76	9.34
6	10.13–11.75	10.98		9.04	
7		11.48		8.94	9.99
8		11.65	11.5	10.37	
9				10.05	
10	11.15–14.26			11.79	

[a]Loban's "random group"

As shown in the table, there is no precise agreement as to the number of words per T-unit that students at a given grade level will use. Crowhurst and Piche provide a range because of the different types of writing used in that study. Hillerich's results tend higher, possibly because the sample was from a suburban school district where writing had been a major emphasis. Although these figures can serve as a basis for comparison, any school district planning to use this technique to evaluate the success of its writing program is advised to develop its own benchmarks in order to determine how students in that district are progressing from year to year and how the program is improving writing skill at each grade level from year to year.

Holistic: General Impression

Many educators in the field of writing instruction see holistic evaluations as the most valid: They measure what they are supposed to measure—the total ability to communicate in writing. On the other hand, they can be the least reliable, since there is so much opportunity for subjectivity on the part of the raters.

"General Impression" evaluations are just that: evaluations based on general impression. The evaluators very quickly read each paper and place it in a rank order, from best to poorest. This may sound much like the traditional scoring that led to wide discrepancies among raters, but it is not. Reliability, in the sense of interrater agreement, is increased in proportion to (1) the speed with which the papers are read, (2) similarity of the background of the raters, (3) use of anchor papers for comparison, and (4) averaging of the ratings of at least two raters.

The procedure will usually begin by bringing together a group of qualified writing teachers who will discuss what they look for in a piece of writing. Such discussion will contribute to some commonality of objectives. Once this is done, each will rapidly read and rank a trial sampling of papers, globally, on a scale. Myers (1980) suggested that the scale have an even number of degrees—1–4, 1–6, or 1–8—in order to avoid the fence-straddling tendency of raters to throw questionable papers into the middle category. Not only do I concur, I suggest also limiting the number of categories to four, since the use of six or eight implies more precision than I think most raters are capable of.

Once an initial ranking has been done, raters are ready to begin their real work. Now they must compare ratings on given papers, discuss reasons for their differences in order to resolve them, and ultimately select "anchor" papers, that is, papers that will exemplify each of the four ranks in their rating scheme. These anchor papers will then serve as the benchmark against which all papers from a new evaluation will be measured.

It is this training that brings raters together with common objectives and ensures greater reliability. Of course, the papers to be evaluated in the final round must be of the same mode as the anchor papers. It would not do to arrive at anchor papers based on expressive writing and then use these to evaluate papers based on transactional writing.

As you see, general impression scoring offers still another means of determining status, whether of the individual or of the group, whether a relative status in terms of other individuals or groups, or as a relative status in terms of the previous status of that individual or group. It offers no diagnostic information and is most useful as a means of evaluating a program, unless one is looking for an arbitrary assessment for promotion or graduation.

Holistic: Primary Trait

"Primary Trait" evaluation has been used in the National Assessment of Educational Progress and is reported very successful. This technique has been fully explicated by Lloyd-Jones (1977), who pointed out its underlying assumption: "...that excellence in one sample of one mode of writing predicts excellence in other modes—that is, good writing is good writing [p. 37]."

As explained by Lloyd-Jones, the first task of the scoring team is to devise writing assignments that will stimulate the best writing of which students are capable within the confines of the type of writing to be evaluated. The assigned writing must specify a topic, a purpose, and an audience. Further, the topic must be within the experience of the writers. He also suggested that proposed exercises be tried out on students to be certain that they effectively elicit the kind of writing intended.

Once the stimuli have been determined, detailed scoring guides must be developed. These will include, among other things, a clear statement of the primary trait to be evaluated, a rubric identifying specific elements for evaluation, preliminary anchor papers scored with the rubric, and subsequent discussion of why each paper was scored as it was.

As you see, primary trait scoring is a complex procedure that most school districts, not to mention teachers, would not find feasible. Results of such scoring might offer little more practical information than the general impression scoring discussed previously.

Holistic: Analytic Scale

In my view, the most promising and helpful of the holistic procedures is the analytic scale. I see it as a refinement of the general impression scoring, a refinement that adds reliability to the scoring and strength to the evaluative team. On a continuum of complexity, it might be placed about midway between general impression scoring and primary trait.

Analytic evaluation is general impression scoring with the prior addition of a rubric, a set of qualities that the evaluating team agrees upon as those to be evaluated in the pieces of writing. Hence, in effect it brings the hidden agenda out on the table. Although general impression scoring recognizes the importance of commonality of background and includes provision for team definition of the sought-for qualities in writing, analytic scoring requires listing of those qualities up front. Admittedly, after a trial run with papers, the rubric agreed upon might be modified, and possibly should be, but at least all readers have a guide to use.

Myers (1980) took no position on this in his discussion of holistic scoring, indicating that a rubric may be developed before or after the scoring. It seems to me a time-saving device to bring the qualities out for discussion *before* an initial evaluation, if not to awaken some new ideas in different team members, at least to avoid the danger of some becoming more entrenched in their preexisting criteria.

Whether consciously or not, anyone who evaluates a piece of writing is using some criterion, be it correctness of mechanics, usage, creative ideas, organization, or even handwriting. The development of a rubric helps evaluators to bring their criteria to a conscious level, to evaluate those criteria with peers, and to arrive at some consensus.

It should come as no surprise that, as I've had teachers develop rubrics in writing groups over the years, there is a remarkable similarity in the rubrics from different groups. Experienced teachers of writing—especially after having discussed qualities of a good writing program—have some common criteria in mind; the rubric is an expression of those criteria. Nevertheless, I would never begin an evaluation of writing by providing the evaluators with a rubric. To do so is to give them a list of words that have no flesh on them, meaningless terms such as *organization, fluency, transitions,* and so on. It is in the process of verbalizing and devising their own rubric that teachers bring meaning to these terms. Hence, the following rubrics are offered only as examples of the kinds of items that make up a rubric; they are not offered as models to be used by any group.

After outlining the major points they were looking for in a piece of writing, one elementary team defined each in terms of the following four degrees of quality:

Organization

1 = lacks sense or organization, unclear, confusing.
2 = disjointed thoughts, doesn't follow topic.
3 = shows thought, focuses on main idea, has a sequence.
4 = well organized, smooth transitions, main idea expanded.

Sentence Structure and Word Choice

1 = lacks any sentence structure.
2 = some sentences incomplete or choppy or all connected with *and.*

3 = complete sentences, but lacks variety and expansion.

4 = complete sentences, variety of sentence beginnings and structures; precision in word choice.

Creativity

1 = dull, uninteresting.

2 = lacks original thought, but clear.

3 = uses concrete examples, has moments of originality but lacks power.

4 = lively, unique, exciting, concrete, and vivid.

Fluency

1 = 0–25 words.

2 = 26–50 words.

3 = 51–75 words.

4 = 76 or more words.

Mechanics

1 = riddled with mechanical errors.

2 = some capitalization and punctuation errors, many spelling errors.

3 = fewer mechanical errors.

4 = nearly perfect.

You will notice in these examples that this group combined sentence structure and word choice. Many prefer to keep them separate. Likewise, fluency was used as a measure of skill in writing. At the primary level, fluency—just the number of words written in response to a topic in a given period of time—is a valid measure of skill.

Other teams have developed very similar rubrics. Without listing the definitions of the four levels for each criterion, let me merely show another outline from a different writing group.

Clarity/Organization: Sequence and Transitions; on Topic

Style to Fit Purpose

Vocabulary: Richness and Appropriateness

Originality/Creativity

Mechanics: Capitalization, Punctuation, Spelling, Paragraphing.

If the evaluative task deals with narrative writing by upper grades, evaluators would also include use of dialogue as part of the criteria, just as persuasive writing would be evaluated in part by the existence of support for arguments. Instead of the all-encompassing rubric, separate criteria can be developed for each type of writing that might be evaluated, thus approaching Lloyd-Jones's primary trait evaluation.

As with general impression scoring, once the rubric has been developed and clarified, readers are to read and make decisions rapidly; they are not to debate or keep score on each item of the rubric. For this reason, if no other, I believe that it is important to keep the rubric short: Longer lists become unwieldly and encourage more debate and score keeping. Likewise, other procedures outlined under general impression scoring apply here. Once an initial reading of a set of papers has been completed, the group of raters will share their ratings and discuss reasons for each rating where they differ. From this discussion, papers will be reevaluated if necessary and certain ones selected to serve as anchors for the scoring of future papers.

It seems that the value of this kind of holistic scoring lies in the fact that the unreliable subjective evaluation based on unstated criteria is replaced by a collection of subjective judgments based on the agreed-upon rubric. A subjective judgment based on six or so specific criteria is made more objective than what might be one subjective criterion in some rater's mind.

Nevertheless, I've found that, even with an agreed-upon rubric, teachers have difficulty in evaluating the writing of their own students. They know those kids! Fred's paper might be classed as a *1* by everyone else, but his teacher gives it a *3* because this is an example of Fred's supreme effort. It is difficult to avoid such biases so evaluation should be blind wherever possible.

Although included under the general classification of "holistic" techniques, some analytic rubrics become so elaborate that they approach the atomistic, providing weighted points for each criterion on the rubric. One such, designed for middle school, provides different weights for each criterion, as shown below:

Creativity

1 = dull, uninteresting.

2 = skeletal, needs excitement and life.

3 = moments of originality, lacks power.

4 = stellar, lively, exciting, different.

Value: _____ × 9 = _____

Organization and Development

1 = confusing, no support or transitions, unorganized, no conclusion.

2 = disjointed, unclear purpose and topic, support weak or unclear.

3 = focused on one idea, but more support and detail needed, some transitions.

4 = clearly organized on topic; logical, smooth transitions.

Value: _____ × 7 = _____

Mechanics

1 = no initial capitalization, no end marks, misspellings of basic words.

2 = some capitalization/punctuation errors, many misspellings.

3 = a few errors, internal punctuation problems.

4 = nearly perfect, no errors in items covered in class.

Value: _____ × 4 = _____

Sentence Structure

1 = many fragments/run-ons, verb tense, lacks subject–verb agreement.

2 = a few fragments/run-ons, errors in pronoun/modifier.

3 = a few usage errors, some sentence variety, needs improved subordination.

4 = good sentence variety with coordination and subordination, correct usage.

Value: _____ × 4 = _____

Legibility

1 = nearly illegible.

2 = carelessly written, poor letter formation.

3 = poor alignment, legible but could be neater.

4 = a joy to read, neatly written.

Value: _____ × 1 = _____

TOTAL SCORE: _____

Any attempt to use this analytic rubric would certainly slow the reader and therefore detract from one of the major points in holistic scoring—rapid reading. On the other hand, such a rubric adds the potential of some diagnostic information if that is the goal. Again, purposes of evaluating should determine the means used.

Holistic evaluation in general is a ranking system and is best used for determining ranks of individuals or groups, either in terms of other individuals or groups, or in terms of that individual's or group's growth over time.

Table 13.3, from Spandel and Stiggins (1980), compares strengths and weaknesses of some of the measures of writing discussed.

Other Techniques

Unlike the sophisticated primary trait evaluation proposed by Lloyd-Jones, a single trait might be evaluated on all pieces of writing. This can be a particularly quick, efficient, and effective tool if an entire school is focusing on one major writing skill during a period of time. For example, if the goal is improving sequencing in writing, a topic that requires some sequencing can be assigned and themes evaluated on that one point only.

Going beyond the rubrics provided in this chapter, which are similar to others used about the country (Whitelaw, 1984), Wilkinson and others (1983) describe a rubric used in the British Commonwealth. Their rubric deals with four much broader areas: cognitive, affective, moral, and stylistic. Theirs is an attempt to evaluate on a broad base the varieties of discourse the child may be using.

Offering what is more likely a research tool than a practical means for teachers to use, Finn (1977) supports a count of mature word choice as a measure of quality in writing. This atomistic measure is the number of infrequent words used in the piece of writing. Although the procedure is suggested for computer use, at least awareness of the influence of unusual words on the part of the teacher can contribute to that teacher's ability to identify well-written papers.

Fluency, number of words written in a given period of time, was mentioned as another means of measuring skill in writing at the primary level. If all one wants is a relative ranking or a measure of growth, this is a quick and effective measure. Use samples of timed writing on a topic and establish "norms" for each grade level. Then, at a later time, posttest children on the same type of topic for the same length of time. In one such study, after a year of intense effort on writing, Hillerich (1971b)

TABLE 13.3. A Comparison of scoring methods for direct writing assessment.

DESCRIPTOR	HOLISTIC	ANALYTICAL
General Capabilities	Comprehensive, general picture of student performance; writing viewed as a unified coherent whole. Applicable to any writing task.	Thorough, trait-by-trait analysis of writing; provides comprehensive picture of performance *if* enough traits are analyzed; traits are those important to *any* piece of writing in *any* situation (*e.g.,* organization, wording, mechanics).
Reliability	High reliability if standards are carefully established and raters are carefully trained.	High reliability if criteria and standards are well defined, and careful training is conducted.
Preparation Time	Up to one day per item to identify range finder (model) papers; up to one-half day to train readers using 4-point scale; full day to train with 8-point scale.	One full day to identify traits; one day per trait to develop scoring criteria (unless traits and criteria are borrowed from another source); one to two days to review results of pilot test and refine traits or criteria as necessary; one-half day to train raters.
Readers	Qualified language arts personnel recommended; high reliability can be achieved with non–language arts readers given sufficient training.	Qualified language arts personnel recommended.
Scoring Time	One to two minutes per paper (experienced readers may read faster).	One to two minutes per paper per trait.
Classroom Use	May be adapted for use in class.	May be adapted for use in class.
Reporting	Allows reporting on students' overall writing skill.	Allows reporting of student performance on wide range of generalizable traits (*i.e.,* the qualities considered important to all good writing).
Group/Sample Size[a]	Primarily usable with a larger sample; with a small sample, responses may be difficult to scale.	Best with smaller samples; extensive scoring time *may* make costs prohibitive with larger groups.

[a]These are very general guidelines. Due to the nature of the scoring-cost/amount-of-information trade-off across scoring methods, readers are urged to seek the technical assistance of a qualified writing assessment specialist if there is a question regarding the appropriate use of available scoring resources.

TABLE 13.3. (continued)

PRIMARY TRAIT	WRITING MECHANICS	T-UNIT ANALYSIS
Highly focused analysis of situation-specific primary trait (and possibly secondary traits); provides specific information on a narrowly defined writing task (*e.g.,* ability to recount details in chronological order).	Can provide either a general or a specific profile of the student's ability to use mechanics properly.	Provides a measure of syntactical sophistication.
High reliability if criteria and standards are well defined and careful training is conducted.	High reliability if given sufficient training time and authoritative, complete, acceptable guidelines (*e.g.,* an English handbook).	High reliability, provided trained and experienced raters are used.
One full day to identify traits; one day per trait to develop scoring criteria (unless traits and criteria are borrowed from another source); one to two days to review results of pilot test and refine traits or criteria as necessary; one-half day to train raters.	One to two days to set up a scoring system (unless borrowed from another source). Minimum of one day to internalize the scoring system and practice scoring.	Half day to full day, depending on raters' previous experience.
Qualified language arts personnel recommended, non–language arts staff may be able to score some traits.	Qualified language arts personnel recommended.	Raters *must* be experienced language arts personnel, preferably those already familiar with the concept of T-unit analysis.
One to two minutes per paper per trait.	Five minutes or more per paper, depending on number of criteria.	Varies greatly, depending on raters' skill.
May be adapted for use in class.	May be adapted for use in class.	May be adapted for use in class.
Allows reporting of student performance on one or more situation-specific traits important to a particular task.	Allows reporting of group or individual data on students' general strengths or weaknesses in mechanics.	Allows group or individual reporting on syntactical sophistication.
Generally more cost-effective with smaller samples, depending on the number of traits to be scored (with one trait, sample size is not an issue).	Best with small samples; extensive scoring time *may* make costs prohibitive with larger groups.	Best with smaller samples; extensive scoring time *may* make costs prohibitive with larger groups.

From *Direct Measures of Writing Skill: Issues and Applications* by Vicki Spandel and Richard J. Stiggins, NWREL, Portland, OR. 1980.

found the average first-grader at the 57th percentile of the base year, the average second-grader at the 66th, and the average third-grader at the 74th percentile.

A variety of sophisticated linguistic analyses is also available for use in evaluating writing. These analyses can offer some diagnostic information in terms of needed language development. Fagan and others (1975) described more than a dozen such instruments.

A Word of Caution

In a summary of research on the subject, Charney (1984) pointed out some weaknesses in the use of holistic scoring. First, one might consider evaluations based on a sample of writing more valid than norm-referenced testing because the latter does not evaluate writing itself. On the other hand, are the criteria devised by one set of evaluators more valid as indicators of writing proficiency than those developed by others? Furthermore, speed of reading is recognized as an important factor in reliability. Yet this very factor precludes any thoughtful evaluation of the piece of writing.

Despite the fact that the evaluation is supposed to be holistic or impressionistic, other research has indicated that quality of handwriting influences even trained raters, as does word choice, length of essay, and spelling errors.

Nonetheless, educators are faced with the need—in fact, the demand—for evaluating writing. Hence, while recognizing the fallibility of existing methods of holistic scoring, at least they have the face validity of being measures of actual writing as opposed to mere measures of correlates of writing skill. Used with this caveat in mind, holistic techniques can be useful in evaluating—if not measuring—skill in written language.

SUMMARY

Because any evaluation ought to be in terms of objectives or goals, this chapter began with such a discussion, suggesting that the purpose of writing is to communicate clearly and effectively on a topic with an intended audience. Hence, the means for evaluating ought to reflect this.

Evaluation is engaged in for a variety of purposes, including reporting, diagnosis, and program evaluation. Reporting requires specifics if it is to be effective, with relative status possibly being reported once each year. Diagnosis, whether of an individual or a group, also requires specifics, whereas program evaluation may be accomplished with a status measure or may also include diagnostic information that will lead to specified changes in the program.

A variety of methods for evaluating writing were discussed, along with procedures for use and the purposes they seem to serve best. All were subsumed under one of two categories: atomistic or holistic.

Atomistic procedures are counts of surface features and provide only a measure of status, either of individuals or of groups. These include standardized tests and counts of the number of words used per T-unit. Of the two, I prefer the latter, which has been found to be the best single measure of sophistication in writing and which comes closer to an evaluation of language skill than does the usual norm-referenced count of mechanics.

Holistic procedures were divided into three types: general impression, primary trait, and analytic scale. All of these are measures of the actual effectiveness of pieces of writing, and therefore, seem more valid. They also all require advance training of the raters to ensure some commonality in criteria used for evaluating, establishment of "anchor" papers to provide examples of each level of writing skill, discussion of results of a trial run to work out differences in ratings, and a final run on the papers to be evaluated.

General impression scoring is done by a fast reading of the papers. Addition of a rubric usually classifies the type of evaluation as primary trait or analytic scale, even though there is not a clear distinction in some cases. Primary trait, reported by Lloyd-Jones, is the most involved, including an extensive set of criteria for each of the modes of writing to be evaluated.

The analytic scale seems to be the most feasible for most schools and for most teachers. This is a matter of developing a simple rubric of four to six major criteria, establishing anchor papers based on fast reading with these criteria in mind, reaching a consensus about papers where there is disagreement, possibly refining the rubric, and then evaluating a set of papers. A four-point scale avoids the tendency to place questionable papers in the middle category.

More intricate analytic scales, with weighted values, were also discussed. These approach the atomistic in their handling but can be of some use for diagnostic purposes.

The chapter concluded with a word of caution. Although great strides have been made in overcoming the lack of interrater agreement traditionally reported in evaluating writing, none of the techniques is perfect. Meanwhile, however, if we are to improve written expression, we must use the best we have at present in order to evaluate our success.

SUGGESTIONS FOR ACTION

1. What method of evaluating do you use in preparing to report to pupils or parents? Try keeping a record of specifics, with example papers, for the next reporting period.

2. How do you evaluate the success of your writing program in your classroom? Do you know whether you are doing a better job each year? Try establishing some baseline data. You might, each year at the same time, merely get a sample of writing from the entire group and evaluate in terms of the number of words used per T-unit. Are students getting more sophisticated in their use of language each year?

3. Is your school engaged in any kind of total assessment of writing skill? You might at least get something started at a few grade levels, or only at your grade if there are several classes at that level. Try, with the other teachers, developing a simple rubric and using it on a sampling of papers. How well do you agree in your evaluations?

4. Have you considered an evaluation of the writing process in your class or in the school? Use the chapter headings and main ideas, or the guide in the Postscript following this chapter, to evaluate how well the appropriate process of writing is being followed. If it is reasonably represented in your class or school, you can rest assured that the product is improving.

5. Some schools that have engaged in holistic evaluation have compiled a booklet of anchor papers for each grade level. This serves as an excellent reference for each teacher to use in comparing the writing in his or her class with the models of the different levels. You might suggest such a compilation for your school or district.

6. With older students, work with them to develop a rubric and have them serve as the evaluators for a set of papers. If you do this, it is advisable to use papers without names, since personal knowledge of the writer biases even teacher judgment.

REFERENCES

CHARNEY, DAVIDA, The Validity of Using Holistic Scoring to Evaluate Writing: A Critical Review," *Research in the Teaching of English, 18* (February, 1984), 65–81. Summarizes research to question the validity of holistic scoring.

COOPER, CHARLES R., "Holistic Evaluation Writing," in Cooper, Charles R., and Lee Odell, *Evaluating Writing: Describing, Measuring, Judging.* Urbana: National Council of Teachers of English, 1977, pp. 3–31. Describes various means of holistic evaluation.

CROWHURST, MARION, and GENE L. PICHE, "Audience and Mode of Discourse Effects on Syntactic Complexity in Writing at Two Grade Levels," *Research in the Teaching of English,* 13 (May, 1979), 101–9. At grades six and ten, compares words used per T-unit in three modes of writing: narrative, descriptive, argumentative.

FAGAN, WILLIAM T., CHARLES R. COOPER, and JULIE M. JENSEN, *Measures for Research and Evaluaton in the English Language Arts.* Urbana: National Council of Teachers of English, 1975, pp. 183–207. Lists and describes devices used in the evaluation of written expression.

HILLERICH, ROBERT L., "Evaluation of Written Language," *Elementary English,* 48 (November, 1971), 839–42. Describes procedures and results of a school district's evaluation of written language.

————, "A Second Evaluation of Written Language," *Illinois School Research,* 7 (Winter, 1971), 28–31. Reports a follow-up of the previous article.

HOLDZKOM, DAVID, LINDA J. REED, E. JANE PORTER, and DONALD L. RUBIN, *Research within Reach: Oral and Written Communication.* Washington, D.C.: National Institute of Education, 1980, pp. 151–60. Describes several methods of evaluating writing: holistic, analytical, primary trait, and per T-unit.

HUNT, KELLOGG W., *Grammatical Structures Written at Three Grade Levels.* Urbana: National Council of Teachers of English, 1965. Reports on the use of words per T-unit.

LLOYD-JONES, RICHARD, "Primary Trait Scoring," in Cooper, Charles R., and Lee Odell, *Evaluating Writing: Describing, Measuring, Judging.* Urbana: National Council of Teachers of English, 1977, pp. 33–66. Describes procedures for primary trait scoring with two examples of its application.

LOBAN, WALTER D., *Language Development: Kindergarten through Grade Twelve.* Urbana: National Council of Teachers of English, 1976. Describes oral and written language development, supporting the use of words per T-unit ("communication unit") as a measure of sophistication in language.

McCaig, Roger A., "A District-Wide Plan for the Evaluation of Student Writing," in Haley-James, Shirley (ed.), *Perspectives on Writing in Grades 1–8.* Urbana: National Council of Teachers of English, 1981, pp. 73–92. Outlines a district-wide plan for evaluating writing.

McCready, Michael, and Virginia S. Melton, "Feasibility of Assessing Writing Using Multiple Assessment Techniques," Research Report, December, 1981, ED 220–871. Reports on the status of assessment and kinds of devices used.

Myers, Miles, *A Procedure for Writing Assessment and Holistic Scoring.* Urbana: National Council of Teachers of English, 1980. An excellent and thorough description of procedures for holistic scoring.

National Assessment of Educational Progress, *Writing Objectives for 1973–74 Assessment.* Denver: Education Commission of the States, 1972. Provides background and listing of the objectives.

———, *Writing Objectives for 1983–84 Assessment.* Denver: Education Commission of the States, 1982. Provides background and listing of objectives.

O'Donnell, Roy, William Griffin, and Raymond Norris, *Syntax of Kindergarten and Elementary School Children: A Transformational Analysis.* Urbana: National Council of Teachers of English, 1967. Reports on oral and written evaluation of language of 180 pupils in grades kindergarten through three, five, and seven, supporting use of words per T-unit as a measure of language development.

Spandel, Vicki, and Richard J. Stiggins, *Direct Measures of Writing Skill: Issues and Applications.* Portland, Oregon: Northwest Regional Educational Laboratory, Center for Applied Performance Testing, 1980. Describes various methods of scoring writing samples, providing strengths and weaknesses of each.

Stiggins, Richard J., "A Comparison of Direct and Indirect Writing Assessment Methods," *Research in the Teaching of English,* 16 (May, 1982), 101–14. Reports relationships in terms of correlation between norm-referenced tests and holistic scoring.

Whitelaw, Nancy, "How Do You Teach the Process of Writing?" *Early Years,* 14 (March, 1984), 52–54. Describes a rubric for writing used by the New York State Department of Education.

Wilkinson, Andrew, Gillian Barnsley, Peter Hanna, and Margaret Swan, "More Comprehensive Assessment of Writing Development," *Language Arts,* 60 (October, 1983), 871–81. Describes a model for evaluating growth in writing based on evaluation of cognitive, affective, moral, and stylistic development.

Postscript

THIS BOOK BEGAN with an overview, a compass pointing direction. As you might have suspected, it never quite got to the road map, indicating specifically which turns to take at what intervals, or even which junction to expect next. So it is with writing. Individuals begin from different points, move at different rates, and even take different routes on their way to becoming proficient—or at least competent—writers. Hence, it seems advisable to recheck that compass briefly as we part.

The guide on the following pages represents some of the highlights of a good writing program, in effect a summary of some of the major points of this book. You are hereby given permission to reproduce this guide for use in your class and are encouraged to share it with your fellow teachers and administrators. If you can agree on many of the points listed, you have a good writing program and, as a result, will have youngsters who can write, who do write, and who enjoy writing.

A GUIDE TO EVALUATING THE WRITING PROCESS

How consistently does your program provide for the following?

	Never	Sometimes	Usually
Prewriting			
1. The classroom environment stimulates writing.	___	___	___
2. Pupils write on topics of their chosing.	___	___	___
3. Prewriting includes time for reflecting on or collecting information.	___	___	___
4. Prewriting activities aid in planning/composing.	___	___	___
5. Prewriting allows for pupil interaction.	___	___	___
Writing			
6. The teacher writes with pupils on the same activity.	___	___	___
7. Oral language is related to print, especially in the case of younger pupils.	___	___	___
8. A workshop atmosphere prevails, with pupils at various stages in their own pieces of writing.	___	___	___
9. Sustained Silent Writing (SSW) is used to increase fluency.	___	___	___
10. Pupils maintain logs or journals.	___	___	___
11. Pupils write daily.	___	___	___
12. Some writing is done without concern for evaluation.	___	___	___
13. Writing is done in the content areas to discover what is known.	___	___	___
14. Writing is done for a variety of purposes.	___	___	___
15. Writing is done in a variety of modes.	___	___	___
16. Pupils write for a variety of audiences.	___	___	___

	Never	*Sometimes*	*Usually*

Conferencing

17. Informal conferences are held by the teacher.

18. Peer conferences are held with early drafts.

19. Peer evaluation is positive.

20. Formal teacher conferences are held on conference drafts.

Skill Instruction

21. Reading experience is related to writing.

22. Models from literature and class are used to illustrate good writing.

23. Procedures for peer evalution are taught.

24. Procedures for revision are taught.

25. Pretests are used for the spelling list.

26. Use of a dictionary for spelling is taught.

27. Mechanics are taught one at a time.

28. Reteaching of skills is done in small groups or individually.

29. Procedures for proofreading are taught.

30. Sentence-combining activities are practiced.

Editing

31. Pupils have criteria for evaluating.

32. Self-evaluation is included.

33. Evaluation focuses on content/ clarity.

34. Criteria for revision are shared.

35. Pupils revise their drafts.

36. Criteria for proofreading are shared.

	Never	Sometimes	Usually
Editing (continued)			
37. Pupils proofread final copy for publication.	—	—	—
Publishing			
38. Sharing of writings takes place in the classroom.	—	—	—
39. Writing is published in books, newspapers, on the bulletin board.	—	—	—
40. Purposeful letter writing takes place.	—	—	—
41. A Young Authors' Conference or other recognition is provided for writing.	—	—	—
Program Evaluation, School-Wide			
42. Provision is made for evaluating the process of writing.	—	—	—
43. Provision is made for evaluating the products of the writing.	—	—	—

APPENDIX: SPELLING LISTS

The placement tests and word lists presented here may be used for a school-wide spelling program, following procedures presented in Chapter 9.

Placement Tests

The following placement tests are representative in difficulty of the spelling words at that grade level. Administer the placement test for your grade in typical spelling-test fashion. The pupil must be able to spell correctly at least 50 percent of the words on pretest (with no previous study of the words) to be placed in that level word list. For example, the grade six pupil who cannot spell correctly at least 50 percent of the words in the grade six placement test should be given the test for grade five, grade four, and so on, until at least 50 percent of the words are spelled correctly. That level is the list level to be assigned.

Word Lists

Word lists are alphabetical, with each preceding grade level containing more frequently used—and therefore more important—words than the next level. The numeral after each word indicates the percent of pupils, from a population of approximately 500 per grade, who missed that word. For example, 1 = 10–19 percent, 2 = 20–29 percent, and so on. If there is no numeral after a word, that word was misspelled by fewer than 10 percent of pupils. Hence, by using this information you can establish weekly lists that are balanced for difficulty.

　　　The complete word lists for each grade are based on a composite developed from Carroll and others (1971), Hillerich (1978), Kucera and Francis (1967), and Rinsland (1945).

　　　Mastery of the words presented here, along with their regularly inflected forms, ensures the ability to spell correctly the following proportions of all words written by children or adults:

	Elementary Pupils (Hillerich)	Adults (Kucera/Francis)
Grade 2 Words	70%	55%
Grades 3–8 Words	28%	43%
Total for Grades 2–8	98%	98%

The remaining 2 percent of words can't be anticipated, and correctness of such infrequent words can be assured only through the *desire* and *ability* to use a dictionary for spelling.

Note that regularly inflected forms have been omitted from the lists. You may want to examine the list from a preceding grade level and include inflected forms of some of those previously taught words. Such a practice can serve as a good review of the base word and as an application of structural generalizations you may have taught about the spelling of inflected forms.

Placement Tests

Grade 3	Grade 4	Grade 5	Grade 6	Grade 7	Grade 8
also	fit	roof	equal	require	signature
chicken	yard	wipe	material	bitter	criticism
grow	reason	imagine	condition	majority	industrial
hadn't	block	return	knot	described	endure
paint	wreck	although	principal	appeal	rural
pretty	highway	straw	depend	flour	construction
Wednesday	nothing	wake	fountain	editor	acquaintance
pool	careful	yourself	chapter	possession	facilities
carry	mirror	pleasant	example	saucers	ability
always	whistle	worse	collar	mischief	stationery
which	fresh	scout	labor	occurred	organize
almost	able	sense	consider	relative	interior
boxes	October	speak	delight	committee	condemn
wear	button	whether	member	official	commerce
afraid	nobody	banana	neighbor-hood	gradually	sufficient
Saturday	cloth	regular	gather	journal	audience
sled	board	borrow	costume	appoint	doubtful
piece	feast	welcome	nickel	scratch	existence
using	plain	ache	effort	oppose	financial
brought	catcher	bar	chest	valued	proceed
	hotel	trunk	native	interrupt	freight
	league	receive	offer	coarse	reasonable
	special	upper	accept	solid	incline
	you're	neighbor	reward	immediate	perceive
	branch	sentence	pure	fortune	mathematics

Grade 2 Word List

a		can		from	3	lake		park		thing	
about	3	candy	3	fun		last	1	paw	1	think	5
after	4	cap		game	1	let	2	pen		this	1
all	1	car		gave	3	letter	6	people	7	three	3
am	1	card		get	1	like	2	pet	1	time	1
an	1	cat		girl	4	little	5	play	2	to	2
and		Christmas	7	give	2	live	1	put	1	today	
any	5	coat	4	glad	2	long	3	ran	1	told	3
apple	3	cold	2	go		look		read	4	too	3
are	2	come	1	good		lot	3	red		took	4
around	6	could	6	got	2	love	1	ride	2	toy	1
as	1	cow		green	2	made	2	ring		train	5
ask	4	dad	1	had	1	make	1	room	1	tree	1
at		daddy	3	hand		man		run	1	try	1
away	2	dark		happy	2	may		said	5	two	2
baby	3	day		has	1	me		Santa	4	up	
back	2	dear	3	hat		men	1	sat	1	us	1
bad	1	did	1	have	1	milk	1	saw	3	use	5
bag	1	didn't	7	he		money	2	say	3	very	4
ball	1	dinner	1	help	3	more		school	4	walk	
balloon	4	do	1	hen	1	morning	5	see		want	4
bang	5	dog		her	1	mother	2	she	1	was	1
bank		doll	2	here	1	mouse	1	sing	2	water	4
barn	1	don't	3	hill	2	much	3	sister	4	way	
be		down	2	him	1	my		sit	2	we	
because	7	dress	4	his		name	1	sleep	2	week	
bed	1	duck		hit		new	2	snow	2	well	2
been	4	eat	1	home	1	next	1	so	1	went	3
before	6	elf	1	house	4	nice		some	3	were	4
best		every	6	how	3	night	4	soon	3	wet	2
big		fast		hurt	6	no		start		what	4
bird	2	fat		I		not		stay		when	4
black	4	father	3	ice	2	now	2	stop	2	where	5
blue	4	feel	4	if	1	of	3	store	3	white	6
book		feet		in		off	2	story	4	who	4
boot	1	find	2	Indian	5	old		sun		will	1
box	1	fire	3	into		on		take	3	wish	3
boy	1	first	5	is		one	2	tell	2	with	3
bring	3	fish	1	it		or	1	that	1	work	3
brother	4	five	1	jaw	4	other	4	the		would	5
bus		fly	1	jump	2	our	4	their	7	year	
but		food	1	just	3	out	1	them	3	yellow	5
by	3	for	1	keep	4	over	3	then	2	yes	
cake		found	1	kitten	1	owl	1	there	5	you	
call	1	four	3	know	4	pan		they	5	your	3
came	1										

Grade 3 Word List

above	2	brown		dish	1	gate		kind	
across	2	bud		does	2	giant	1	king	
add	1	bug		doesn't	4	gift		kiss	1
afraid	3	bunny	1	done	2	gone	1	kite	
afternoon	1	burn	1	door		good-by	2	knew	2
again	4	buy	2	downstairs	3	grade	1	laid	3
ago		cage		dream	1	grass	1	lamp	
air	1	camp		drink		gray	1	land	
almost	2	cannot	1	drive	2	great	3	large	3
along		can't	1	drop	1	ground	2	late	2
also	2	carry	3	each	1	grow		lay	1
always	4	cart		ear		guess	3	learn	3
animal	4	catch	4	Easter	4	gun		leave	3
another	3	caught	4	egg		hadn't	3	left	1
anything	3	cent	1	eight	2	hair		leg	
arm	1	chair	2	end		hall		let's	2
art		change	2	even	1	ham		light	
ate	1	chicken	3	ever	1	hard		line	
aunt	3	chief	3	everybody	3	hay		lion	3
band		child	1	eye	1	head	1	lip	1
bark	1	children	2	face		hear	1	littlest	4
basket	2	church	3	fair	2	heard	4	lock	
bat		city	1	fall		hello	1	log	
bath		class	1	far		hid	1	lost	
bear	1	clay		farm	1	hide	1	loud	2
became		clean	1	fed	2	high	1	lovely	4
bee		clock	1	feed		hold	1	low	1
began	3	close	1	fell		hole	1	lunch	1
begin	2	clothes	4	few	2	hop		mad	
behind	1	color	3	fight	1	hope		mail	1
bell		cook	1	fill		horse	2	many	2
bet	2	cookies	3	fine		hot		mark	
better	2	corn	1	flag		hunt	1	mean	3
birthday	2	country	4	flat		ice cream	3	meat	1
bit	1	cream	1	floor	1	I'd	3	meet	2
blow	1	cry		flower	1	I'll	1	melt	
boat	1	cup		foot		I'm	1	merry	2
body	1	curl	4	fox		ink		met	2
bone		cut		Friday	1	inside		might	3
born	1	dance	1	friend	3	its	1	mile	1
both	2	dart		frog		it's	1	mine	
bread	1	deep	1	front	2	jar		miss	1
bright	1	desk	1	full	1	kept	3	mix	1
broke	3	dime	1	funny		key		Monday	1
brought	4	dirt	2	garden		kill		moon	

most		place	2	seed		storm	1	town	
move	1	plant	1	seen	2	stove		tribe	3
Mr.		please	1	sell	1	street	1	trip	1
Mrs.	2	pole		send		strong		truck	1
mud		pond	1	sent	1	summer	2	Tuesday	3
must		pony	1	set	1	Sunday		turn	1
near	1	pool		shall	2	supper	1	uncle	4
neck	1	poor	1	sheep		swim	1	under	
need		pretty	3	ship		swing		until	4
nest		pull		shop		table	1	upon	3
net		puppy	2	shot	1	talk	1	visit	4
never		push		should	3	tall		wait	2
nine		rabbit	2	show	1	tan		warm	1
nose	1	race	1	sick	1	teach	3	wash	1
number		rain	1	side		team	1	wasn't	3
nut		raw	3	six		ten		watch	4
oh	1	rest	1	skin		tent		wear	5
once	1	right	1	sky	1	test		Wednesday	7
only	2	river		sled	2	than	1	weed	2
open		road	1	slide		thank		we'll	3
outside		robin	1	small	1	that's	1	which	5
own	1	rock		snowball	1	these	2	while	2
paint	1	rope		soap	1	they're	6	why	2
pair	2	rose		someone	1	thick		win	
paper	1	round	1	something	1	third	4	window	1
part	1	rug	1	sometime	1	those	1	wing	
party	1	salt	1	song		thought	3	winter	1
pencil	4	same		sorry	1	throw	2	won	1
pick	1	sand		sound	1	Thursday	3	wood	
picture	3	sang		south	2	tiger	3	wool	
pie		Santa Claus	4	spell	1	tire	1	word	1
piece	5	Saturday	5	spring	1	tired	3	world	1
pig		says	4	stand		tonight		write	2
pin	1	sea		stick	1	top		yet	1
pink		second	2	still	1				

Grade 4 Word List

able	2	bike	1	chocolate	6	dug	1
act	2	bill		chop		during	3
age		bite	1	circle	2	dust	
agent	2	blew	2	circus	3	early	3
ahead	1	block	1	climb	2	earth	2
airplane	1	bloom	2	cloth	1	east	
airport	1	board	4	clothing	2	easy	2
alike		bottle	2	club	1	eighteen	3
alive		bottom	2	coal	3	either	3
alone	1	bought	3	coffee	5	else	4
already	3	bow	1	coin	1	engine	4
America	4	bowl	2	company	3	enjoy	2
amount	1	brain	2	cool	1	enough	4
angel	4	branch	1	corner	2	enter	1
ankle	5	brave		cost	1	escape	3
answer	3	break	2	cottage	2	eve	1
ant		breakfast	2	cotton	4	evening	4
anybody	2	brick		couldn't	4	everyone	2
anyway	2	brush	1	cousin	5	everything	1
April	2	bubble	3	cover		everywhere	2
aren't	2	build	3	crash	1	fairy	3
army	1	bullet	6	crew	1	family	3
arrow	1	bunch		cross	1	famous	3
asleep		bush	1	crown		farmer	1
attack	3	business	6	date		feast	
August	4	busy	3	daylight	1	feather	1
awake		butter		dead	1	February	7
awhile	3	button	4	death	2	felt	2
bake	1	cab		December	1	fence	1
bare	3	cabin	1	decide	3	field	3
barrel	3	cabinet	5	deer	1	fifteen	3
base	1	candle	2	desert	2	fifty	3
baseball	1	captain	3	diamond	7	finger	1
beach	1	care		die		finish	2
bean	1	careful	3	different	3	fireplace	1
beat	2	case		dig		fit	
beautiful	7	cast		dirty	1	fix	1
become		cattle	1	dive		flew	2
bedroom		cause	3	doctor	4	follow	3
beg	2	cave		dollar	4	forest	2
believe	7	certain	7	drank		forgive	
belong		chase	2	draw	1	forgot	
belt		cheese	3	drew	2	fort	1
beside		chew	1	drove	1	fourth	4
between	3	chick	1	dry	1	free	

Grade 4 Word List *(continued)*

freeze	2	interesting	2	midnight		phone	1
fresh	2	invite	2	mighty	4	picnic	3
fry	1	isn't	3	mind	1	pipe	1
fur	1	I've	3	minute	6	plain	4
ghost	2	jail		mirror		plan	
glass		January	4	Mister	3	plane	1
goat		jet		monkey	2	planet	3
gold		job		month	3	playground	1
grand		join	1	moss	3	plenty	1
grandfather		July	1	mostly	2	pocket	2
grandma	1	June	1	mountain	5	poem	3
grandmother		junk		mouth		point	1
grandpa	1	kid		movie	2	police	2
grew	2	kitchen	3	myself	1	pop	
gum		knee	2	nail		porch	1
gym	2	knife	2	nap		post	
half		lady	1	nearly	2	pot	
Halloween	3	lamb	1	newspaper		potato	3
hang	1	laugh	3	nobody	1	pound	2
happen	2	lawn		noise	2	present	2
hasn't	3	lead		noon	1	princess	3
haven't	2	league	9	north		probably	8
health	2	led	3	note		problem	2
heart	3	less		nothing	1	program	2
heat		library	3	November	1	purple	1
heavy	2	lie	1	nurse	1	queen	
held	1	life		oak	2	quick	3
herself		list		ocean		quiet	3
he's		listen	3	o'clock	1	quit	4
highway	1	load	2	October	1	quite	4
himself	1	loose	2	often	3	rainy	
history	1	luck		oil		raise	3
holiday	2	magic	2	orange	3	ranch	
honey	1	map		pack	1	rang	
hook	1	March		page		rather	1
horn		marry	6	paid	4	reach	1
hotel	1	match		pants	3	ready	2
hour	1	math	1	pass	1	real	1
huge	1	May		past	1	reason	4
hundred	3	maybe	2	patch	2	recess	3
hung	1	meal	1	pay		reindeer	6
hungry	3	mess	1	pear	3	remember	4
hurry	1	mice	1	peas	1	report	
inch		microscope	6	penny	1	rice	
instead	4	middle	3	person		rich	

Grade 4 Word List *(continued)*

rocket	1	sleigh	6	such	2	twenty	1
rode	1	slept	2	sudden	5	unless	
roll	2	slid	1	sugar	2	upstairs	2
row		slip		suit	1	vacation	2
rubber	1	slow		sunny	2	valley	2
rule		smart		sure	3	voice	2
sack		smell		surprise	5	wagon	2
sad		smile		sweet	1	wall	
saddle	3	smoke		tail	1	war	1
sail		snake	1	tea	1	weather	1
sale	1	sock	1	tear	1	west	
scare	2	soft	1	teeth	1	wheat	2
seal	1	sold		telephone	3	wheel	
seat	1	somebody	2	thankful	1	whistle	4
secret	4	somewhere	3	Thanksgiving	3	whole	3
seem	1	son		there's	2	whose	6
self	2	sore	1	thin		wide	
September	2	space	1	thirty	4	wife	1
seven	1	special	5	though	5	wire	
seventh	1	spelling	1	thousand	1	witch	3
sew	4	spend	1	threw	5	without	
shape		spent		through	5	woke	1
share	2	spider	1	ticket	1	wolf	
sharp		spoke		tie	1	woman	3
shell		spoon	1	tight	3	women	5
shirt	1	sport		till		wonder	1
shoe	1	spot		tiny	1	won't	3
shoot	4	spread	2	tip		wooden	1
shore	1	spy	1	together	3	wore	3
short	1	squirrel	8	tomorrow	6	worn	2
shouldn't	4	stage	1	tooth	1	worry	3
shout	1	stairs	2	toward	6	wouldn't	3
sight	3	star	1	track	1	wreck	5
sign	4	state		trade	1	wrong	2
silk	1	station	2	trap		wrote	3
silly	1	step		treat	1	yard	1
silver	2	stock	1	trick	1	yesterday	1
single	2	stood	3	trouble	3	you'll	4
sir	1	strange	1	true	1	young	2
size	1	stuck	2	turkey	2	you're	7
skate	2	study	1	twelve	4	zoo	
sleepy	1						

Grade 5 Word List

accident	8	blond	3	choose	3	electric	2
ache	4	blood		chose	1	elephant	1
acre	2	blouse	3	citizen	5	eleven	2
action	1	blown	1	clear		empty	4
address	2	bold	1	closet	2	enemy	2
adventure	1	booklet		cloud	1	especially	9
against	4	borrow	4	clown		except	2
agree	1	boss		coach	2	excited	2
aid	1	bother	1	coast	1	excuse	2
aim	3	brake	2	comb	1	expect	2
allow	4	bravery	1	congress	1	explain	3
although	2	breath	1	contest		explore	1
American	2	breathe	4	continue	3	extra	2
among	2	breeze	1	copy	2	fact	1
angry	1	bridge	1	count		factory	2
anyhow	2	brook		county		fail	2
anyone	2	broom		couple	1	faint	4
anywhere		bucket	1	course	4	farther	1
apart		buffalo	2	court	2	favor	1
appear	2	built	3	crack	1	favorite	3
apron	2	bulb	2	crackers	3	fear	1
artist	2	bull		creek	3	fellow	1
awful	4	butterfly		crowd	2	fifth	2
ax	2	canoe	4	crumbs	2	figure	2
background	3	cape		cute	1	finally	3
bacon	2	capital	3	danger		flash	
bait	2	capture	2	dangerous	2	float	
banana	5	carefully	5	dare		flood	1
bar		careless	3	daughter	2	fog	
basement	1	cash		deck		fold	
basketball		celebrate	4	deliver	1	folks	2
bathing	1	cellar	5	destroy	4	fool	1
battle	1	cement		dew	2	foolish	1
beauty	4	center	1	discover	1	force	3
begun	1	certainly	5	distance	2	forever	
below		chain	2	ditch		forgotten	6
bench		chalk	1	double	1	fork	
bend		chance		dozen	2	form	
bent		charge		drill	1	forty	2
bicycle	4	check	1	drown	3	forward	2
birth	1	cheek	3	drum		fought	2
blame		cheer	1	duty		freedom	1
blanket	1	chimney	3	earn	1	frost	1
blast		choice	3	easily	6	froze	1
blind	1	choke	2	edge	1	fruit	2

262

Grade 5 Word List (continued)

furniture	4	jolly		nature		price	
future	2	journey	6	navy		prince	
garage	2	joy		neat	1	prize	1
gasoline	1	juice	2	needle	2	promise	3
gay		kick		neighbor	5	protect	1
geese	2	knit	2	niece	7	proud	1
general	4	knock	3	none	1	prove	1
gentle	1	known	2	nor	1	puddle	2
glove		lace	2	northern	1	pump	1
golden		lad		notice	1	pumpkin	3
goose		ladder	1	obey		purse	2
government	3	language	4	office	1	quarter	2
gown		laundry	2	officer	1	queer	2
grant	1	law		onto		question	3
grape		lazy		order		quickly	2
group	1	leaf	1	ought	4	quietly	3
grown	1	lean	1	oven		radio	1
guard	6	leap	1	package	1	raft	1
guide	1	least	1	pail	1	railroad	
hammer	2	leather		pain		rainbow	
happiness	5	lesson	1	pal	1	rake	
harm	1	lift		pale	3	receive	7
hate		lonely	2	pasture	1	regular	5
haul	5	lonesome	2	path		remind	
heel	4	lose	3	peace		repair	2
helicopter	4	lying	5	peach		restless	2
he'll	1	machine	2	perfect	2	return	1
hike		maid	2	perhaps	1	rid	
hobby	1	main		period	2	rise	
hockey	1	march		piano	3	roar	1
honest	2	market		pile	1	roof	
honor	3	mask		pillow	1	rotten	5
hose		master		pilot	3	rough	4
hospital	2	matter	1	pitch	1	safe	
husband	1	message	2	pitcher	4	sandwich	3
idea	1	metal	3	plate		sank	
ill		mill		pleasant	5	saucer	7
imagine	7	million	3	poison	4	scene	4
important	1	mistake	1	polite	2	science	
industry	2	model	4	possible	3	score	
invent	1	modern	1	powder		scout	1
iron	1	moment	1	power		scream	4
island	1	monster	1	practice	3	screen	2
jelly		motor	2	president	3	search	4
joke		nation	1	press	1	season	1

Grade 5 Word List *(continued)*

seek	3	speed		thief	4	usually	1
sense	6	spoil		thirteen	3	verse	2
sentence	2	square	1	thorn	1	view	3
seventeen	1	stake	2	thread	1	village	1
seventy	1	stamp		throat	2	vine	
several	4	stare	2	thunder		wake	
shade		steal	2	toast		Washington	1
shake		stole	2	toe		waste	1
sheet		stomach	5	tool		wave	
shelf	1	stone		tore		weak	
she'll	1	straw	1	torn		we'd	1
shine		stream	1	toss	3	weigh	2
shook	2	strike	2	touch	1	weight	2
shut		struck	2	tough	4	welcome	
sidewalk		stuff	2	trace	1	weren't	4
signal	1	subject		trail		western	1
since	3	submarine	4	travel	1	what's	1
sincere	5	suffer	2	trunk	1	whenever	1
sink	1	suggest	5	trust		whether	3
sixteen		sunshine		truth	2	whom	1
sixth		supply	4	tune	1	who's	2
sixty	1	suppose	5	turtle	1	wild	
skirt	1	surround	4	twice	1	wipe	1
slave		sweater	1	ugly	1	wonderful	1
slippery	4	sweep	1	understand	1	worse	2
sneeze	2	tank		unfair	2	worst	4
softball	1	taste	1	unhappy		worth	2
soil		taught	2	united	1	wrap	4
sort		tax		United States		wrist	4
soup		television	3	unknown	3	yell	
sour	1	terrible	3	unusual	6	you'd	2
spare	1	theater	2	upper	2	yourself	
speak	1	themselves	3	useful	2	you've	3
speech	5						

Grade 6 Word List

accept	8	avoid		collar	3	depend	
accidentally	2	awoke	1	collect		design	
accomplish	2	balance	1	college	5	dessert	4
according	1	barely	5	comfort		developed	
account	5	batteries	2	comfortable	1	difference	2
actually	5	bay		command	1	difficult	2
admire		beard		compare	1	direct	
admit		beneath	3	complete	1	direction	
advance	4	beyond		composition	2	disappear	4
advice		blink		computer		disease	4
afford	1	blizzard	1	condition		divide	
agreed	1	blossom	1	conduct		division	5
aisle	5	boil		conquer	2	doubt	5
alarm		boom		consider	1	drag	
allowance	2	border	1	contain	1	drift	
all right	2	bounce		control	3	dull	1
altogether	2	bound	1	conversation		dumb	1
A.M.	1	brakes	3	copper		eastern	2
amazed	1	buildings		correct	3	education	2
ancient	1	burst	2	costume	4	effort	
angle		bury	2	cough	2	eighth	1
angrily	6	calendar	3	council	2	electricity	1
announce	2	calm	2	courage		embarrassed	3
anxious	2	camera	2	create		empire	2
apartment		canyon		creature		energy	1
appointment	2	capitol	1	creep	2	entire	2
approach	3	capsule	2	crime		entrance	
area		castle	1	crop		envelope	1
argument	1	ceiling	2	cruel	1	equal	
arrange	2	cell	1	curious	1	equipment	2
arrive	4	central	1	curtain	4	etc.	8
article	4	century		daily	3	Europe	1
ashamed	2	channel	1	dairy		event	1
assembly	2	chapter	1	damage		evidence	2
assignment	7	character	3	daring	1	evil	2
association	2	cheap		deal		exactly	5
astronaut	5	cheerful	1	declare	1	examination	1
attempt	2	cherry		decorate	1	examined	2
attend	3	chest		deed	1	example	3
attention	6	chorus	2	defeat		excellent	3
attic	3	chosen	1	degree		excitement	2
author	4	civilization	1	delight		exciting	2
automatic	1	claim		demand		exclaim	3
autumn	2	clerk		dentist	1	excused	3
average	4	cliff		department		exercise	3

experience	2	immediately	4	mount		plastic	
experiment	2	improve	1	movement		pleasure	3
explorer	2	include		muscles	1	P.M.	
extremely	3	indeed		museum	2	popular	
fasten	3	innocent	3	music	2	population	2
fault	1	insect	1	mystery	1	port	
fever	1	instance	2	narrow	2	portable	
fierce	3	intelligent	3	national	3	position	4
file		interest	2	native		pour	1
final	2	invention		natural		powerful	1
flame		itself	1	naughty	6	practically	4
flight		judge	1	necessary	9	praise	2
flow		jungle		neighborhood	5	pray	
foreign	3	junior	1	neither	4	prefer	1
forget	1	knight	1	nickel	7	prepare	2
forth	3	knock	4	nineteen	2	prevent	
fountain	6	knot	2	ninety	3	principal	6
fourteen	1	knowledge	3	ninth	5	principle	7
friendship		labor	2	noble	2	print	
frightened	2	lack		nuclear	2	private	
frozen		later	1	object	1	professor	4
fuel		lazily	5	occurs	1	project	1
furnish		length	3	offer		property	
gain	1	lettuce	4	operation	1	protection	1
gang	1	level	1	opinion	2	provide	3
gather		liberty		opposite	3	public	2
gravity		lightning	2	orbit		pupil	4
greet		limb	1	ordinary		pure	
grocery	6	liquid		organ	2	purpose	
guest	2	located	1	organization	1	quality	
habit		loss	2	original	1	quarrel	3
handkerchief	6	magazine	2	ourselves		realize	1
handle	1	major	1	owner	1	recently	1
handsome	2	male		pajamas	3	recognize	2
harbor	1	manage		palace	3	record	
haunted	2	manner	1	parent		refrigerator	4
healthy	3	manufacture	1	particular	1	refuse	
heaven		mate		partner		relief	2
heavily	5	material	5	passage		remain	
height	2	meanwhile		passenger	1	removed	1
hers	2	measure		pattern	3	reply	2
hollow		medicine	6	peanut		rescue	2
holy	1	member	1	pearl		restaurant	8
however		mention	1	perfume	3	result	
human	2	method		pirate	4	reward	

ribbon	2	similar	2	succeed	2	unable	
route	2	simple		success	1	union	2
rush		ski	3	support		university	1
safety		slice	2	surface	2	usual	6
sailor		slight		swept		valuable	1
salad	1	smooth	1	swift		value	
sample		social	3	sword	2	various	1
scenery	2	society	2	system		vegetable	1
scientist	1	soldier	1	tablet		vote	
secretary	3	southern	1	tale	2	voyage	1
section		spirit	1	temperature	2	waist	2
series	2	split		temple	1	wander	2
serve	2	statement		terribly	1	we've	
service	2	steak	1	thousands	7	whale	
settle	2	steel	1	thrown	3	whatever	
settlement	1	stiff	2	thumb	1	wherever	2
shadow	2	stir	2	timber		whisper	
shed	1	straight	1	title	1	willing	
shoulder	1	strangely	5	tongue		wise	
shovel		stranger	1	transportation	1	within	
shown		strength	1	treasure		wound	
sigh		struggle	2	troop	1	written	1
silence		student		tunnel		yield	2
silent	1	style		type		zero	1

Grade 7 Word List

aboard	approximate	cabbage	cozy
abolish	arise	cadet	crisp
absent	arithmetic	calf	crowed
abundant	arose	calves	crust
abuse	arrangement	canal	cure
academy	arrest	cane	current
accomplished	ash	cease	custom
accurate	aside	cedar	dawn
accuse	assistance	changeable	debt
achieve	assistant	chart	decision
acid	atom	chiefly	declaration
acquaint	attract	childhood	decline
acquire	authority	chin	decoration
active	autobiography	civil	defend
activity	automobile	claimed	defense
actor	avenue	classroom	delicate
actual	await	coarse	democratic
addition	aware	code	deny
adjective	bandage	colony	depart
adjust	banquet	column	describe
administration	barber	combine	desire
adopt	battery	commission	destination
advantage	beautifully	committee	detail
adverb	beef	common	determine
advertise	behave	community	development
advertisement	benefit	companion	devote
advise	berry	compass	dictionary
affair	biography	compel	difficulty
afterward	bitter	completely	digest
alley	blade	concern	disappointed
aloud	blank	conclude	discuss
amend	bleed	conductor	display
amusement	blockade	confidence	distant
ancestor	boast	connect	distinct
anchor	boiler	conscious	district
anger	boundaries	consent	dread
announcement	boyhood	considerable	drug
annual	brace	consist	due
anxiously	brand	constant	eager
apparently	brief	contact	economic
appeal	broad	contained	editor
applied	bump	contract	effect
appoint	bundle	convention	elected
appreciate	bunk	corps	election
approve	burglar	correctly	element

employ	goal	local	pine
engage	golf	location	plow
English	governor	lodge	plural
enlargement	gradually	lower	poet
enormous	grain	lumber	political
entertain	grave	lungs	portion
entirely	greatly	machinery	possession
error	growth	majority	possibly
established	gymnasium	maple	practical
exact	hail	marble	prayer
excellently	harmful	meant	precious
exchange	harmless	mere	predict
exist	harvest	merely	presence
expense	haste	mild	pressure
express	hawk	military	pride
expression	hero	minister	privilege
extend	highly	mischief	process
faith	horseback	mixture	profit
false	identify	mobile	progress
fame	immediate	motion	proper
familiar	importance	murmur	proportion
fancy	impossible	musical	propose
fashion	incident	mysterious	punish
fate	increase	naturally	punishment
fattened	independence	nerve	purchase
feature	indicate	nervous	quantity
figured	individual	nevertheless	rank
film	inform	noun	rapid
firm	information	numerous	rate
flesh	injured	obtain	recent
flour	intend	occupy	recover
former	interrupt	odd	reduce
fortune	invitation	official	reflects
founded	issue	onions	regard
fraction	jacket	opportunity	relative
frame	jewel	oppose	religious
friendly	journal	pace	remarked
fully	jury	parade	render
further	justice	paragraph	representative
gaze	justify	partly	require
generally	kindly	paste	respect
given	laboratory	permit	reveal
glance	lawyer	photograph	revolution
glory	likely	physical	ridge
glow	limited	pierce	rifle

Grade 7 Word List *(continued)*

ripe	spite	throne	victory
root	steady	thus	virtue
sake	steam	tobacco	volume
scale	steer	toil	wage
scarcely	strict	total	warfare
scratch	successful	towards	warn
secure	sum	traveler	wealth
seize	superintendent	treatment	wealthy
selfish	supposed	treaty	weave
senate	surrender	trial	wedding
separate	swiftly	truly	welcomed
serious	sympathy	tube	whip
shelter	talent	typical	wicked
silently	tape	understood	wisdom
situation	target	unit	wit
slightly	telescope	urge	witness
solid	tender	utter	wives
sorrow	tennis	vast	worker
soul	territory	vessel	worship
source	therefore	veto	youth
spin	thrill	victim	zone

Grade 8 Word List

abandon
ability
abroad
absence
absolute
abundantly
abused
academic
acceptance
accomplishment
accustomed
achievement
acquaintance
actively
additional
adequate
administrative
adult
advising
affection
agencies
agreement
alphabet
amazement
ambition
amendment
analysis
annually
apparent
appearance
application
apply
appreciation
appropriate
approval
approximately
aquarium
arc
arrival
artificial
aspect
assert
assume
assumption
assure

atmosphere
atomic
attach
attain
attendant
attitude
attractive
audience
awakened
ballet
ballot
bargain
based
basic
basis
behaved
behavior
belief
betray
billion
bind
briefly
brilliant
budget
burden
bureau
camel
campaign
candidate
capable
capacity
career
carpenter
carved
celebration
cereal
certificate
characteristic
charter
chemical
circumstance
citizenship
climate
cloudless
collection

colonel
combination
comedy
comment
commerce
commercial
commit
communication
comparable
comparison
competition
complex
composed
conceal
concentration
concept
conclusion
concrete
condemn
conference
conflict
confusion
connection
consciously
consideration
constantly
constitution
construction
continual
contrary
contrast
contributed
converse
convince
copyright
corporation
correction
courageous
creative
credit
crept
crisis
criticism
cube
culture

curve
data
deceive
definite
delicious
delightful
dense
deposit
depth
descend
desirable
destined
detect
detective
device
diagram
digestion
dignity
disaster
discussion
disguise
dismal
dispute
distinction
distribution
domestic
doubtful
dramatic
duplicate
dwell
earnest
edition
educate
effective
electronic
emotional
emphasis
emptiness
encourage
endlessly
endure
engineer
enormously
entertainment
environment

erect
essential
estimate
evaporate
eventually
evidently
executive
existence
extent
facilities
federal
female
fertile
financial
fiscal
fond
forehead
formula
fracture
freight
frequently
fright
function
funds
funeral
generation
gentlemen
geography
glimpse
glorious
govern
graph
grateful
grease
grind
gross
guilty
harness
hedge
hemisphere
herd
historic
historical
horizon
humor

Grade 8 Word List (continued)

ideal	logical	origin	professional	rhyme
identification	magnet	orphan	prominent	rhythm
idle	maintain	otherwise	protein	risk
idol	manhood	oxygen	provision	role
illustrated	mantle	pane	psychological	royal
image	marine	parallel	publication	rural
impact	marriage	particularly	published	salary
imperfect	mathematics	patient	pursue	satisfactory
impression	maximum	peculiar	radiation	satisfied
improvement	meadow	per	range	scheduled
incline	medical	perceive	rare	scheme
income	medium	percent	reaction	scientific
independence	memory	percentage	readily	security
index	mental	performance	rear	seldom
industrial	mineral	permanent	reasonable	selected
infection	minimum	personal	recall	senator
influence	minor	personality	reception	senior
initial	mischievous	phantom	recognition	session
injury	missle	pierced	recommended	signature
inn	mission	platform	recreation	significant
inner	modify	pledge	reduction	simply
insisted	monarch	plunge	reference	site
institute	moral	plus	reflection	skill
institution	murder	poetry	region	slope
instrument	musicians	policy	regret	solar
intellectual	necessarily	positive	reign	solution
intensity	negative	possess	relation	somehow
interfere	neglect	possibility	relieved	somewhat
interior	nephew	postage	remarkable	sought
internal	neutral	potential	repeated	sow
international	nodded	precisely	replace	species
investigation	normal	precision	represent	specific
involved	noticeable	preparation	republic	spiritual
irrigation	notion	pressurize	request	spray
items	novel	presumably	research	staff
jazz	numerals	previous	reservation	standard
jealous	oblige	primary	reserve	starch
judgment	observation	prime	residential	stationary
latter	obvious	primitive	resistance	stationery
legal	occasion	prior	resolution	statue
legislation	occupation	prison	resources	status
liberal	operator	procedure	response	steep
literary	orchard	proceed	responsibility	strait
literature	orchestra	produce	restore	stress
logic	organize	production	review	stretch

Grade 8 Word List *(continued)*

strip
structure
stumbled
stylish
substance
substantial
sufficient
summon
superior
supreme
syllable
symbol
tariff
task

technical
technique
tendency
tension
term
testimony
text
theme
theory
thoroughly
threat
throughout
timid
tissue

tone
topic
torch
tour
tower
tradition
traffic
tragedy
transfer
treasury
tremendous
trend
triangle
triumph

tropical
typewriter
ultimate
unconscious
unfold
uniform
unique
universe
urban
vanish
vapor
variety
vary
vehicles

venture
version
vertical
via
violence
virtually
vision
vital
vocational
weakness
weapon
welfare
wherefore

GLOSSARY

ABBREVIATION: a shortened form of a word, ending in a period (Mr., Ms.). *Contrast:* ACRONYM; CLIPPED FORM; PORTMANTEAU.

ABSTRACTION, LEVELS OF: *See:* LEVELS OF ABSTRACTION.

ACCENT: *See:* STRESS.

ACRONYM: a coined word—it must be pronounceable—formed from the first letter(s) of each word in a compound term (for example, NATO from North Atlantic Treaty Organization).

ACROSTIC: a square of letters in which each row and column forms a word.

AFFIX: a bound morpheme attached either before (prefix) or after (suffix) a base word in English. *See:* PREFIX; SUFFIX.

ALLITERATION: a literary device making use of repeated initial sounds (example: seven silly snakes). *See:* ONOMATOPOEIA; RIGMAROLE.

ANALYTIC SCALE: a type of holistic evaluation of writing samples using a rubric or scale of criteria.

ANTONYM: a word that has the opposite meaning of another word (for example, *hot* and *cold*). *Contrast:* SYNONYM.

AUTOMATIC SPELLING VOCABULARY: *See:* SECURITY LIST.

BASE: a free morpheme, unencumbered by affixes: the base of *runs* and *running* is *run.* Distinguished from ROOT or STEM only in the case of compounds, where *lighthouse* is a BASE made of two ROOTS or STEMS.

BLEND: *See:* PORTMANTEAU. (Often inappropriately used to refer to a CONSONANT CLUSTER.)

BORROWING: the practice of adding words from another language, with spelling and/or pronunciation sometimes changed.

CINQUAIN: a nonrhyming poem consisting of five lines: 1 word = title, 2 words = description, 3 words = action, 4 words = feeling, 1 word = retitle.

CLIPPED FORM: a shortened version of a word (*gas* for *gasoline*). *Contrast:* ACRONYM; PORTMANTEAU; ABBREVIATION.

COINED WORD: an invented word, often from a trade name *(zipper).*

COLLOQUIALISM: a word or expression characteristic of a regional dialect and considered too informal for use in formal standard English. *See:* SLANG; DIALECT; JARGON.

COMBINING FORM: a Greek or Latin root used to form English words *(uni-, -ology).*

COMBINING SENTENCES: *See:* SENTENCE COMBINING.

COMPOSING: those acts involving thinking through and organizing ideas for writing, including dictating such thoughts.

COMPOUND: a single unit formed by combining two or more free morphemes as "closed compounds" *(rowboat),* "hyphenated compounds" *(law-abiding),* or "open compounds" *(lead pencil).*

CONCRETE POETRY: writing in which the shape or form reflects the content (a well-pɔuɹnɪ phrase). Also called SHAPE POETRY.

CONNOTATION: the emotional impact of words that goes beyond the denotation or dictionary meaning *(hamburger* and *ground beef* denote the same substance but have different connotations). *See:* DENOTATION; SEMANTICS.

CONTRACTION: a word formed by shortening through omission of phonemes (in speech) or letters replaced by an apostrophe (in writing). *Contrast:* ABBREVIATION; ACRONYM.

DECODING: the basic reading process of converting the printed "code" into its speech forms or directly into the meaning units conveyed by the speech forms. *Contrast:* ENCODING.

DENOTATION: the lexical or dictionary meaning of a word *(home* and *house* both denote abodes). *Contrast:* CONNOTATION.

DERIVATION: a process whereby the grammatical functon of a base is changed by the addition of a prefix or suffix. *See:* DERIVATIONAL AFFIX. *Contrast:* INFLECTIONAL AFFIX.

DERIVATIONAL AFFIX: a prefix or suffix that changes the grammatical function of a word (from the noun *friend* is derived *friendly, befriend). Contrast:* INFLECTIONAL AFFIX.

DERIVATIVE: a word formed by adding a derivational affix to a base.

DETERMINER: a member of a group of structure words in English, serving to "mark" or signal a noun *(the, a, many, some). See:* STRUCTURE WORD.

DIACRITIC: *See:* DIACRITICAL MARK.

DIACRITICAL MARK: a mark or symbol used with a letter in order to represent a sound as opposed to either a spelling or a letter name (ā represents the vowel sound in *make).*

DIALECT: form of a language as spoken by a social or geographical group within a language community. Dialect may vary from the "standard" in pronunciation, vocabulary, or syntax, but not sufficiently to distinguish it as a separate language. *See:* COLLOQUIALISM; SLANG; JARGON.

DIAMANTE: a nonrhyming poem consisting of seven lines, often on a dual or contrasting subject (hot/cold, love/hate); 1 noun, 2 adjectives, 3 -*ing* verbals, 4 nouns (2 representing a shift in subject), 3 -*ing* verbals, 2 adjectives, 1 noun.

EDITING: the final polishing of a piece of writing, consisting of revision and proofreading. *See:* REVISION; PROOFREADING.

ENCODING: the process of representing the spoken language with visual symbols; in English, the process of writing/spelling. *Contrast:* DECODING.

ENTRY WORD: the word in the alphabetical listing in a dictionary.

EPONYM: a person's name used to designate the entity named after that person *(sandwich* for Earl of Sandwich, *macadam* for John McAdam).

ETYMOLOGIST: one who specializes in tracing the history of origins of words.

ETYMOLOGY: the linguistic specialty dealing with the history or origins of words. *See:* ETYMOLOGIST; LINGUISTICS.

FIGURATIVE LANGUAGE: words or expressions used metaphorically or nonliterally for emotional or stylistic effect. *See:* IDIOM; METAPHOR; SIMILE; SLANG.

FORM CLASS WORDS: sets of words that take certain affixes. There are four form classes: nouns, verbs, adjectives, adverbs. *Contrast:* STRUCTURE WORDS.

FUNCTION WORD: *See: STRUCTURE WORD.*

GRAMMAR: the study of word classes, inflections, and syntax.

GRAPHEME: the minimal unit in writing (a letter or letters) used to represent a phoneme (sound): *(b* in *bat, th* in *thumb).* Spelling involves the accepted sequencing of graphemes to represent morphemes or meaning units. *See:* ENCODING; MORPHEME; PHONEME.

GRAPHEME–PHONEME CORRESPONDENCE: a decoding skill establishing the relationship between a letter (grapheme) and the sound (phoneme) it usually represents. Also referred to as "letter–sound association." *See:* DECODING. *Contrast:* PHONEME–GRAPHEME CORRESPONDENCE.

HAIKU: a three-line word picture, usually related to nature. Lines consist of five, seven, and five syllables.

HEURISTIC: a device, such as the 5 *W*'s *(who, what, when, where, why),* to aid in exploration or discovery of a topic.

HOLISTIC EVALUATION: an impressionistic sorting or ranking of written pieces by trained evaluators, based on fast reading and avoiding any count of surface features. *See:* PRIMARY TRAIT; ANALYTIC SCALE.

HOMOGRAPH: one of two or more words with the same spelling that may differ in pronunciation and/or meaning and/or origin *(pool* for swimming and *pool* table; *read,* pronounced as /rēd/ or /red/). *Contrast:* HOMOPHONE; MULTIPLE MEANINGS.

HOMONYM: a general term sometimes applied to homographs, homophones, or words with multiple meanings.

HOMOPHONE: one of two or more words with the same pronunciation that may differ in spelling and/or meaning and/or origin *(pare, pear, pair). See:* HOMOGRAPH; MULTIPLE MEANINGS.

IDIOM: in any language, an expression whose meaning cannot be determined from the literal meaning of the individual words *(lose your head).* Idioms may be peculiar to a specific dialect or common to the entire language community. *See:* DIALECT.

INFLECTED COUNT: a method used in tabulating the number of different words whereby each different inflected form of a word is counted as a separate word *(play, plays, played* would be counted as three different words*). Contrast:* LEXICAL COUNT.

INFLECTION: (1) a change in the pitch or volume of the voice; (2) a change in a base word to reflect number, tense, and so on, but with no change in that word's grammatical function. *See:* INFLECTIONAL AFFIX.

INFLECTIONAL AFFIX: those prefixes and suffixes that change the tense, number, and so on of a base but do not change its grammatical function *(-s, -ed, -ing). Contrast:* DERIVATIONAL AFFIX.

INTONATION: *See:* INFLECTION, definition #1.

JARGON: the vocabulary—technical or idiomatic—peculiar to a specific group (educational jargon, medical jargon).

JUNCTURE: the degree of pause in speech. Linguists usually identify four `levels, ranging from the minimal pause to distinguish "ice cream" from "I scream"; to the final pause at the end of a statement. *See:* PITCH; STRESS; PHONEME, SUPRASEGMENTAL.

LANGUAGE: a system of communication, never clearly defined by linguists, consisting of common elements and mutually intelligible to its users; a broader category than dialect. *See:* DIALECT.

LEVELS OF ABSTRACTION: semanticist's term for the varying degrees of specificity in communicaton, from the particular to the general; a concern in reading and writing persuasive material, where one may not jump from the specific ("Tabby scratches") to the general ("Cats scratch").

LEVELS OF USAGE: degrees of formality or informality used in speaking or writing; for instructional purposes, the distinction of three levels should be adequate: (1) extreme formal, (2) standard, (3) informal. *See:* DIALECT; JARGON; SLANG.

LEXICAL COUNT: a method used in tabulating the number of different words whereby all "regular" inflected forms are considered repetitions of the same word *(play, plays, played* are counted as three occurrences of *play). See:* INFLECTION; BASE WORD. *Contrast:* INFLECTED COUNT.

LEXICAL MEANING: the "dictionary" or semantic meaning of a word as distinguished from its structural meaning as part of a syntactical unit. *See:* STRUCTURAL MEANING.

LEXICON: the collection of words in a language. The English lexicon is divided into two groups of words, structure words and form class words. *See:* STRUCTURE WORDS; FORM CLASS WORDS.

LIMERICK: a five-line nonsense poem with a fixed rhythm and rhyme pattern.

LINGUIST: one whose discipline is the study of human languages. *See:* LINGUISTICS.

LINGUISTICS: the scientific study of languages, dealing with phonology (sounds), morphology (structure and meaning), syntax (grammar), and etymology (origins).

MALAPROP: a confused usage of words (a *neon*—for *nylon*—shirt). *See:* spoonerism

MAPPING: *See:* WEBBING

MECHANICS: those elements of writing that deal with correctness of capitalization, punctuation, spelling, and format.

METAPHOR: figurative language in which comparison is implied between normally unlike things or actions (The game was a circus.) *See:* FIGURATIVE LANGUAGE. *Contrast:* SIMILE.

MINIMAL PAIR: any two utterances containing only one significant difference in phonemes *(toy/boy, bat, bet). See:* PHONEME, SEGMENTAL.

MINIMAL TERMINAL UNIT: *See:* T-UNIT.

MNEMONIC: a device intended to assist memory. (A mnemonic device for avoiding confuson of *there/their* is to remember *heir* as a person and *here* as a place.)

MORPHEME: the smallest unit of meaning in language. "Free" morphemes stand alone *(boy, play)* whereas "bound" morphemes must be attached to other morphemes *(-s, -ed)*. Hence, *boys* and *played* are two-morpheme words.

MORPHOPHONEMIC ALTERNATIONS: shifts in pronunciation—with no change in spelling of the base—that often accompany derivational changes in words *(angel/angelic). See:* DERIVATIONAL AFFIX.

MULTIPLE MEANINGS: most English words have more than one meaning; not to be confused with homographs, which have the same spelling but are listed as separate entry words in the dictionary. *See:* HOMOGRAPH.

NEOLOGISM: a newly coined word, developed by invention or by using an old word with a new meaning. *See:* COINED WORDS.

NONSTANDARD ENGLISH: variations in the use of English—vocabulary, pronunciation, or syntax—that differ from the "norm" or standard. May include DIALECT; SLANG; JARGON; COLLOQUIALISMS.

NOUN: one of the four form classes of words in English. Clues to its recognition include the possible existence of a noun marker before it, its ability to take a plural or possessive marker, or the existence of a noun-forming suffix, as well as its position in a sentence.

ONOMATOPOETIC WORD: a word that sounds like the noise it refers to *(hiss, crash)*.

PALINDROME: a word or sentence that reads the same forward and backward *(madam)*.

PHONEME: the individual units of sound in a language. English contains about forty-five phonemes: twenty-four consonant phonemes, nine vowel phonemes, and twelve suprasegmental phonemes. *See:* PHONEME, SEGMENTAL; PHONEME, SUPRASEGMENTAL.

PHONEME–GRAPHEME CORRESPONDENCE: an encoding skill establishing the relationship between a sound (phoneme) and the letter (grapheme) usually used to represent it *(laugh* is composed of three phonemes, where /l/ is represented by *l,* /a/ by *au,* and /f/ by *gh*). Also called "sound–letter association." *See:* ENCODING; PHONEME; GRAPHEME.

PHONEME, SEGMENTAL: the smallest significant unit of sound in a language *(laugh* is made up of three phonemes—/l/, /a/, /f/—and differs from *calf* by only one phoneme—the initial phoneme). *See:* PHONEME, SUPRASEGMENTAL; MINIMAL PAIRS.

PHONEME, SUPRASEGMENTAL: the elements of pitch, stress, and juncture imposed on the segmental phonemes (sounds) of the language. Linguists identify four levels of pitch, four of stress, and four of juncture in English. *See:* PHONEME, SEGMENTAL; PITCH; STRESS; JUNCTURE.

PHONEMICS: a specialty within the linguistic area of phonology that deals with the study of phonemes. *Contrast:* PHONETICS; PHONICS.

PHONETICS: the study of the speech process, that is, the production, transmission, and reception of speech sounds. *Contrast:* PHONICS; PHONEMICS.

PHONICS: a method used in teaching beginning reading to establish letter–sound associations. *See:* GRAPHEME–PHONEME CORRESPONDENCE.

PHONOGRAM: a pronounceable unit or syllable of language, whether or not meaning is attached *(-at, -ick, -et);* used to provide practice in word patterns by adding initial consonants or clusters.

PHONOLOGY: study of the sound structure of language, including phonemics and phonetics. *See:* PHONETICS; PHONEMICS.

PITCH: tonal quality in English speech that signals meanings. Linguists usually define four levels of pitch, from very high to low. *See:* PHONEME, SUPRASEGMENTAL; STRESS; JUNCTURE.

PORTMANTEAU WORD: a word created by the combination of existing words or word parts (*motel* from *motor hotel*).

PREFIX: an affix (bound morpheme) added to the front of a base and altering the meaning of that base (*un-* reverses the meaning of *lock*). *See:* AFFIX; MORPHEME, BOUND; BASE WORD.

PRETEST: in spelling, a test of unstudied words to determine which words need to be learned by study. *See:* TEST–STUDY METHOD. *Contrast* STUDY–TEST METHOD.

PREWRITING: activities involving the collecting and organizing of thoughts for writing; may continue during the writing process.

PRIMARY TRAIT: a holistic evaluation method based on prior construction of a detailed scoring guide in relation to a specific writing task. *See:* HOLISTIC EVALUATION; ANALYTIC SCALE.

PROOFREADING: the act of checking printed or written language to identify and correct mechanical errors, such as in capitalization, punctuation, spelling, or format. *Contrast:* REVISION.

PSYCHOLINGUISTICS: a sub-area of linguistics dealing with the psychology of language.

READING: a process, vocal or subvocal, of reconstructing and reacting to ideas or information presented in visual form; most often restricted to printed form. *See:* DECODING. *CONTRAST:* SPELLING, ENCODING.

REBUS: a written statement using pictures for some or all of the words ("The [picture of ball] is on the [picture of table].")

REVISION: the editing act of reworking written material, changing words, expressions, style, organization, and so on, in order to make it more clear or interesting. *Contrast:* PROOFREADING.

RIGMAROLE: a medieval roundelay, consisting of alliterative phrases or sentences, all beginning with ordinal numbers (one weeping wayfarer watching wanderers, two tiny turtles tasting turnips,...).

ROOT: *See:* BASE WORD.

RUBRIC: a classification or listing of criteria to be used in the holistic evaluation of a piece of writing. *See:* HOLISTIC EVALUATION; ANALYTIC SCALE; PRIMARY TRAIT.

RUNNING WORDS: in a word count, every word and every repetition of every word; all of the words in a sample of speech or print. ("The big boy found the little boy" contains seven running words but only five different words.)

SCHWA: the symbol ə or the sound it represents. The most frequently used vowel sound in English, it is the sound heard at the beginning of *about.*

SECURITY LIST: the basic list of the most frequently used words, which should be learned for spelling to the point of automatic response; usually considered to be about 3,000 words. Also referred to as the "automatic spelling vocabulary."

SEGMENTAL PHONEME: *See:* PHONEME, SEGMENTAL.

SEMANTIC WEBBING: *See:* WEBBING.

SEMANTICS: the study of human communication as it influences human interaction, usually going beyond the denotation (lexical meaning) of words to consider their connotations (emotional effects). *See:* CONNOTATON; DENOTATION; LEXICAL MEANING.

SENTENCE: best exemplified rather than defined. Mechanically a sentence is a word or group of words beginning and ending with double cross juncture; in print, beginning with a capital letter and ending with end punctuation. Syntactically, a sentence usually consists of a subject (noun phrase) and a predicate (verb phrase). *See:* JUNCTURE; SYNTAX; SENTENCE PATTERNS.

SENTENCE COMBINING: a technique for developing sentence flexibility through experience in the various ways of combining related simple sentences or ideas into complex sentences.

SENTENCE PATTERNS: the classification of sentences according to structure, using the form class words as a basis (N–V, N–V–N, N–Vl–Adj, etc.).

SHAPE POETRY: *See:* CONCRETE POETRY.

SIMILE: figurative language wherein a comparison is stated literally between unlike things or events. (The game was as funny as a circus.) *See:* METAPHOR.

SLANG: informal, nonstandard vocabulary used by a particular age or social group; usually consisting of coined or changed word meanings or figures of speech; similar to jargon, but usually less lasting; different from dialect in that dialect is more geographic and more a matter of pronunciation. *See:* JARGON; DIALECT; COLLOQUIALISM.

SLANTING: a writing technique whereby the author deliberately selects emotion-loaded words to achieve a desired effect on the reader.

SLASH MARKS: the marks "/ /" used in writing by linguists to indicate that symbols so enclosed refer to the phoneme (sound) as opposed to the grapheme (letter); (/e/ refers to the vowel sound in *head* or *bed*). Slash marks are technically called *virgules.*

SOUND–LETTER ASSOCIATION: *See:* PHONEME–GRAPHEME CORRESPONDENCE.

SPELLING CONSCIENCE: an attitude or desire on the part of a writer to spell correctly. Apparently accompanied by a necessary awareness of uncertainty about certain words.

SPELLING: a process of stringing together in proper sequence, orally or visually, the appropriate letters (graphemes) in order to represent desired sounds or words. *See:* ENCODING. *Contrast:* READING.

SPOONERISM: a confused juxtaposition of sounds in words. ("It's kisstomary to cuss the bride.") *See:* MALAPROP.

STANDARD ENGLISH: the broad "norm" of English as spoken and written by most American English speakers; includes agreement on vocabulary, pronunciation, and syntax to some extent. *See:* DIALECT; SLANG; JARGON; COLLOQUIALISM.

STEM: *See:* BASE WORD.

STRESS: the degree of force or emphasis with which a sound or word is pronounced. Linguists usually identify four levels, from primary to weak; often combined with pitch to signal meanings and also important in pronouncing homographs such as *re-cord'* and *rec'-ord. See:* PHONEME, SUPRASEGMENTAL; PITCH; JUNCTURE.

STRUCTURAL ANALYSIS: the process of examining a word for its component parts, either morphemes or syllables. *See:* MORPHEME; SYLLABLE.

STRUCTURAL MEANING: knowledge of the function of a word as based on understanding of the syntax of the language. (The English speaker has structural meaning for *gleap* and *glipped* in "The gleap glipped," even though these words have no lexical meaning.) Also called "syntactic meaning." *Contrast:* LEXICAL MEANING.

STRUCTURE WORD: any word not a member of the four form classes. Structure words (determiners, prepositions, connectives, modals, etc.) have little or no lexical meaning; they serve to tie together the form classes into meaningful syntactic patterns, thereby providing structural meaning. Also called "function words." *See:* LEXICAL MEANING; STRUCTURAL MEANING.

STUDY–TEST METHOD: the traditional approach to spelling instruction in which pupils are given a list of words—usually weekly—to study for spelling. *Contrast:* TEST–STUDY METHOD.

SUFFIX: an affix (bound morpheme) added to the end of a base word to alter meaning or form class. Suffixes may be inflectional *(-s, -ed)* or derivational *(-ful, -able). See:* DERIVATIONAL AFFIX; INFLECTIONAL AFFIX.

SUPRASEGMENTAL PHONEME: *See:* PHONEME, SUPRASEGMENTAL.

SYLLABICATION: the process of determining the point of division between syllables. There are at least three different standards for such division: visual or entry word syllabication *(yel-low),* which is the writing convention; speech syllabication *(/yel-ō/); and morphemic or meaning syllabication (bomb-ard* vs. *bom-bard). See:* SYLLABLE; SYLLABLE, OPEN; SYLLABLE, CLOSED.

SYLLABIC CONSONANT: a final consonant phoneme that constitutes the entire final syllable in a word, thereby denying the "rule" that every syllable has a vowel sound. (In *certain* and *battle,* /n/ and /l/ are the final syllables, as opposed to *captain* and *capital).* Some dictionaries show this final syllable with a vestige of *schwa:* a superscript *schwa* preceding the consonant sound.

SYLLABLE: the next larger unit of sound beyond a phoneme, consisting of at least a vowel sound or syllabic consonant and usually one or more consonant sounds. *Syllable* contains three syllables: *syl-la-ble).* *See:* SYLLABICATON; SYLLABLE, CLOSED; SYLLABLE, OPEN.

SYLLABLE, CLOSED: any syllable ending in a consonant sound (the first syllable in *babble* vs. that in *baby*). *See:* SYLLABLE; SYLLABICATION. *Contrast:* SYLLABLE, OPEN.

SYLLABLE, OPEN: any syllable ending in a vowel sound (the first syllable in *baby* vs. that in *babble*). *See:* SYLLABLE; SYLLABICATION. *Contrast:* SYLLABLE, CLOSED.

SYNONYM: a word whose denotation (lexical meaning) is similar to that of another word *(sour* and *tart* are synonyms). *See:* DENOTATION; LEXICAL MEANING. *Contrast:* ANTONYM.

SYNTACTIC MEANING: *See:* STRUCTURAL MEANING.

SYNTAX: that portion of grammar which deals with the way words are strung together to form meaningful phrases, clauses, and sentences. *See:* GRAMMAR.

TANKA: a haiku with two added lines of seven syllables each. *See:* HAIKU.

TEST–STUDY METHOD: a research-supported approach to spelling instruction in which pupils are pretested to determine what words they need to study for spelling before they begin studying the word list. *Contrast:* STUDY–TEST METHOD.

TRANSCRIBING: the process of mechanically getting thoughts onto paper, either through writing, printing, typing, or similar functions. *Contrast:* COMPOSING.

T-UNIT: any independent clause with all of its subordinate clauses and modifiers. The number of words used, per T-unit, is a good measure of sophistication in expressive language. Technically called a "minimal terminal unit."

VERB: one of the four form classes. "Verb" belies the traditional definition as an "action" word. Clues to the identification of a verb include the ability to take certain inflections, possible precedence by modals, and the position in a sentence. *See:* NOUN; FORM CLASS WORDS.

VIRGULES: *See:* SLASH MARKS.

WEBBING: a technique often used in content areas or vocabulary development to plot visually the interrelationships between words or ideas; a form of outlining.

Subject Index

Author Index